TARNISHED SCALPELS

TARNISHED SCALPELS

The Court-Martials of Fifty Union Surgeons

Thomas P. Lowry, M.D.
and
Jack D. Welsh, M.D.

STACKPOLE
BOOKS

Published by
STACKPOLE BOOKS
5067 Ritter Road
Mechanicsburg, PA 17055
www.stackpolebooks.com

Printed in the United States of America

10 9 8 7 6 5 4 3 2 1

FIRST EDITION

Library of Congress Cataloging-in-Publication Data

Lowry, Thomas P. (Thomas Power), 1932-
    Tarnished scalpels: the court-martials of fifty Union surgeons / Thomas P. Lowry and Jack D. Welsh.—1st ed.
        p. cm.
    Includes bibliographical references and index.
    ISBN: 0-8117-1603-1
    1. Courts-martial and courts of inquiry—United States. 2. Trials (Military offenses)—United States. 3. United States. Army—Surgeons—Malpractice.
    I. Welsh, Jack D., 1928- II. Title.

KF7641 .L693 2000
343.73'0143—dc21   99-087411

For Michael P. Musick:

Friend, Mentor, National Treasure

CONTENTS

ACKNOWLEDGMENTS

We express here the central role of Beverly A. Lowry, who not only found half of our surgeons but who has entered tens of thousands of Civil War court-martials into the computer, done all the keyboard work to create the manuscript for this book, and acted as hostess and chef during our many days of conferring over stacks of papers.

No serious work on the Union army can be done without the help of Michael P. Musick of the National Archives. To him and to his colleagues at that magnificent repository we owe a limitless debt.

Three librarians provided invaluable help: Ms. Nancy Eckerman, of the Indiana University School of Medicine; Ms. Carol M. Spawn, of the Academy of Natural Sciences in Philadelphia; and Mr. Christopher Stanwood, of the College of Physicians in Philadelphia. We are also deeply indebted to several medical colleagues: Clyde B. Kernek, Sheperdstown, West Virginia; John Porter, Beatrice, Nebraska; William Sharp, South Orange, New Jersey; Tom P. Sweeney, Republic, Missouri; and Bruce A. Evans, Rochester, Minnesota.

William C. "Jack" Davis, our editor, crystallized the book's organization with a single Olympian thunderbolt. Robert K. Krick and Robert E. L. Krick answered many questions regarding Virginia history and geography. Rev. Albert H. Ledoux and Professor Robert Barnett straightened out our Latin.

Any errors, omissions, or unwarranted opinions remain the responsibility of the authors.

THE SOURCE MATERIAL

The original source for every story is the court-martial file. The approximately 80,000 general court-martials held by the Union army are in Record Group 153 at the National Archives. These files are no particular order other than being vaguely chronological. There is an 1885 name index; the only subject index is one currently under construction by Thomas and Beverly Lowry. For every doctor's story, we searched the same files and references. In addition, in some cases we found further sources. Rather than cite the same sources fifty times in fifty chapters, the reader can safely assume that at a minimum, for every doctor, the authors searched the following.

Record Group 153, Civil War Court-martial files, National Archives.

Record Group 94, Entry 561, Medical Officers Files, National Archives.

The Compiled Military Service Records, National Archives.

The Pension Index and Records, National Archives.

Record Group 94, Entry 360, Records of the Adjutant General of Colored Troops. (These records were consulted only for surgeons of U.S. Colored Troops.)

The Official Records of the War of the Rebellion.

The Medical and Surgical History of the War of the Rebellion.

The Directory of Deceased American Physicians, 1804–1929 (Chicago: American Medical Association, 1993).

Medical Obituaries: American Physicians' Biographical Notices in Selected Medical Journals Before 1907. (Boone, N.C.: Holloway, 1996).

FOREWORD

Jesus and "the wily Pharisees" open the introduction. The Japanese movie *Rashomon* launches Chapter Three. A headless Private Benjamin Anderson of the 23rd United States Colored Troops introduces Chapter Fifteen. Nine chapters cluster under the heading "Wine and Women" (a Lowry book is certain never to stray too far afield from either of those intoxicating reagents). Readers would be badly mistaken to expect a quotidian experience as they delve into the wide array of remarkable tales that comprise *Tarnished Scalpels.*

Dr. Thomas P. Lowry and his long-suffering consort, Beverly, have become institutions at Washington's National Archives. The diligent couple has become at least as familiar a cultural landmark among serious researchers as are the archives' impressive facade and dreadful canteen. This book is one manifestation—not the first and surely not the last—of the historical riches that the Lowrys have mined at 7th and Pennsylvania.

Unfortunately, the official transcripts of Confederate court-martials do not survive in any large volume. (Private copies of a few exist in collections of personal papers.) The only two notable examples are from the ineffectual hounding of General Richard Brooke Garnett by "Stonewall" Jackson after the battle of Kernstown and James Longstreet's disingenuous attempts to shift blame for his pathetic Knoxville fiasco onto the shoulders of Lafayette McLaws. Other Confederate court papers are gone—not With The Wind, but rather With The Fire that consumed much of Richmond in April 1865. Synopses of some Southern court proceedings do exist, but they usually are disappointingly terse. The good news is that Unionist court-martial records survive, in full scope and great volume. Some 80,000 cases are on file at the National Archives for the period of the Civil War. The Lowrys have, incredibly, processed 61,000 of them at this writing. If it is safe to assume that not all (likely not even *most*) Federalist perfidy came formally to trial, then it is unmistakably clear that the Northern armies misbehaved energetically and often.

The Lowrys' dogged examination of the mountains of paper surviving from those court-martials has uncovered much of interest and importance in many realms. The courts reveal a great deal about mid-19th-century military matters, needless to say, but they also contain invaluable subtexts on subjects societal, political, racial, sexual, criminal, sectional, medical, and (perhaps most of all) dipsomaniacal: An astonishingly large segment of the Federalist soldiery evidently spent right much time in the fond embrace of Demon Rum. This book is constructed from the most striking of the court records dedicated to medical and surgical misbehavior.

Civil War books continue to spew from presses far and near, as though induced by an insidious publishing emetic. Amazingly few bother to indulge in anything so complex and challenging as original research, and not many more essay to cover new ground, even ineptly. *Tarnished Scalpels* flouts both of those unlovely tendencies by using exclusive manuscript material to shed entirely new light. Any book that achieves those two ends—on *any* Civil War topic—deserves the most perfervid sort of accolades. That the subject is interesting and the writing lively only serves to gild the lily and make this a splendid piece of work. Strike up the band—a big brass one—for the Lowry-Welsh collaboration.

Almost everyone who pays attention to the Civil War has come across the era's most daunting statistic, which goes something like this: More Americans died in uniform between 1861 and 1865 than in all of the nation's other wars combined, starting with the earliest Indian quarrels in 1607 and running up into the midst of the Vietnam War. That encompasses more than three and a half centuries of conflict including several worldwide wars, two World Wars, and decades of frontier strife. In the shadow of the 1860s' butcher bill of such horrendous proportions, medical services became of central importance to millions of Americans. Attention to that aspect of the war has been sparse. A handful of fine studies (including earlier work by coauthor Welsh) examine the medical establishments of the contending armies, but they mount up to only a tiny fraction of what the subject warrants. Although Drs. Lowry and Welsh have not undertaken a broad analysis of medical affairs, their tales amassed from primary sources surely broaden and enrich the body of available knowledge in that realm.

One of the best parts of *Tarnished Scalpels* is a thoughtfully conceived and skillfully drawn introduction that summarizes the state of medical knowledge, training, and practice in 1860. It is hard to exaggerate the degree to which each of those things stood in utter darkness by comparison to modern protocols. The authors then proceed to admonish readers—entirely aptly—to avoid feeling smug about *current* knowledge "with a wholly unearned sense of omniscience." The erudite doctors cite a number of medical discoveries that have recently shattered firmly held beliefs, and they remind us that men of every era have ample cause to look back with horror on the primitive superstitions of their ancestors. The soothing sense of superiority so often assumed by casual modern observers, over all manner of now-outmoded behavior patterns and long-dead people, constitutes intolerable intellectual arrogance. Lowry and Welsh offer a guideline that would serve well for Civil War study of any stripe: "In order to judge whether a doctor [substitute general, politician, author, thinker, social architect, ad infinitum] has failed to practice his art correctly, it is necessary to understand what he should have known, not by *our* standards but by his." Obeying that dictum would serve us all well, even if it would—especially *since* it would!—put a battalion of polemicists out of business.

Having said all of that, it must be admitted that the fifty surgeons cavorting under the operating-room light in this book hardly serve as a representative sample. Doctors with gaudy and outrageous transcripts make for far better copy than do those following the caduceus in more businesslike fashion. Their travails, however, provide clear evidence of the continuum of history upon which we all exist. The men examined in *Tarnished Scalpels* are familiar antecedents to modern Americans we know or know of. Some of them would fit comfortably in the current White House, under the present popular-culture notion of what makes an appropriate denizen of that once-august place. There is, as someone already has noted, nothing new under the sun.

Tarnished Scalpels serves as an admirable companion volume to Lowry's *Tarnished Eagles* (Stackpole, 1997). Together the two books yank the shroud from intensely human Civil War figures, seen heretofore through a glass darkly. The view thus unveiled is fascinating.

Robert K. Krick
Fredericksburg, Virginia
April 1999

INTRODUCTION

Jesus' reply to the wily Pharisees—"Render therefore unto Caesar the things which are Caesar's; and unto God the things which are God's"—shows with perfect clarity the concept of dual responsibilities. So, too, did the Civil War surgeon answer to two different authorities: the principles of medical tradition and the regulations of the army.

In the former realm, it was his duty to follow the customs and ethics of his profession, and his responsibility to maximize his skills in the diagnosis and treatment of wounds and sickness. In the latter arena—a world unfamiliar to most doctors—he was to learn and follow the Articles of War, the Regulations of the Army, and the customs of military life.

The court-martials of the fifty doctors presented here therefore fall into two general groups: failure to practice proper medicine and failure to follow the procedures and administrative rules that govern life in the army for all men, medical or not. (Since many doctors faced multiple charges, with multiple specifications, some overlap inevitably exists between the various groupings. The six sections into which the book is divided reflect the dominant themes of each court-martial.)

Let us consider medical issues first. In order to judge whether a doctor has failed to practice his art correctly, it is necessary to understand what he should have known, not by *our* standards but by his.

In all branches of military history, there is a temptation for the observer today—who may have read a dozen analyses of a long-ago battle and walked the field himself (without the annoying distractions of flying bullets, exploding shells, blinding smoke, screaming wounded, and disemboweled horses)—to feel smugly superior to old General Dunderhead, who should have kept his reserves at Point A, sent his cavalry to Point B, and anticipated the arrival of flanking enemy troops at Point C. In the elegant words of the scholar Bruce A. Evans, such thinking "puffs up the observer with a wholly unearned sense of omniscience." We should observe a similar degree of diffidence in understanding Civil War medicine.[1]

Our Civil War doctor did not think of bacteria because *no one* thought of bacteria. He did not strive for a sterile operating field because that concept would not arrive for another twenty years. For the same reasons, he did not x-ray his patients or order transfusions or examine their blood for parasites or prescribe antibiotics. We know of these things, but no one in 1861–1865 did.

And are we that much more clever today? Only a decade ago duodenal ulcers were "known" to be caused by "stress"; today the baleful effects of a microbe, *Helicobacter pylorii,* seems a more likely cause. Twenty years ago Alzheimer's disease was "caused" by cooking in aluminum kettles; now it seems that even Chlamydia might be the culprit. So, too, with obsessive-compulsive disorder: A generation ago it was caused by rigid toilet training and treated with psychoanalysis; today, it is related to overactive brain structures and is treated with certain antidepressants. With these recent examples of changing knowledge to lend us humility, we may proceed to examine what a Civil War doctor realistically could and should have known—and how he might have learned it.

Today the journey from high school to a Fellowship in the American College of Surgeons is a fifteen-year path, under intense scrutiny and regulated by many agencies. In 1861 medical school consisted of nine months of lectures. To graduate, the student attended the same lecture series for a second time. There was little or no practical clinical experience. After receiving his diploma, the young doctor with money would visit clinics and hospitals in Europe for a few months to complete his education. Those without the means to travel might apprentice themselves to local practitioners. Medical schools existed to make money; if they raised their entrance requirements or flunked out students, there was less profit, so the natural consequence was to admit anyone and graduate everyone.

Were there institutions outside of the medical schools that would assure some degree of quality? The answer is a resounding, "No!" Neither the patients nor the army could look to state licensure as a measure of quality. Since the members of the medical profession themselves rarely agreed on the principal points of medical theory and practice, there was no rational way to set standards, and the states had almost totally abandoned trying to regulate or license medical practice.

The lack of a clear theoretical basis for diagnosis and treatment gave rise to sects. The homeopaths believed that materials that duplicated the symptoms of a disease, when administered in extremely small doses, were curative of that disease; in that theory they were strongly supported by the well-known editor, Horace "Go West, young man" Greeley. The naturopaths relied upon herbal remedies, while the hydropaths utilized baths, enemas, and the consumption of various mineral waters to effect a cure.

Mainstream doctors in 1861 were dubbed allopaths and relied upon observations of diseased conditions. Some illnesses were associated with inflammation, increased blood flow, fever, rapid pulse, agitation, and excited delirium.

These were termed "sthenic" diseases. The opposite conditions, the so-called asthenic illnesses, were forms of depletion and exhibited torpor, decreased energy, wasting away, quiet delirium, and a slow, weak pulse.

These concepts of a duality of illnesses led, logically, to a system of treatment. Sthenic illnesses, which revealed an excess of tissue excitement, were treated with bleeding, powerful laxatives, and violent emetics all to remove the excess vitality. When this treatment for sthenic conditions proved too strenuous for the patient, less violent measures, such as cupping, mustard plasters, and vegetable diets, were used to draw the excess vitality away from the diseased area.

Conversely, the asthenic patients needed building up and were dosed with tonics, alcohol, and diets rich in animal products. As might be expected, this sthenic-asthenic balance could change as the patient's condition improved or worsened, and the physician was faced with a confusing set of choices. For example, should he employ digitalis to slow the pulse? Should he use a mercurial to restore the tongue to a normal appearance? (The color and coating of the tongue fascinated doctors in the 1860s.) Should he use a diuretic to improve a scanty flow of urine? Should he use a vegetable astringent to reduce fluid loss from membranes? These were the types of conceptualizations that occupied the best minds in medicine. From the vantage point of today's knowledge, we can see that the concepts of sthenia and asthenia were of little help in understanding the underlying pathophysiology of disease—and therefore the possibility of a rational approach to treatment.

What *was* certain in medical knowledge 140 years ago? Without invoking any hindsight, we today could reasonably expect a Civil War–era physician to know at least five things. The first was the prevention and cure of scurvy. In 1795 the Royal Navy, based upon decades of experience, mandated the use of lime juice to prevent scurvy. The life-and-death importance of fruits and vegetables in a soldier's diet was no secret.

The second certain area was malaria, usually called the Ague, or intermittent fever. The first cure of malaria by "Peruvian bark" was published in 1642. In 1861, summarizing over two centuries of experience, the U.S. Sanitary Commission, in a widely publicized communication, strongly recommended quinine sulfate, three to six grains (1 grain = 60 mg.) a day, as a *preventive* for malaria, and urged that the Secretary of War instruct the Surgeon General to place sufficient quinine in the hands of every surgeon.

A third area where there seemed little room for doubt was that of vaccination against smallpox. Edward Jenner had clarified its usage in the previous century, and George Washington himself had ordered vaccination for his troops in the American Revolution. Fifty years later, vaccination, too, should have been common knowledge among medical men and done universally.

Syphilis, as well, had a long history and a specific remedy—mercury—first recommended by Paracelsus in 1530. Three centuries later, even with all its toxic side effects, the salts of mercury remained the standard remedy for a disease that affected at least 80,000 Union soldiers.

Finally, there was the control of pain. Opium and its various derivatives had been in use for many centuries, probably many millennia. For the specific acute pain associated with surgery, two general anesthetics were usually available: chloroform and the less widely used ether. The uses of both had been widely publicized fifteen years before the war. While many doctors entering the army had little practical experience in the use of anesthetics, they soon had ample chance to gain such knowledge.

In the more mechanical aspects of medical work, such as operative surgery, nearly every doctor had studied anatomy—although few, if any, had been confronted with the necessity of amputating dozens of limbs in a single afternoon (or hundreds in the wearying days following the great battles). The inexperienced doctors soon found that there was more to amputation than just sawing through the bone: There were arteries to locate and tie; there was the creation of a flap that would heal smoothly; and there was the necessity of administering sufficient chloroform to numb the patient without killing him.

The Civil War was so vast and so prolonged that an attempt to simplify any aspect of it is likely to be disappointing. As an example, in the purely military realm, for every easy-to-understand organization like the 54th Pennsylvania Infantry, there was at least one or two idiosyncratic organizations, such as Paddy Graydon's Spy Company or the Mississippi Marine Brigade, each of which today would require a huge footnote of explanation.

So, too, with army surgeons. Most of the Union army were volunteer troops, organized by the individual states; most surgeon's commissions were issued by state governors. There were as many sets of standards as there were states. During the course of the war, some 12,000 Union doctors had served in the field or in hospitals. At least seven different categories of military doctors served the cause of the North:

1. Surgeons and Assistant Surgeons of the U.S. Army. Most of these men had long army experience and during the Civil War were assigned to administrative and staff positions.
2. Surgeons (and Assistant Surgeons) of U.S. Volunteers, a category created by Congress to augment the regular army men serving in staff positions.
3. Regimental Surgeons (and Assistant Surgeons) who were commissioned by the governors of the various states, not by the President of the United States. These state-appointed doctors formed the largest single category, totaling almost 6,000 men.
4. The so-called Contract Surgeons, with the title of Acting Assistant Surgeon, U.S. Army. They held no commission, but received the pay of a first lieutenant. There were 5,500 such men, who served mainly in the general hospitals in the north.

5. Medical officers of the Veterans Corps.
6. Acting Staff Surgeons.
7. Surgeons (and Assistant Surgeons) of U.S. Colored Troops, who were commissioned by the President.[2]

In addition to these seven categories, there were the "civilian volunteers," men who flocked briefly to a battle site for the opportunity to hone their surgical skills. Many were appointed by regimental commanders; some just got off the train and announced their presence. In 1862 their work did as much harm as good, but under a revised scheme of organization, they proved their worth in the campaigns of 1864 and 1865.

The subject of examinations for prospective army surgeons is a complex one. A five-hour examination was required for men aspiring to a Federal commission in the medical corps, but many states required no examination at all. Some authorities placed great reliance upon book knowledge, while others thought that "practical" experience was more relevant. The medical officer files at the National Archives contain many examples of such examinations. Most of the questions relate directly to medical practice, although some examinations had general-knowledge questions, such as naming the royal families of Europe.

Many different written examinations were administered to surgeons applying for appointment, commissioning, or promotion. Their formats changed as the war progressed and were different for the various levels of responsibility. A complete study of the questions, and an analysis of the responses, would require a separate book, so it should be clear that this a random sampling. In some of the cases presented here, only the answers appear in the doctor's file; however, it was not hard to recreate the questions.

The level of difficulty in these examinations may cause some readers to see Civil War surgeons in a more positive light and have greater respect for the "primitive" medicine that they practiced. One can only speculate about the purpose of the general knowledge and historic questions.

William F. Hutchinson had served with the 22nd New York Infantry and sat for the examination for Assistant Surgeon, U.S. Volunteers. Here are a few of the questions he was to answer:

> Describe the surgical anatomy of the parts involved in the operation of tracheotomy. Describe the various fractures which may affect the femur, the appearances presented, and the proper treatment of each variety. Suppose a musket ball [was] to enter the forearm, shattering the head of the radius, splintering the ulna, and opening the joint. Would you amputate or resect? Give the reasoning that would influence your decision in either event. What is meant by cataract? Describe the different varieties of the disease, and the various operations for its relief. Describe the operation for the removal of the superior maxillary bone of the left side; give the after treatment, in detail.

Describe the anatomy of the heart, including muscles, chambers, arteries, valves, and surrounding structures. Describe the pattern of cardiac circulation. Give the cause and treatment of secondary hemorrhage in previously operated wounds. Describe the [body's] reaction to vaccination, and the value of this procedure. [Hutchinson's response included a note that he had vaccinated 780 men.]

N. S. Drake had served with the 16th New York Cavalry and wished promotion to Assistant Surgeon, U. S. Army. He was confronted with these questions:

Describe the superficial and deep palmar arches of the hand. Describe the essential points in ligating the common carotid artery. Give the origin, action, and insertion of the Bicep Flexor Cruris Muscle. Describe the anatomy and function of the spleen. Describe the path and branches of the Great Sciatic Nerve. Give the anatomy and function of the Sterno Cleido Mastoid Muscle. Give a brief history of the reign of King Henry IV of France. Describe the origin and use of artesian wells. What is a Lymphatic Temperament? Which nationalities are most prone to suffer from Nostalgia? How many cubic feet of space should be provided for each hospital patient? What are the physical and mental effects of extreme cold? Give the pathology and differential diagnosis of pericarditis. Distinguish between typhoid fever and typhus. Define and discuss rubeola. Describe the pathology and symptoms of Bright's disease. Contrast the healing processes of incised wounds and gunshot wounds. Describe the diagnoses and treatments of fractures of the fibula.

Alonza Eisenlord of the 7th New York Infantry presented himself for the examination to be an Assistant Surgeon of U.S. Volunteers. Here are a few of the questions he faced:

Give the history of the union of Scotland with England. What were the causes of the American Revolution? Describe the different types of clouds and how they predict weather changes. What are the effects of temperature and humidity on disease? How does one select a location for a hospital tent? Describe the pathological effects of overeating. What are the clinical signs for diagnosing pulmonary tuberculosis and how may it be treated? Give the same for diphtheria. And for rupia. Describe the superficial musculature of the forearm. Describe the diagnosis and treatment of a fracture of the coracoid process of the scapula. Describe the points to be considered in treatment of a gunshot wound of the bladder.

Dr. A. C. Benedict of the 1st New York Regiment of Infantry ran into difficulty with his first question: how to treat remittent fever (malaria). He suggested mercury, when quinine would have been a more likely answer. However, he did better with the three layers of meninges surrounding the brain, the symptoms of chronic alcoholism, and the multiple branchings of the brachial artery.

Many states did not administer a written examination to applicants for appointment as a surgeon; one of the states requiring an examination was Illinois, which asked the applicant 113 questions, including the following:

> How can you tell smallpox from measles? What do you do in a case of poisoning by arsenic? What is the dose of chloral? How many kinds of Peruvian Bark are used in this country? How would you prepare Dovers Powders? Are the diseases most prevalent in Illinois sthenic or asthenic in character? What are the dangers to the mother in a breech presentation? What is the length of the longest diameter of the superior strait? Give symptoms and treatment of morbus coxarius. Where are the glands of Meibomius, and what is their function?

The remaining 102 questions were of equal difficulty. Considering the brevity of formal medical training in 1861–1865, it is a tribute to the absorptive qualities of the human mind that so many doctors successfully answered such questions as these.

Although this book focuses on doctors who ran afoul of the system, it should be noted that at the close of 1861, the Sanitary Commission, based on its inspections of many medical facilities, rated 64 percent of the doctors as having "discharged their duties with creditable energy and earnestness." A mere 2 percent were rated as out-and-out "incompetent," while the remainder fell in an intermediary category. In brief, two-thirds of doctors performed well by the standards of the day. Given the enormous disruption inherent in mobilizing a peacetime, largely rural population to fight a modern, industrial war across a whole continent, the two-thirds figure most likely reflects a high level of dedication in the physicians who flocked to the Union cause.[3]

When they arrived to perform that duty, they met a challenge for which their medical training could not have prepared them: doing things the army way. And not just any army but one officered almost entirely by men with as little military experience as the doctors. The difference was that the doctors knew something about doctoring, while in general the volunteer officers knew nothing about officering. Thus, it was the blind leading the myopic.

The line officers, as students of the war have long known, soon sorted themselves into two groups: one composed of men willing and able to learn their new craft, and another group composed of political opportunists, bullies, cowards, drunks, and the merely stupid. A gradual weeding process removed the latter, while death in battle tended to reduce the ranks of the brave and the competent. Newly appointed officers knew little of military rules and regulations, but the doctors seem to have known even less. This brings us to the second set of categories for which doctors were court-martialed: purely military or administrative offenses, as opposed to those based upon shortcomings in medical performance.

The first set of guidelines for military life were the 101 sections of the Articles of War. Many of these rules, such as those mandating good behavior in church, did not have a direct bearing on the doctors' duties. Articles 83 and 99 were ones often invoked in the trials of surgeons. The former, "conduct unbecoming an officer and a gentleman," and the latter, "conduct prejudicial to good order and military discipline," were "all-purpose" provisions and could be used to describe a wide variety of offenses. Article 39 stated that any officer guilty of embezzlement should refund the money and be cashiered (dishonorably discharged), while Article 42 stated that no officer may sleep out of camp without permission. Officers drunk on duty would also be cashiered (Article 45), though those guilty of fraud would not only be dismissed but have the crime published in the offender's hometown newspaper, this latter punishment being described in lurid detail in Article 85. Thus the fledgling army surgeon was admonished to avoid a great number of obvious crimes; but the Articles of War afforded him precious little guidance as to what he was *supposed* to do, just what *not* to do.

The Regulations of the Army were another potential source of guidance for the fledgling military surgeon. However, a perusal of the 455 pages of text and 22 pages of index of the 1861 printing shows only 41 pages devoted to medical matters—and 30 of those pages are sample forms for the guidance of those submitting reports and requisitions! In the remaining 11 pages we learn a number of things of doubtful utility, such as: "The senior medical officer of each post will on June 30 make requisition for supplies for the coming year, if stationed on the upper lakes, upper Mississippi River, or west of the Mississippi River. All other posts will submit their requisitions on September 30." We also learn that after an Assistant Surgeon had served for five years that he must take the promotional examination for Surgeon. If he failed, he left the service. These same 11 pages detail the number of beds, books, saws, scalpels, kettles, and so forth to be issued to each post. Frequent reference is made to economy and frugality. It is clear that these guidelines were meant for a penurious time, an era of small forts and isolated posts, scattered across a vast land, an army that saw little action. Even a cursory reading shows an enormous chasm between what the Medical Corps was ready for in 1861 and what was to be the actual whirlwind, the cataclysm of biblical proportions, the rain of fire and death, that swept the country in the succeeding four years. And it was certainly no guide to a new doctor first entering the service.[4]

A few texts were prepared specifically for the use of Civil War medical men. Surgeon General William Hammond, whose own career was cut short by a highly political court-martial, had written a text on military hygiene and sanitation, and coauthored a manual for hospital stewards, but neither provided the guidance needed by a neophyte army doctor about the army itself.

Late in the war, several books appeared that were intended to aid this medical audience. Charles A. Greenleaf's *A Manual for Medical Officers of the U.S. Army* is concerned mainly with administrative matters that would be relevant to a medical director: pages of forms to be filed in triplicate. A doctor following the author's guidance would have no time to see patients. William Grace's *The Army Surgeon's Manual* contains reprints of the army and medical department regulations and pages of general orders, but it was hardly the practical, down-to-earth book that a beginner needed. There were many different books on the technical aspects of medicine—hygiene, orthopedics, recruit examination, and gunshot wounds—but nothing that would have been much help to our fifty doctors. Useful as a book entitled *The Essential Things to Know While Serving as a Doctor in the Union Army* might have been for 12,000 doctors, it simply did not exist.

As an example of the manifold subjects whose clarification might have prevented many court-martials was that of food. The crucial issue here was not one of nutrition but the administrative source of the food and how it was paid for. Doctors were officers. In the Civil War, as in today's army, the enlisted man had his food provided by the federal government; he did not, and still does not, pay for his meals. Quite the opposite was true for officers—they were responsible for the costs of their food. The origins of this dichotomy lay in the past. The officers' mess (a word that may mean a specific building or merely an association of men) was where gentlemen gathered to eat, drink, smoke, and associate with their social equals. They often had in common the same schools (West Point, Sandhurst, St. Cyr) and some degree of literacy. They usually owned their own horses and brought their own servants. Their uniforms were often the products of the finest tailors.

Enlisted men—at least in Europe—were recruited from the lower ranks of society, could not read or write, and had few privileges, but they were entitled to be fed at government expense, even if it was only hardtack. Officers were to see to their own food supply, not just because it was assumed that they might be more particular in their choice of cuisine, but also for the practical reason that they were paid more. (War in America was unique: Many privates were as well educated as officers—and were their former neighbors, as well.)

At a fixed base, such as a long-established post, the surgeon ate with the other officers and contributed to a mess fund. The enlisted men had their separate "chow hall" (to use a post–Civil War term), or if they were in a hospital, they were fed from the hospital kitchen. But on the march life was different. In a countryside that may have been pillaged by troops of both sides—as well as bushwhackers, bummers, and refugees—there might be no food to buy. If the doctor (or any officer) ate food intended for the enlisted men or the hospital patients, he was guilty of a crime. Such infractions ranged from clear abuse, where the doctors ate the "luxury foods" (such as fresh vegetables, chicken, milk, and butter) and left the remains for the enlisted men, to much more benign situations, where the surgeon in question had used his own money to buy food for his nurses and patients, which he then shared with them. However, in both cases he could be indicted for "messing with enlisted men." Here, too, both the Articles of War and Regulations of the Army are silent regarding enlisted men and officers sharing a table or a food supply.

The customs of the army depended on an oral tradition, a learning by experience, but a vast citizen army raised almost overnight had no collective memory—and therefore no way to inform itself. This ignorance was the basis of several court-martials, as will be seen in the section of the book devoted to the misuse of food and money.

The problem of doctors and food was equally vexatious in the huge hospitals, both Union and Confederate, when it came to feeding the night staff. (A clothing store can close at night, and no harm is done; but emergency services, such as police stations, fire departments, and hospitals, can never close, and therefore must have one or more night shifts: "swing," "graveyard," and so forth.) The needs of the sick were no less during the Civil War, and the hours of darkness were tended then, as now, by certain hospital staff. An ongoing survey of Confederate records by one author (J.D.W.) has revealed an attempt to solve the twin problems of night staffing and night feeding of medical staff. The writer of this Confederate directive correctly anticipated that whether or not the doctor paid his way, he would be *suspected* of stealing and eating the rations of the sick, especially the better foods. The following order and directive was issued February 9, 1863, by Dr. E. A. Flewellen, Medical Director of the Army of Tennessee.

> The sleeping of a sufficient number of medical officers in or about the relative hospitals to which they are attached is regarded as a matter demanded by the interest of the service and necessary, provision therefor should be made, even should it require the construction of rude shanties for cooking and messing purposes, but they [the doctors] should provide their own mess and purchase their own supplies.
>
> In some Hospitals, Medical Officers have boarded; paying the commutative price of rations. To this I cannot consent[,] for should they not consume an under proportion of the luxuries and better articles of diet[,] they cannot avoid such an interpretation on the part of the patients and the public[;] it would be sure to give rise to complaints and great dissatisfaction, and might culminate in serious disturbance."[5]

Flewellen's directive conjures up visions of the doctors of the Army of Tennessee, huddled near their "rude shanties" in the chilly winter of 1862–1863, trying to solve the problems of shopping for food in a damaged economy. The customs of the times dictated that a Negro be hired as a cook, and it seems likely that the doctors muttered things like "You can't find good help these days," as they turned up their collars against the wintry blasts and waited for dinner to be served.

Since the men who headed the Confederate army and its medical corps were alumni of the same schools as their Union counterparts, it is not surprising that the rules and regulations, forms and procedures were almost identical in the two armies. Officers and food remained a contentious issue to the end of the war, and neither the North nor the South seems to have found a workable solution to the problem.

The "hospital fund" was a frequent source of mystification, especially for the volunteer surgeon. This may be because the "fund" was based upon an assumption so wrong, so cruel, and so unworkable as to render nearly senseless any physician not immersed in years of experience with the old army, with its penny-wise and pound-foolish economies, partly a product of half-senile peevishness and partly the residue of a niggardly Congress.

This startling "fund" assumption was that a sick or wounded man needed less nourishment than a well man on active duty. Since less food was issued to a hospitalized soldier, the surgeon was expected to render an exact accounting of the money "saved." An early attempt to clarify this issue is seen in the testimony of the regimental quartermaster at the trial of Dr. Boemer: "The hospital fund is formed as follows: the hospital rations are commuted at 13 cents and the difference between the 13 cents, and the 30 cents regularly allowed, forms the hospital fund." The two court-martials of Assistant Surgeon Nelson Isham of the 97th New York both focused on his illegal eating of hospital rations. In the course of one of Isham's trials, a witness gave this clarification: "We did not draw full rations for the sick. We drew only what we supposed we would need. The difference remained as hospital fund, in the hands of the commissary. We drew on it [the fund] for articles purchased of the sutler, delicacies for the sick, such as milk and chicken."

George W. Adams's classic *Doctors in Blue* notes, "It was supposed that a sick man ate less than his normal ration, and the surgeon was expected to keep account of the difference. This provided a fund which could be used to buy delicacies, when obtainable." The final word may be a key. If "delicacies" were not obtainable, this could mean that the sick soldier received much less food than the well soldier.[6]

Consider the patient, sick on his straw mattress, weak with blood loss and/or diarrhea. His almost unchewable hardtack is reduced below the starvation level. What salt pork he gets is mostly fat, cooked over a fire, and nearly indigestible. His coffee ration is cut—a horror not just because of the loss of a cheering stimulant, but because coffee was boiled, which killed the dysentery bacteria found in most water supplies. What the Civil War establishment called "delicacies," with the implication of sybaritic luxury, were the building blocks for recuperating tissue: protein and vitamins. One might think that the dried vegetables developed during the war would have provided some fraction of the B vitamins needed every day, but a memo found in the medical officer file of Anthony E. Stocker states: "Portable Soup [a dehydrated concoction] is to only be given to patients in battle." While this statement contains at least one internal contradiction, it certainly suggests that the wounded man convalescing over many months would be unlikely to receive such a item of luxury as "Portable Soup."

Even the liberal and beneficent Sanitary Commission seemed convinced that the Union soldier was overfed. In their *Rules for Preserving the Health of the Soldier*, published July 12, 1861, we see: "The articles of food composing the rations issued by the United State Commissary Department have been proved, by sound experience, to be those best calculated for the food of the soldier. The amount allowed for each man is greater in quantity than the similar allowances for any European soldier. If he understands his duties and manages well, any commissary of subsistence can save from 15 to 30 percent, out of the rations furnished by the Government, and with the money thus saved, fresh vegetables, butter, milk, &c., may be procured."[7] In fairness, it should be noted that the report was issued before the movement of huge armies in the field and the attendant supply problems; one looks in vain in Civil War photographs for chubby infantrymen.

Returning to the somewhat incoherent testimony in Boemer's trial, it would appear that the government spent 30¢ a day to feed a man when he was well and 13¢ a day after he was wounded. The 17¢ difference (the surgeon was supposed to be a bookkeeper, as well) was to be used to buy nourishing items *if they could be found*. The sutler, who could supply only what his wagon could carry—and those items at a high price—was one potential supplier. Another was the Southern farmer's wife. Her husband was usually absent or dead. Each army passing through had bought or stolen any surplus crop plus much of what she and her children had hidden to keep death away. Neither the farm wife nor the sutler (much less the mythical prudent commissary of subsistence, with his butter and milk) could reasonably be seen as a source of nutrition for the thousands of sick and wounded that filled every hospital.

One additional possible source of food for patients was the multitude of private benevolent associations, usually organized on a community or regimental basis, with names like the Lancaster Lancers Ladies Association, which would send by express, boxes of "delicacies," such as preserved meat, canned fruit, cheese, and wine. While these efforts were well intended and often successful, spoilage, and the difficulties of private shipments in a war zone, made them unreliable sources of consistent nutrition.

Surgeon General William Hammond, in Circular Number 3, dated January 30, 1863, reported on studies of the hospital fund at "well-regulated hospitals, as to the capacity of the hospital fund to support a proper diet table for the sick." The results were unanimous: "[T]he cost of supplying such a diet exceeds the value of the hospital ration."

However, even a reformer like Hammond did not suggest ending the tradition of the hospital fund and merely ordered that it be used entirely for food and food preparation, and not diverted to other uses.

The hospital fund concept seems to have had its origin in the prewar fixed army base, with a viable civilian economy in the surrounding countryside. The surgeon who administered such funds had often been at the same post for years and had the time to keep account books. The hospital fund was something uniquely unsuited to the vast mobile armies that swept from Pennsylvania to Texas. Keeping the hospital fund concept in place surely ranks as one of the most boneheaded, numskulled, dimwitted decisions in a war richly supplied with such administrative brilliance.

These fifty stories of doctors shed light upon many aspects of life in the 1860s: the state of medical knowledge, the hardships of warfare, the wide range of human character, and the difficulty of making 2 million individualists into a coherent military machine.

The records of the Civil War are so vast, their organization so complex, that no one person can read or comprehend more than a fraction of them—much less write all there is to say about even that fraction. Every Civil War story is a small part of a larger picture, like the individual stones in a mosaic: Viewed one by one, they may seem to be only brightly colored bits of glass or tile, but put in their proper places, and viewed from a greater distance, they suddenly blend into a pattern, and a picture emerges where before there had been only random chips and glints of light. So, too, with our fifty doctors. Each story may have its own unique merit, but taken as a whole, these trials and tribulations can inform us more broadly of the human condition in 1861–1865; give us once again the sights, sounds, and smells of the debris of battle; and show us once more the swathes of sick, cut down by the invisible scythes wielded by enemies that lurked in the fetid water and the swampy air.

These stories can further tell us that some doctors, men of bad character, would sacrifice their patients' welfare for personal benefit, while others, made of better stuff, would go far out of their way to help the sick and wounded. These court-martial records show us men groping in a fog of ignorance and frustration, the last generation of physicians who had to function without the basic knowledge of physiology and disease now familiar to every high-school biology student.

The great majority of Civil War surgeons did their duty. Even those who fell short raise the question: Could we, with the same challenges and the same limited knowledge, have done better?

In our own reading of these cases, we have come to have a deeper and richer understanding of the complexities of that enormous convulsion that shook our nation five generations ago and brought us to sense an increased empathy with our distant colleagues as they struggled to serve both the medical and the procedural needs of their country. Even those who failed to meet this dual challenge can be torches in the dark corridors of history, bringing us further along the seemingly endless path that leads to complete understanding of the Civil War.

PART ONE

Care of Patients

Chapter One

Eben Jackson

As New Years Day 1865 dawned, the South had only one major port still open to receive its life-preserving blockade runners: Wilmington, North Carolina. The chief protection for the harbor entrance was Fort Fisher, with its fifty heavy guns and 1,500-man garrison—a fort so crucial that Robert E. Lee himself had said it had to be held at all costs.

After several unsuccessful tries, a joint operation headed by Adm. David D. Porter and Maj. Gen. Alfred H. Terry crushed the defenders, and Fort Fisher fell on January 15, 1865. Among the troops under Terry's command were the 30th Regiment of U.S. Colored Troops (USCT).

Four days after the victory, a reconnaissance party of the Union Sharpshooters Battalion (3rd Division, 25th Army Corps) was on night patrol, and one of its members was shot in the chest. (The records do not tell how he was wounded.) Through a dark and stormy night Maj. Philip Weinman and his men carried their bleeding comrade to the camp of the nearest Union regiment, which was the 30th USCT. After ordering his men to put the wounded sharpshooter on the ground, Weinman walked through the dark and found the tent of Dr. Eben Jackson. It was now close to midnight.[1]

Weinman asked Jackson to treat the wounded man; Jackson said, "Send the man to the hospital." This was the basis for the charges filed a few days later by Weinman—that Jackson was guilty of "inhumanly and utterly neglecting his duty, by positively refusing to attend a wounded man." The trial, held at Federal Point, South Carolina, within sight of the shattered remains of Fort Fisher, was presided over by Bvt. Brig. Gen. A. M. Blackman. Here, the many versions of the same story were revealed.

Major Weinman testified first. "I thought that the wounded man would die, although he did survive. Dr. Jackson was the first surgeon that I could find, and when I arrived, he was doing sick call. [At midnight?] The doctor did not even inquire about the nature of the wound, but simply told me to take the

At Fort Fisher, North Carolina, Dr. Eben Jackson (far left, seated) was accused of "inhumanely neglecting" a man shot in the chest. Was Jackson's explanation sufficient?
MASSACHUSETTS COMMANDERY, MILITARY ORDER OF THE LOYAL LEGION, USAMHI

man to the hospital. He did not even tell me how to find the hospital. The wounded man was only 400 yards from the doctor's tent."

Two officers of the 30th USCT testified. Lt. Col. H. A. Oakman described Dr. Jackson as "an energetic and prompt officer." He recalled that the doctor had told Weinman exactly where to find the hospital, which was in the nearest house. Col. J. W. Ames praised Jackson, noting that "on the expedition to Wilmington, on the steamer *General Lyon,* the doctor was attentive to his duties." Ames did recall, however, that Surgeon Jackson had said of the wounded man that night, "I don't want him in my camp."

The defendant then gave his version of the story. "I was already in bed when Major Weinman arrived and asked my help. It would have been an injustice to the wounded man to lie in the rain and mud at 11:00 P.M. while I dressed and found my hospital steward to dress the wounds, when the wounded man was so near the hospital. God knows this is the first time in three years that I have even been reprimanded. I could not operate in the dark, in the rain. It would have been foolish to try." He concluded, "If there is an error, it is of the head, not the heart. I feel that you will do me justice and that the honorable name I have tried to establish will not be blasted."

The court was unsympathetic to this plea and sentenced Dr. Jackson "to be dismissed [from] the service of the United States." Colonel Ames recommended mitigation, and the reviewing officer, Maj. Gen. John M. Schofield, concurred. The final outcome: Jackson was "reprimanded for want of professional pride and care for the well-being of the wounded." He was released from arrest and returned to duty.

General Terry's comments on the court-martial, written at Fort Fisher a day later, were more in Jackson's favor: "Respectfully forwarded with the suggestion that the testimony in the case proves neither inhumanity nor neglect of duty. It cannot be considered the duty of a regimental surgeon to attend to the sick and wounded of all the regiments of the division in which he is serving, unless he is specially ordered to do so. Nor is it inhuman to direct that a man shall be sent to a neighboring hospital instead of attending to him in bivouac."

These words do not seem to have soothed Jackson's feelings. On February 14, 1865, he submitted his resignation, citing "pecuniary embarrassments at my home, which involve the interest and comfort of my family." His request passed upward through channels and received these comments: Lieutenant Colonel Oakman noted, "Approved—believing it to be for the benefit of the Service," while Colonel Ames merely said, "Approved." Brig. Gen. Charles J. Paine added, "I know little of this officer. From inquiries, I think the interests of the Service will be advanced by his resignation." General Terry seems to have struck a more sympathetic note. He recalled the court-martial records and stated, "The sentence in the case appears to me utterly unsupported by the testimony. I respectfully recommend that his resignation be approved." Jackson was honorably discharged the following month.

What was Jackson's past record, and what did his future hold? He received his M.D. from Castleton College in 1856. He had been mustered into the 17th Wisconsin in July 1862 as assistant surgeon and spent November and December of that year on detached service at Holly Springs, Mississippi, and April of 1863 in similar service at Providence, Louisiana. In July 1863 he resigned his commission, citing conflict with the surgeon of the regiment, sickness from the tropical climate at Vicksburg, and business problems in Wisconsin. Seven months later, in Baltimore, Maryland, he was mustered into the 30th U.S. Colored Troops as surgeon, with the rank of major. He was thirty-nine.

Federal records tell us little of his postwar life until 1891, when he applied for a pension on grounds of inguinal hernia and senile debility. The examiner noted that Jackson was 5'4", with blue eyes and light complexion, plus a prominent hernia. Jackson received twelve dollars a month until his death in 1898, at Somerville, Massachusetts.

><+>+O+<+><

COMMENT: The overt problem leading to court-martial is one of "triage"— where and when to treat a wounded man with the facilities available at that place. Treating a gunshot wound of the chest at night in the rain, without light, equipment, or anesthesia, would have indeed seemed foolish when a building, presumably with these facilities, was only a few hundred yard away. In this case the "line" officer's opinion prevailed over that of the medical officer. Was this undue interference in the doctor's province or a valid criticism of the doctor's priorities? Perhaps Jackson was exhausted and irritable from treating the wounded of a great battle only four days earlier, or maybe his resignation from both his regiments reflects an undue touchiness. Lieutenant Colonel Oakman, who knew him well, believed that Jackson's departure would be "for the benefit of the service." And that is as much as we will ever know.

Chapter Two

George A. Spies

Barely three weeks after they were mustered in, the men of the 47th Ohio saw their first blood—at the battle of Carnifex Ferry, fought on the steep hills above the Kanawha River, in what is today Fayette County, West Virginia. Three months later they moved upriver to Gauley Bridge and stayed there until April 1862.

In February 1862 it was not Confederate bullets that laid low the men of the 47th Ohio; their sickness and death was placed at the door of the regimental surgeon, the charge being "conduct prejudicial to good order and military discipline." The first specification read, "George A. Spies, Surgeon, 47th Regiment Ohio Volunteer Infantry, did, on or about the fifth day of February, A.D. 1862, at the hospital of the said 47th Regiment, located at Camp Gauley Mount, County of Fayette, State of [West] Virginia, neglect to treat Private Samuel A. Gordon, of Company K, 47th Regiment of Ohio Volunteer Infantry, then and there confined by disease in said hospital, from which neglect the said Samuel A. Gordon, became filthy and lousy [i.e., covered with lice], and the said Samuel A. Gordon did, on the eighth day of February, A.D. 1862, die." Almost identical words charged similar neglect in the deaths of Pvt. William Hammer (Company K), Fifer Anthony Miller (Company D), and Pvt. Cautious Sturtevant (Company E).[1]

Dr. Spies was also charged with having allowed the regimental hospital to become "filthy and lousy," which impaired "Private Samuel A. Gordon and diverse others" in their recovery, and that Spies also failed in his duty to keep the hospital "properly cleaned and purified." Only one witness appeared, Acting Hospital Steward Daniel Sykes, who "had studied medicine before he came out to Virginia." He had much to say.

> I have been hospital steward since October 9, 1861, and am familiar with the treatment of the soldiers. Private Gordon was well treated. The hospital was kept as clean as possible under the circumstances.

The condition of the hospital was in good order, in some respects. We kept the floors and beds clean, but the patients were not clean. All the time that Gordon was there, he did not have his clothes changed. I don't remember how long he was in the hospital. The hospital had a few sheets and pillows and ticks [mattress sacks], but there were not any shirts. The surgeon ordered me not to change the patient's clothes. [There were none to replace the clothes in which they arrived.] I don't know whether Gordon was lousy or not, but when men came in lousy, they were left so, since we had no medicine to take off the lice.

The hospital consists of three log houses. I worked at the hospital and gave out medicine. We generally had washing done for the sick. I think the doctor paid all the attention he could, and I heard no complaints on the part of the sick as to their condition.

Sykes was now cross-examined by the defendant: "How often did I visit the hospital and how often did I prescribe for the patients? Did I order their diet? Did I order you to write it down and make out a diet table? Did I not always order that the hospital be kept clean? Did you not go to the sutler's to get empty cigar boxes for the men to spit in?" Sykes responded that the doctor usually visited the hospital twice a day, sometimes more often, and when the cases were bad, Spies made three visits a day. He agreed that Dr. Spies prescribed for the patients, ordered their diet, and ordered the hospital steward to write down the diet and make out a diet table. "You never used to speak about keeping the hospital clean, but I always understood that it was your wish that it be clean." He agreed with the doctor that he had gone to the sutler to get some cigar boxes for the patients to spit in. He recalled that the only flaw in nursing care was that the bedpan was not always taken out after a "passage" [bowel movement] because of the "carelessness of the attendants."

In response to further questions, Sykes recalled that many patients showed up with only the clothes they were wearing and that the mattress sacks were not washed after the patient recovered. When queried about how long patients lived after being admitted to the hospital, Sykes told the Court that "William Hammer was in the hospital four days and died; Anthony Miller was admitted on the ninth of February and died on the 26th and Cautious Sturtevant was admitted on the 28th of February and died on the 14th of March."

The court found Dr. Spies not guilty of all the charges and did "therefore honorably acquit him." They also made a finding that the charges and specifications "in this case were malicious and unfounded." Spies resigned his commission as soon as the trial ended.

More than most Civil War veterans, Dr. Spies is absent from the records: no pension application, no medical officer file, no mention in compilations of physician obituaries.

⊱─┼─◈─◦─O─◦─◈┼─⊰

COMMENT: The thirty-eight-year-old surgeon was probably not feeling very well himself in February 1862. A letter from surgeon Augustus Hoeltze of Spies's own regiment described "a left scrotal hernia from a fall with a horse on the road to Carnifex Ferry, September 14th, 1861."

The testimony of Acting Hospital Steward Sykes tells us much about life in 1862. A hospital was not a shining brick-and-glass edifice but instead a tree, a tent, a barn, or an old farmhouse. The men were crawling with lice. There were no clean clothes. (The army seemed to expect that the regimental surgeon had both the power and the facilities to establish a laundry.) The beds were stuffed with straw—if any could be found. The sacks that held the straw were not washed between patients. Since most wounded men drained pus and most sick men had uncontrolled diarrhea, the condition of these mattress sacks, and the straw inside them, can well be imagined. (True history is not for the sqeamish.)

The defendant was pleased to tell the court that old cigar boxes were supplied as spittoons. Were the men spitting tobacco juice—or tuberculosis residue or the infectious mucus of pneumonia or bronchitis? Whatever was being expectorated, the man with a cigar box was getting better and more elegant nursing care than the man who spat on the floor.

Today, if a doctor or a nurse needs to wash, there is hot water in the tap and soap in the dispenser. Dirty linen is taken away in color-coded sacks, sterilized, washed, and returned. Autoclaves churn out packs of sterile instruments. Jars of disposable needles and scalpels are everywhere. For such luxury, such sanitation, the Civil War doctor, north or south, no matter how well supplied and trained, might well have been on Mars.

To paraphrase Gilbert and Sullivan, "Taking one consideration with another, a surgeon's life is not a happy one."

Chapter Three

Luther G. Thomas

The Japanese movie *Rashomon* tells the same story through the eyes of several different witnesses—and lets the audience decide what is "truth." The trial of Dr. Luther Thomas has parallels: The court, the commanding general, the president—even the authors—have their conclusions. The reader may have yet a different one.

The 26th New Jersey Infantry was a nine-month regiment that saw a lot of battles in three-quarters of a year: twice at Fredericksburg, once at Chancellorsville, four days in the infamous Mud March, and skirmishes elsewhere. Their surgeon was a Princeton man who went on to the College of Physicians and Surgeons in New York, where he received his M.D. in 1852. Ten years of practice puts most doctors at the peak of their careers; with Thomas, it found him facing a court-martial.[1]

The scene of his alleged misdeeds was White Oak Church, Virginia. (The church can still be seen today, on Route 218, six miles east of Fredericksburg.) The time was December 13 through 15, 1862—days that exactly coincided with the first battle of Fredericksburg. Thomas was charged with being drunk on duty; with telling a hospital steward, "I don't give a damn for the sick anyway"; with ordering sick men to join their regiments when they were too weak to march; with telling a patient, "You are no more sick than the Devil is"; and with failing to provide his patients with food, medicine, shelter, and medical attention, all at the hospital of the 2nd Division at White Oak Church. Now begins the parade of witnesses, with many a contradictory story.

Lt. Anthony Davis of the 7th Massachusetts said: "Dr. Thomas appeared as if he had been taking ardent spirits. He could not sit his horse without reeling. He rode a short distance and then fell off, then he got on again and rode off. He couldn't talk straight. I don't think that six hours afterwards he would know what he had done." Capt. H. B. Masters, Commissary of Subsistence, 3rd Brigade, 3rd Division, VI Corps, said, "Our commissary stores were within 100 yards of White Oak Church, and we had enough food to feed 100 men."

At White Oak Church, Dr. Thomas was asked to care for more than 300 patients without food, medicine, blankets, mattresses, or heat. This photo, taken later, shows a United States Christian Commission sign above the door. Library of Congress

This 1999 photograph of the southeast wall shows that, except for a good coat of paint, White Oak Church has changed little in 138 years. Author's Photo

S. J. Allen, surgeon of the 4th Vermont, and medical director of the 2nd Division, told the court, "Dr. Thomas reported for duty on the afternoon of December the 10th. I ordered him to establish a hospital at White Oak Church. On December 18th, I ordered him and all the surgeons of the division to select the men [patients] who were able to do duty, and send them across the river to their regiments. [Note: This would put these barely convalescent men on the south bank of the Rappahannock, from whence the Union Army had withdrawn its troops after a disastrous defeat. Clearly there is some confusion.] Dr. Thomas told me that he was short of medicines and food for the sick. I told him to get them from someone else. The commissary of the 2nd Brigade was within 100 rods. At no time did I think he was intoxicated."

Capt. James McNair of the 33rd New York gave his recollections of hospital conditions at White Oak Church:

> I was in the vicinity from the 10th of December to the 24th, looking after boys in my regiment. [It is probable that McNair was also a patient.] When I went there at midnight on the 10th, there was no accommodation; a third of the men lay by the road until morning. The next morning, I went to a private house across the road and remained some two weeks. After being there about five days, I visited the hospital every day. The morning of the 15th, it was bitter cold. Our boys were two or three under a single blanket, shivering. One said that he was dying, so I moved him into my place across the street.
>
> I found a sutler and got bread for our regiment. Those who could walk came to me for it; the others crawled and offered me any amount of money for it, saying they were starving. Some who found no room in the hospital went into the woods and built bough houses; one from our regiment died there. I went to Dr. Oliver, but he was out of every medicine except for opium for three days. The lady of the house fed fifty men for two days. The 6th Maine had a regimental cook who was very attentive, and they fared better.
>
> Four men froze to death for want of shelter. I'd seen them the night before in the church; they all had the typhoid fever. I went over the next morning and found two of them dead. There was no fire, and it was so cold I could only stay five minutes. Both the church and the barn were full, which is why the bough shelters. I think the night they froze to death was the 16th of December.
>
> Dr. Thomas afforded me all the facilities at his command, and Dr. Black and Dr. Oliver attended me. I saw Dr. Thomas nearly every day, usually at the barn. He thought the barn more comfortable for the men, and I agreed. He had been to Aquia for supplies, but had been unable to get any.

H. P. Waldron was hospital steward of the 77th New York. "I went to Dr. Thomas and asked him where to find the sick men of the 3rd Brigade. He said they were at the barn, but I could not find them. When I went back, he told me again to look at the barn, but I still could not find them, and went back again. That was when Dr. Thomas told me, 'If you'd look, you'd find them! I'm not the keeper of the sick; I don't care a damn for the sick anyway.'" On cross-examination, Waldron described a man of the 77th New York lying outside the barn "on some cornstalks, sick with rheumatism and dropsy."

Pvt. William McCall of the 77nd New York had worked at hospitals for a year and seemed better informed than most:

> The third day of the fight [Battle of Fredericksburg], there was a rush of patients coming in, and Dr. Thomas wished to forward some of the previous patients on to their regiments. He picked out fifty or sixty and gave them in my charge, to take them to their regiments across the river. He gave me thirty diarrhea pills and, as we had no rations, an order to get provisions from the first commissary I met. We went about half a mile, and several men could go no further, so we camped for the night.
>
> The next morning, the men would go no further without food, so I took one or two of the smartest to the river, to get rations from a commissary. We were sent from one place to another, but received no rations. While I was absent, several of the sick had gone in search of provisions. The next morning, we started for the landing. When we set out, we went very slowly, stopping every 200 yards. Two men were so weak with diarrhea that they could not attend to themselves and had to be attended to [apparently, meaning wiping or cleansing them]. A few men had brought a cracker [hardtack square] with them. I had given away my own provisions. That was all the food we had. Of our whole party, maybe five were really fit for duty with their regiments.
>
> Back at White Oak Church, food had been scanty. A few boys [patients] had rations that they brought with them. The third day the hospital was open, there were two crackers and a cup of coffee for each man. I was sent out with a written requisition for rice and whisky. The commissary had no rice or whisky, but plenty of bread, but because bread was not listed on the requisition, they would give us nothing."

In answer to a question by the court, Eldridge denied that Dr. Thomas was ever abusive or insulting.

Capt. H. B. Wetherell, assistant quartermaster for the 2nd Brigade, stated that there was food available one and a quarter miles from the hospital and that Dr. Thomas had been furnished with a team of horses and a wagon on

December 12th. Lt. Charles Eccelston of the 36th New York, and provost marshal of the 3rd Division, described a quarrel with Dr. Thomas over a horse stable. The doctor said that he needed the stable to shelter wounded patients; the lieutenant insisted that he needed it for his horse. "I instructed the sentinel to shoot the doctor if he took my horse out of the stable. Surgeon Thomas talked thick, as if his tongue were edgewise in his mouth. I think he was drunk." (It would seem that Dr. Thomas never got his stable; here, the horse took precedence over patients.)

Pvt. William Wyatt of the 77th New York saw the doctor fall off his horse and need help getting back on, and he considered the doctor to be intoxicated. "Of course, the ground was wet and slippery." Wyatt, who was in White Oak Church hospital for nine days, said that for the first three days he had two crackers and a cup of coffee per day, but after that he had four crackers a day, coffee twice a day, and sometimes soup at lunch. Pvt. Charles Whiteneek, who looked after the doctor's horse, said that Thomas had bought a saddle at Hagerstown, Maryland: "The leather of the stirrup has been cut. I often help him to mount, as the leather catches his foot; his horse is frequently restless." Private Whiteneek had never seen Dr. Thomas drunk.

Pvt. William Godber, 26th New Jersey, a hospital nurse, recalled:

> Dr. Thomas was ordered to White Oak Church hospital the evening of December the 10th. He arrived at midnight, with a good stock of medicines. [A medicine chest will not suffice for 250 sick men for five days.] The church was very dirty, with no accommodations, only the bare floor. The doctor ordered hay from the barn to make the men more comfortable. The patients were divided into rows, with a nurse assigned to each row; soon, the church and the barn were filled with sick and wounded and the doctor ordered us to build the bough shelters. I slept in the barn with Dr. Thomas every night. He was usually up before daylight to see to the sick. I never saw him drunk.

Pvt. Francis Ames of the 6th Maine worked at the White Oak Church hospital from December 10th to December 20th. "On December 12th, we procured our first provisions: 200 rations of pork, 200 of coffee, 200 of rice, 200 of desiccated potatoes, 200 of hard bread, and 200 candles. I went with Dr. Thomas to get a hospital tent and camp kettles. We would have had the tent up earlier, but the doctor had a several-hour argument with the provost marshal about the stable. I was with the doctor the entire time, and I never saw him drunk."

Pvt. Ezekial Emerson of the 5th Wisconsin was a nurse at Thomas's hospital. Emerson told the Court that there had been eleven deaths there: nine from typhoid and two from "inflammation of the spine." He was certain that none had frozen to death and that he had never seen Dr. Thomas drunk. Pvt. David McGallon of the 43rd New York, who had served as a nurse, not only denied the freezing-to-death story but said that the church "had got very hot and stuffy."

Four more witnesses spoke for the defense, reiterating Thomas's sobriety and describing an open box of hardtack in the barn, arranged so that any patient could help himself at any time.

In Dr. Thomas's long written defense, he shed more light on Civil War medicine. In summary, these were some of the high points: The patients were divided into squads of twenty, with a nurse for each squad. One chest of medicines is not enough to establish a divison hospital. Artificial heat is detrimental to fever patients. The crucial element in recovery is good ventilation. Patients recovering from protracted fevers have increased appetite and will eat things that are fatal. Apples, cheese, pickles, and preserved fish are all dangerous to fever patients. The White Oak Church hospital between December 10th and December 18th had an average of 250 patients at any one time, with a maximum of 320 on one of those days. There were six deaths; four from typhoid, one from dysentery, and one from "nostalgia." In a final note, Thomas added that he himself had become jaundiced around December the 18th.

The judge advocate of the court prepared a rebuttal to Thomas's defense, saying, in brief, that he believed the prosecution witnesses but not the hospital workers who testified for the defense. The judge advocate's argument concluded, "Should he be guilty of any part of the charges, I know this general court martial will allow no mistaken feeling of mercy to prevent justice from being done." With that ominous admonition, the court voted.

They found Thomas guilty of most of the charges and ordered him cashiered. The reviewing general disapproved the sentence and forwarded the case to the President, with a recommendation for remission. Lincoln restored Thomas to duty.

He was mustered out in June 1863 but was the object of criticism once more in April, when Maj. Gen. John Sedgwick wrote, "Surgeon Thomas has recommended Thomas Osborne to the Governor of New Jersey as assistant surgeon for the 26th New Jersey Infantry. Osborne is an engineer, without medical training, and entirely disqualified for medical duties. Dr. Thomas' conduct shows an utter disregard for the interests of the service and the commanding general desires an explanation." No explanation appears in the records. Dr. Luther T. Thomas died in 1864.

⊱┄✦┄•◯•┄✦┄⊰

COMMENT: Most histories of the battle of Fredericksburg emphasize the deaths from gunfire, but at White Oak Church bacteria were the killers. The tasks assigned to Civil War doctors would certainly tax the strengths of a physician today: They were expected to successfully treat 300 men, housed in a church, a barn, and "bough shelters," without effective medicines, with very few blankets (much less beds, sheets, or pillows), while being forced to beg food from unsympathetic supply officers.

The court-martial board certainly chose to believe the line officers and discount the testimony of the medical personnel, whether doctor or nurse. The court ignored what seems the underlying problem: asking a doctor with three months of military experience to establish a division hospital in the middle of winter, with not only a complete lack of administrative support but active hostility from those responsible for food, shelter, and police aid.

In understanding this case, it is also important to consider the doctor's own jaundice. Turning yellow is usually a sign of hepatitis; before the jaundice appears, there are many days of nausea and extreme fatigue—not what a man with 300 patients needs.

Was Dr. Thomas drunk? Was he unsympathetic? Was he slow to provide food and shelter? Opinion was divided in 1863. Ours is not; Thomas was asked to accomplish a difficult task with minimal resources, against active opposition. He did as well as most men could have done.

Chapter Four

Anthony E. Stocker

Brig. Gen. George A. McCall was ten years old when the British burned Washington, D.C. In 1861 he became one of the oldest West Point graduates to serve in the field. He was also the first witness in the court-martial of Dr. Anthony Eugene Stocker, a brigade surgeon in McCall's Division. To understand Stocker's trial requires a brief digression into the geography of Virginia.

Fredericksburg, site of two battles, lies on the south bank of the Rappahannock River. Falmouth is on the north bank, about two miles upstream. Aquia Creek is an indentation in the west bank of the Potomac River, about fifteen miles northeast of Falmouth. Belle Plain is on Potomac Creek, which enters the Potomac River about three miles south of Aquia Creek, and almost due east of Falmouth.

It was not an easy area for travel. The marshy bottomlands of Aquia Creek made transportation difficult (and continued to do so up until the 1930s). The railroad bridge between Fredericksburg and Potomac Creek had been badly damaged during the Confederate withdrawal in April 1862. As much as possible, Union forces relied upon the relatively swift and comfortable steamboats, but that required reaching the steamboat landing at either Aquia Creek or Belle Plain.

In early May 1862, Dr. Anthony Stocker was put in charge of a train of horse-drawn ambulances, which were to take sick men by road from Falmouth to the boats at Aquia Creek, and then see them on their way to hospitals in Washington, D.C. In the words of the charge of "neglect of duty," we see the outcome of his mission.

> Brigade Surgeon Anthony E. Stocker, having been directed to take charge of the sick belonging to McCall's Division, and conduct them to the general hospital at Washington City, D.C., did fail to conduct the ambulances containing said sick on the road from the camp of the division near Falmouth, Virginia, to the landing at Aquia Creek and did not proceed with them to said landing and entered at once upon

the boat without waiting the arrival of the sick he was charged to conduct, in consequence of said neglect, one of the ambulances strayed from the road and went to Belle Plain, where they were provided for by the orders of the general commanding the department. All this on or about May 8, 1862.[1]

In the writings of the Civil War, Ulysses S. Grant and Abraham Lincoln were justly famous for clear and precise communication. The text of Dr. Stocker's trial suggests that little such clarity, and even less conciseness, existed at Falmouth in May 1862. The court began with a question to General McCall: "Who was in charge of the sick and what were their directions?"

> Dr. Stocker came to my tent on May the 7th and said that there were a number of sick that had to be transported to Washington or Alexandria before the division could proceed on. Stocker wanted to go as far as Aquia Creek Landing, where he would confer with the medical director of the corps, and, if considered necessary, would proceed with them to Washington or Alexandria, where his presence was required to procure capital stores. I told Dr. Stocker that the division might move at any time and the faster this move was done the better. Subsequently, he sent a pass for himself to go to Washington to the Adjutant General of the Division, which although not exactly within the meaning that he had first proposed. I granted it, my understanding was that the sick would go under the direct supervision of Dr. Stocker. I went the same day to Washington on the steamer *North America* and met Surgeon Stocker on board. He told me that the sick had not arrived in time for that boat, but that he had made arrangements for them to be sent forward on another boat.

Speaking of himself in the third person, Dr. Stocker now asked the witness: "Has not Surgeon Stocker, on previous occasions, asked for the sick to go in a similar manner, without it being expected that he go along?" McCall replied, "I cannot recall any occurring at this camp." (With the double negative in the question, it is unclear what McCall could not remember.) The next question was of similar construction: "Were not [the] sick sent by Stocker, acting medical director of the division, from Manassas and from Catlett's Station, on his application in the same manner?" Again, General McCall replied, "I cannot recollect." The defendant, still referring to himself in the third person, asked the witness, "Has not Dr. Stocker, as acting medical director of the division, applied to you at various camps for removal of [the] sick to general hospitals, and the carrying out was left to his discretion, without it being understood that he would accompany the sick?" General McCall agreed that such had been the case when they were at Camp Tennally (probably in Washington, D.C.).

Continuing the cross-examination, Dr. Stocker asked, "Was any distinct order given to Surgeon Stocker, or was it a conversation only, on May 7th, the time referred to in the charge?" The answer was also framed in the third person, "The subject was brought up to me at my headquarters by Surgeon Stocker, who verbally stated to me that the principal object of his visit to Washington was the transfer of the sick to the general hospital, and my reply, if he thought it necessary, he would be authorized to accompany the sick."

Paraphrasing the continuing cross-examination, the main themes were as follows: If Dr. Stocker did not go beyond Aquia Creek, who was supposed to take care of the sick? Apparently that would be left to the discretion of the medical director of the corps. There seemed to be agreement that Dr. Stocker had discretion to accompany the sick as far as Aquia Landing; beyond that point, the medical director would make the decision. On the steamboat headed from Aquia Creek to Washington, D.C., General McCall met Dr. Stocker but did not, at that time, in any way criticize or reprimand him for being there. And a final point was established that on two previous occasions of transporting the sick, Dr. Stocker did not require a pass in writing but merely asked permission.

The court now proceeded on to Captain H. E. Biddle, who was Assistant Adjutant General of McCall's Division. The court asked him what he knew about a pass for Stocker to go to Washington. "Dr. Stocker came to my tent on the 7th of May and said that he had a conversation with General McCall about removing the sick to Washington, and that he needed passes for ambulance drivers, sick [men], and nurses, to proceed to Aquia Creek, [and] also desired a pass for himself. He stated with respect for the pass for himself, after it was written, that it might be necessary for him to proceed to Washington with the sick. I think I added to the pass such words as 'and to accompany them to Washington, if necessary.'" Now, it was Stocker's turn again: "Are you sure that Dr. Stocker called to see you, or did he go right to his tent and subsequently enclose the pass to you?" Captain Biddle replied, "I can't say that he came to my tent right after seeing General McCall. I do think that when I signed the passes, I gave them to Dr. Stocker in person." Now the defendant asked Captain Biddle, "Have you the note in your possession that Dr. Stocker enclosed with the passes to you for signature subsequent to his interview with General McCall, and did you not return them at once with signature?" Answering one part of this compound question, Biddle said, "I don't recall any such note." Here Exhibit A was shown to the witness, who examined the paper and said, "This is not the original pass, it does have my signature, but the date is May the 3rd. It does not agree with my recollection of the pass." The final question and answer established that at division headquarters, no record was kept of passes issued.

Next up was Lt. D. W. Cutting, aide de camp to Gen. Irvin McDowell. His understanding of the matter was as follows, "It was said that there were some sick on the steamer at Belle Plain, and General McDowell asked me to find out who they were. I could find no one who had any charge of them.

They were put on the boat without anybody taking care of them, and the captain of the boat knew of no one in charge. This group of very sick men went as far as Aquia Creek, where they were left off. I had to go on a different steamer, but before I left, I asked that Captain Biddle send his own surgeon to look after them."

Captain Biddle returned to the stand, and described his review of the paperwork. "I have found the paper asked for by Dr. Stocker, the request for passes, dated May 2nd, 1862. My recollection now is that the doctor was at my tent the evening before. I prepared passes, but there was problem with the spelling of one nurse's name, and the final pass was not sent until the next evening." Although the sick departed on May the 3rd, when the charges were drawn up, the date of May 8th was selected because "when General [John] Reynolds drew up the charges, he picked up some of the papers and saw a letter from Dr. Magruder and thought it was the 8th." Stocker now returned to cross-examination: "When you state that you prepared passes on the previous day for Stocker, Vogel and so forth, do you mean that you did so at Dr. Stocker's request and handed them to him, and that one of them is not the pass indicated?" By now, the circles of confusion were gradually widening. "I mean that Dr. Stocker applied for passes, I drew them up, to the best of my recollection, I inserted the words 'to proceed or accompany them to Washington, if necessary,' but I am not sure if the doctor picked up the passes or not because I have so many of these that I get confused at times." The doctor had one final question of the long-suffering Captain Biddle. "Is not your recollection at fault; are you not confusing the sending of patients from Manassas, when you refused to sign a pass previously made out with the number of patients blank?" The court ruled that this question was improper. At this point, Dr. Stocker admitted what everyone else seemed to know already: Some of the sick men who got on the boat at Belle Plain Landing were part of a group that had gone astray on the road from Falmouth to Aquia Creek.

The first defense witness, a mere private, seemed far more coherent than the officers who preceded him on the witness stand. This was Joseph Vogel, of Company G, 1st Pennsylvania Artillery, who seemed to be quite familiar with ambulance trains.

> We started with six ambulances. I sat in the front ambulance. We came to a very bad place in the road, got over it, and moved on. After a while, I looked around and saw there were only two ambulances, so I told the driver to stop and we could go back and see what was the cause of the other ambulances staying behind. I walked back and saw an ambulance stuck in the mud over the hubs of the axles, so we worked the ambulances and at last got them up. Then we went about a mile and got stuck again in a bog. After we got clear there, we went on down to the creek. I didn't see the others there, and I thought they had gone on

and when we came to Aquia Creek, we found that there were only three ambulances and the other three had gone on a different road.

There was a sergeant there at Aquia Creek who had brought a lot of sick from Alexandria. [Why the sick were being brought *from* Alexandria instead of *to* Alexandria is unexplained.] I believe the sergeant provided as far as was in his power for those sick. Me and him drew the rations and divided as well as we could. I went to Captain Biddle and asked him if he couldn't get me a doctor to prescribe for these men, if anything was needed. He did so, and got me a doctor. I was pretty much exhausted by then and went and laid down and appointed a man to watch over these sick men. The sergeant took the doctor's horse and went to look after the other ambulances. It was between 11:00 and 12:00 o'clock when the boat came up from Belle Plain. Dr. Stocker had gone on [apparently to Washington] and had left word that I was to fetch the sick on, as soon as they came, [and] that he had made provisions for them at Washington.

The next day, we started on at 5:00 in the morning, got all the sick together, and when we got to Washington, the ambulances and everything was ready to move them to the hospital at Mount Pleasant. [It is clear that Private Vogel was functioning as commander of the train of six ambulances, and seems the most responsible and enterprising person in the Falmouth to Aquia Creek trek.]

In the next set of questions, Dr. Stocker appears to be trying to take the credit for any coherence in this adventure in transport and, using his standard third-person interrogation style, asked, "Did you receive orders from Dr. Stocker [that is, himself] to take charge of the ambulances to Aquia Creek on May the 3rd?" Private Vogel said, "I cannot say positively that I did, but as soon as the doctor went ahead to hunt out the road, I took charge of the ambulances." In further questioning, it turns out that Vogel on three previous occasions had been in charge of an ambulance train. Vogel then helped Stocker's case by stating that the sick had not suffered in any way because of the absence of the doctor. (If Stocker had no medical function on this trip, and seemed useless as a wagon master, it is unclear what function he served.) Stocker returned again to the form of the leading, compound, double-negative question so dear to the hearts of Victorian cross-examiners: "Private Vogel, are you not in error in stating as a fact that the sick required no attention from Dr. Stocker, when you were separated from a portion of them?" [In other words, How do you know that the people you didn't see didn't need a doctor?] Vogel replied that he had no idea what happened at Belle Plain because he wasn't there; he only knew what he had been told.

The subject suddenly switched from doctoring to railroads. Stocker asked Private Vogel, "Did you see some platform [flat] cars where the common road crosses the railroad, on which the sick could have been placed?" Yes, Vogel had seen these railroad cars. Stocker now wanted to know why Vogel had not placed the sick onto the railroad cars and "taken proper care of them." Vogel replied, "I did not know they were there for that purpose."

Surgeon Henry Colston of the 3rd Pennsylvania Reserve Corps made a very brief appearance, in which he said that he had worked three months with Private Vogel and found him to be a reliable person.

The aide de camp to Gen. Reynolds, Capt. Henry Spears, told the Court that he had met Dr. Stocker on the road. "But I was going the wrong way." He recalled that he had told Dr. Stocker that there was no time to spare because the boat was going to leave Aquia at 1:00. However, Spears seemed to have little information on any other subject.

The man who was in charge of a group of sick soldiers coming from Alexandria to Fredericksburg was Sgt. William Oaks, of the 7th Pennsylvania Reserve Corps. "I started from Alexandria with twenty-five men to take back to the reserves. I had a pass to Fredericksburg. Coming off the boat, I met Dr. Stocker. Our group had been sent away from Alexandria without any provisions. Dr. Stocker got provisions for the men in my group, and also for the sick that were to go to Washington [presumably the original six ambulances under Stocker's care]. At the same time that Dr. Stocker was ordering provisions, he sent the [railroad] cars up to meet the ambulances, but there was a misunderstanding and they missed them. Three of the ambulances came into Aquia Creek about sundown, and Dr. Stocker [had] made arrangements [beforehand] for quarters for the men for that night."

There was a final appearance by General McCall, who had found the papers in his office and told the court that he should have said May 2nd, rather than May 7th. He also described Dr. Stocker as "zealous and thorough in discharge of all of his duties."

Among the many papers submitted with the transcript was a letter from Dr. Stocker to Dr. Magruder, Medical Director of the Army of Rappahannock. In it, he says,

> I had been told that the distance to Aquia Creek was about 15 miles, that the roads were good, and the time to get there between two and three hours. We planned to leave at 8:30 to allow plenty of time, since the boat was scheduled for departure at 2:00 P.M. The ambulances of the first brigade were late at the rendezvous time and we did not 'get away' until 9:30 in the morning. At the time we were trying to get one of the wagons out of the bog, confusion arose. I sent [railroad] flatcars to intercept the ambulances, and since there were only three ambulances and not six, the lieutenant in charge just let them go by. When I realized that our ambulances filled with sick could not be there in time for the ship to depart [from Aquia Creek],

I made provisions for shelter for the men. I then wired directions to the transport officer at Washington to have ambulances waiting for the sick of our group, who were immediately taken to Mount Pleasant Hospital.

In his written defense, Stocker made several points. He believed himself to have been without any orders directing him to stay by the ambulances. Every provision was made for the comfort of the sick, and no proof has been offered that any man was neglected or in any way was the worse for the ambulances going astray, which was caused not by him but by the bad conditions of the roads. Finally, he left on the steamboat only after he had received many assurances that his group of sick would follow shortly and be well provided for.

Stocker was found guilty of neglect, sentenced to be reprimanded and then returned to duty. But he apparently was a lightning rod for litigation. A year and a half later he was relieved of his command at Chesapeake Hospital, Fort Monroe, Virginia, based on charges made by a Surgeon Gilbert. However, the commanding general suspended the order, considering that the charges were "frivolous and dictated by unworthy motives." In July of 1866, Dr. Stocker was living in the town of Linden, St. Francis County, Arkansas. He died in 1897. There the written record stops.

>‑‑◦‑‑‑‑‑‑‑◦‑‑‑‑‑◦‑‑‑◦‑‑‑‑<

COMMENT: Amidst all the confusion, Stocker seems to have done his best for the ambulance train. He sent a railroad train after them, a plan that failed because of lack of curiosity and enterprise on the part of the lieutenant in charge. Stocker also made provision for the lost and delayed men at Aquia Creek and had the correct transportation awaiting them dockside in Washington, D.C. In a swamp with no road signs, no military police directing traffic, no machinery for hauling wagons out of the mud, it is hard to know what more he might have done.

It is not difficult to sympathize with the sick men in the six ambulances, whose opinions were never consulted. A soldier had to be quite unwell to be sent from Falmouth to Washington, D.C., so these were serious illnesses. A section of the country that continually flooded should not have presented any surprises to men who had seen many mud-soaked dirt roads. Why the apparently functioning railroad was not brought into the plan much earlier is not made clear. And why, when three flatcars were sent, was no arrangement made to notify Private Vogel? This enterprising young man seems to emerge as the hero of the drama, being clearer-headed and more productive than the doctors and officers who outranked him. It is such men who are the real heroes of any war.

Chapter Five

James R. Riley

Is it lawful for a board of line officers to try a doctor on a question of medical practice? Surgeon James R. Riley, who toasted a dead soldier's passing with the words, "I hope he is in a better world," raised the issue of who may stand in judgment of a doctor's decisions.[1]

All the protagonists in this drama were members of the 127th Pennsylvania, a nine-month regiment that was raised in Harrisburg, Pennsylvania, and spent the last four months of 1862 in the Defenses of Washington, D.C. In mid-December of that year, they were rushed to Fredericksburg, Virginia, and joined the rest of the Army of the Potomac in General Burnside's ill-starred uphill battle. Two weeks later, New Years Eve 1862, Pvt. Daniel Britz of Company H lay very ill. What happened next is the crux of the trial, held on January 5th, 1863, in the bitter cold of a Virginia winter.

The first charge, "neglect of duty," had four specifications:

1. Surgeon Riley [also spelled Reily], on the 31st of December, 1862, did neglect to visit Private Daniel Britz of Company H, 127th Pennsylvania, although called upon by several members of the company to do so, who informed him that the said Britz was in a dying condition; nevertheless, Riley neglected to visit him and the said Britz died shortly afterwards; all this at Camp Alleman between 3:00 and 4:00 o'clock P.M.;

2. Riley did neglect to provide hospital accommodations for Britz, and permitted him to die in company quarters [usually meaning a two-man tent], without either professional aid or attention;

3. Riley has neglected and continues to neglect to procure and furnish medicines for the sick;

4. Riley neglects to attend to the police [cleaning] arrangements of the camp, neglects to visit the company streets and quarters, and neglects entirely the sanitary condition of the camp.

Under a second charge, "conduct unbecoming an officer and a gentleman," it was specified that at 4:00 P.M. on December 31st, on being informed that Private Britz had died, Dr. Riley grasped a bottle containing whiskey, took a drink, and remarked, "Here is hoping that Britz is in a better world." He pleaded not guilty.

Maj. Jeremiah Rohrer, of Riley's regiment, recalled that on New Years Day he met Dr. Riley, on horseback, on the road leading to Maj. Gen. Oliver O. Howard's headquarters, and they both halted. "The doctor told me that a man in Company H had died suddenly. As to the question of the cleanliness of the camp, I have never known the doctor to visit the street of the regiment in the ten days since our quarters were finished." Capt. Lorenzo Greenawalt was also of the opinion that Riley inspected the cleanliness of the camp about once in two weeks and that there had been some shortage of medicine.

Lt. Isaiah Willis recalled having sent a man for the doctor, about Britz, and the doctor had replied, "Well, fetch him up here." He sent another messenger to the doctor, saying it was not possible to move Britz, as he was dying. Dr. Riley still did not come, and the messenger brought another surgeon. "I do know that Britz had been sick from about the first day of September but had been on duty about three weeks in spite of being sick."

At this point Dr. Riley asked for counsel, and he chose Dr. Nathan Hayward of the 20th Massachusetts to represent him. His new counsel entered the following protest: "The charges and specifications against Dr. Riley are of a professional character, requiring for their adjudication, a board of medical men. This Court is composed wholly of military men, and we protest against being tried by it." The court found in the regulations no authority for such an objection and suspended the trial while seeking consultation. On January the 12th the court reconvened and stated that the authority that had appointed the court had decided that such a case came within the jurisdiction of a military court-martial.

Capt. James Henderson knew that Dr. Riley had had no quinine about two weeks earlier, but Henderson had no information as to the reason for the shortage. Chaplain John C. Gregg was able to shed a little more light on the death of Britz.

> I was on my way to the quartermaster's department and I saw a man going to the hospital in a hurry. I inquired what was the matter and he told me that a man was thought to be dying. I went immediately to Britz' quarters. I entered his tent, and he breathed only once after I got there. I had been there two or three minutes when Dr. [Edward] Horner came in. About twenty minutes after the death, Dr. Riley confessed to me that he did have a drink and had used the words, "I hope he is in a better land." He also told me that he meant

no harm, and meant no disrespect to the dead, it was just that his profession renders men more callous than other professions, and that it was customary for physicians thus to speak. The regiment had lost thirty-five men in nine months.

Cpl. Henry Willis told the court, "I was the first man that called upon Surgeon Riley and his reply to me was that I should bring him up. I replied that the man seemed to be dying. The only reply he made was, 'Bring him up and I'll take care of him during the night.' Dr. Riley did not come down to see the patient. This was about fifteen minutes before Britz died." Pvt. Joseph Snyder had been with the dead man earlier that day. "Britz and me were sitting together close to the fire. I spread my gum blanket down and him and me sat down. I got asking him what was the matter with him and he told me that he was very weak and was not getting any better. He told me he did not wish to go into the hospital." On the subject of not procuring medicines for the regiment, Snyder had this recollection: "I saw the doctor shortly after he came from attending to the wounded. I asked him for medicine and he said he hoped to have some in a couple of days. When he did get the medicine, it did me good."

Pvt. Grafton Fox was present at the regimental hospital the afternoon of Britz' death.

I was sitting in the doctor's office when a man came running in saying that a man was very sick and thought to be dying. Dr. Horner was in the hospital, and he told the man that Britz should go to Dr. Riley, as Dr. Riley had prescribed for Britz. Then a second and a third man came up, all saying that Britz was dying. Dr. Riley was not present at that time and Dr. Horner went down to company quarters, soon came back and said that the man was dead. Right after that, Dr. Riley arrived and was told that Britz had died. I remember that Dr. Riley said, "What! Britz dead! Britz! Britz! That is very sudden, indeed." Dr. Riley then sat down on the couch and seemed surprised at the suddenness of the death, that he had told the messengers to bring him up to the hospital, where he would make him comfortable. Then the doctor went to a box at one side of the tent, lifted up a bottle, and said, "Poor fellow, I hope he is in a better world," and took a drink.

This ended the testimony because the court announced that it was not necessary to call defense witnesses. "We find the case against Dr. Riley is not sustained and that the evidence has been trivial and unsupported. Valuable time of the Court has been taken up with investigation of charges without foundation. The charges are dismissed." This decision was confirmed by Maj. Gen. Oliver O. Howard.

As soon as the trial was over, Dr. Riley transferred to the 179th Pennsylvania. No reason is recorded for the transfer. In July 1863, the 179th Pennsylvania, with Dr. Riley, was mustered out of service. He made no pension application and is absent from the army records after his mustering out.

>─┼─♦─O─◄─┼─◄

COMMENT: If a soldier in his tent was reported to be dying, should the doctor go to him or have the man brought to the hospital? In the absence of a recorded diagnosis (or even symptoms), it is hard to answer that question. It is also likely that seen or not seen, hospital or no hospital, the outcome would have been the same. What troubled the regiment was the doctor's failure to do *something,* if only as a manifestation of concern.

Death was everywhere in the camps of the Civil War. Malaria, diarrhea, smallpox, measles, and typhoid went through the camps like a scythe through grain. The Confederate guns at Fredericksburg had piled Union bodies like bloody windrows. This harvest of death overwhelmed the emotional strength of doctors, yet the wounded and the sick still longed for a touch of compassion, a sense that they were noticed, not left to die invisibly. This fear seems to be the root of such proceedings.

As to Riley's toast to Britz's passing, it is not unreasonable that it was a genuine wish for the patient's well being in an afterlife. The doctor's brief salute can be seen as a miniature form of an Irish wake, with the consumption of liquor and the raising of toasts to the departed. From the testimony, it appears that Riley was as shocked as anyone that this young private had passed so swiftly from life to death.

Chapter Six

George H. Oliver

Florence Nightingale encountered stubborn and opinionated doctors in the Crimean War. George H. Oliver could have been have been one of them, had he not served on the Russian side in that conflict. While little is known of his life in 1853–1856 on the shores of the Black Sea, his contributions to American medicine are well documented. From the green hills of Maryland to the desert banks of the Rio Grande, he remained a stormy petrel, always at the center of some contention and, in his own opinion, never wrong.[1]

Dr. Oliver began his American service as a surgeon of U.S. Volunteers in the Department of West Virginia. In November 1861 he was attached to Brig. Gen. Robert Schenck's brigade, and the following month he went on eight weeks of leave. Upon his return, he was physician in charge of a camp for Confederate prisoners; then, in March 1862, he began the sixteen-month assignment where controversy first appeared: Director of the Cumberland Hospital in Maryland.

Cumberland was a transportation hub, ideal for receiving patients. The major portion of the hospital was at the cooler elevation of Clarysville, about eight miles west of Cumberland itself. The Clarysville Inn, erected in 1807 and still used today, served as the main building, and it was there that Oliver reported for duty at Clarysville on March 14, 1862.

In July 1862 David Tod, governor of Ohio, sent this telegram to Surgeon General William Hammond: "I have reliable information that the brigade surgeon at Cumberland, Maryland, is a drunkard and hence unfit for his post." That same week, Charles R. Fosdick wrote from Cincinnati to John A. Gurley—Ohio congressman, Universalist minister, and associate of John C. Frémont:

> I arrived home last evening and deem it my duty to make known at once a fact I discovered at Cumberland, Maryland, on my way from Washington, and I present the matter to you in hopes you may be able to place it before the proper authority.

Dr. George H. Oliver was a center of controversy in Maryland, New Mexico, and Texas. Here, in his elegant uniform, he hardly seems to be the drunk his enemies described. Massachusetts Commandery, Military Order of the Loyal Legion, USAMHI

As a member of the U.S. Sanitary Commission, I desired to look through the hospitals. The request was granted by the stewards in charge of the different hospitals, every facility afforded me. The physicians were also attentive, but the surgeon in charge of the hospitals, Dr. George H. Oliver, Post Surgeon (or majordomo, as he styles himself) is the person of whom complaint is made. From the stewards, physicians, sick soldiers, and numerous citizens I learn he is most of the time intoxicated and in this condition I found him on Saturday night, so much so he was entirely incompetent for duty or even conversation. He is reported as rough and brutal in his treatment of the sick. The condition in which I find him warrants the charges thus made. At one of the hospitals, on Saturday morning last, he ordered the surgeon to have 30 men got ready to be removed to Clarysville Hospital, eight miles from Cumberland. Knowing the condition of the men better than the post surgeon, the doctor informed him that they were too sick to be removed. Dr. Oliver swore that they should go and they were accordingly brought downstairs and placed on the sidewalk. No ambulances were ready and after some time, the post surgeon made his appearance and ordered the men back to the hospital, being under the influence of liquor when both orders were given. The day before, he ordered 50 wounded men to be sent to the same place. The surgeon of the ward remonstrated and he was threatened with the guard house. The men were accordingly sent off. No necessity existed for their removal and nothing but the whim of the drunken surgeon caused it.

These facts can be substantiated if necessary, but that alone of his being found so much intoxicated as he was on Saturday last should, in my opinion, cause him to be removed. Our brave boys, after enduring the trials of a campaign, should not be subjected to such treatment as too many have already received at his hands. I heartily wish Secretary [of War Simon] Cameron could be made acquainted with these facts and knowing the interest you manifest in the welfare of our soldiers, I have thus taken the liberty of writing you at length.

Following this letter, nothing changed. Dr. Oliver remained at his post. In January 1863 the governor of West Virginia, F. H. Pierpoint, wrote to General Schenck:

Dear Sir:
I have heard so many reports of the wretched culpable neglect of the hospital keepers at Cumberland that I am compelled to ask for the removal of Dr. Oliver, the surgeon. I am convinced that from some cause, he wants [lacks] interest in the concern. That soldiers are dying

and have died from neglect. I have had my agents there. Governor Tod has had his. All concur in opinion that Dr. Oliver ought to be removed.

This last message seems to have stimulated the authorities to look into the situation at Cumberland Hospital. In response to the query of Surgeon J. Simpson, Medical Director of the Eighth Army Corps, Dr. Oliver wrote on January 24, 1863:

Sir, In compliance with your verbal request, I have the honor to submit the following statement in regards to the accusation of negligence of the attending surgeons which I pronounce to be untrue. On the 7th of December last, there were by the morning report 474 patients then in the hospital, that night 119 patients were admitted from New Creek, Virginia, on the 8th, 32, on the 9th, 37, on the 10th, 49, on the 11th, 95, on the 12th, 165, on the 13th, 75, on the 14th, 55 patients were sent to this place, in some instances without one minute's notice and many of them exceedingly sick and in most wretched condition.

Many of these were kept at New Creek until they were moribund. Among the number was a lieutenant who died in less than 48 hours after his arrival here. I visited him and consulted with all my medical assistants in this case and all that could be done was merely to protract his life a few hours. Here you will perceive that 631 patients were admitted into general hospital in the space of eight days. Buildings had to be taken, emptied of the tenants, their contents to be removed, bunks and beds to be provided, kitchens built and furnished, privies erected and other necessaries for hospital use to be provided as best they might. At that time, the medical assistants I had at this point consisted of Dr. Ober, Skilling and Beerbowen (contract physicians).

With every disposition to make the most ample allowance for the condition of invalid and convalescents in hospitals away from home, relatives and friends, without perhaps even an acquaintance, I think any man acquainted to moderate degrees with such things who will take into consideration the number of patients suddenly and summarily thrown on our hands, who will look at the premises taken and the work done, the results accomplished cannot for a moment permit the idea to be entertained that any avoidable neglect was perpetrated.

It is no difficult matter for those who are ignorant of the labor required to fit up a hospital, who are accustomed to the luxuries of home, and the superintending care of the good housewife especially if more disposed to find fault, than to assist in removing faults and difficulties, to make a complaint from their home habits, from their own morbid fastidiousness, they may very readily come to the conclusion that men are neglected because the attending surgeons do not, three, four or half-dozen times every day visit 2- or 300 bedsides, hear over the same complaints, answer the same questions, promise furloughs and discharges, and say he will grant them because of a dying child, sick wife, and the many excuses and pretexts offered to accomplish a furlough or discharge. Nor is it more difficult for such persons to go into a building just scrubbed and fitted with new-made bunks and beds and fires recently lighted, with bare brick walls freshly white-washed, to imagine that the "atmosphere was really so offensive as to make a well man sick." It will be a less difficult matter for these persons to find fault with the ventilation, if they will for one 24 hours take the place of a patient in one of these buildings and find that he has one or more windows left open at the top during the whole of that time though there may be 30 or 50 other persons beside himself in that ward.

If the persons, be they state agents or other agents, will do the labor already named, they will not be disposed to find faults, that in eight days with these accommodations provided for over 600 men with the limited facilities then existing here, with the fact that each man had not a spitoon, a chamber [pot] or bedpan and a drinking cup. Let them add to all this the scores of daily applications of relatives and friends, inquiring where A or B is to be found, his condition, his prospects, can't I take him home with me, or to a private house, or furlough, or discharge, where and what are his effects, and a score of other questions repeated perhaps half a dozen times to the assistant surgeons, then to the surgeon in charge, inquiries after dead men and their effects, when, where and how they died, if after he has answered these and other questions three or four times to the same person, he should at the last say, 'I have already answered these questions and informed you that furloughs are positively forbidden by the Secretary of War and I have not time to answer you again,' they would hardly think it uncivil even to a state agent to let him take a seat in your office alone after placing into his hands your books and allowing him to copy therefrom what he pleased while you went out and attended to other matters.

This frantic and disjointed letter certainly indicates that there are two sides to every dispute. It would appear that there were 200 patients per doctor, very little in the way of what we today would consider a hospital, and that the flow of anxious relatives and inquiring politicians had very much set Dr. Oliver's teeth on edge. That he felt hard-pressed is evident; he also felt that any fault lay entirely with others than himself. The man in charge of the investigation, Dr.

Simpson, wrote to his own superiors that "I could find no substantiation of the charges against Dr. Oliver."

Oliver was cleared—but not for long. Two months later, in April 1863, he was court-martialed not once but twice. In the first trial he was charged with being drunk on five different occasions at Cumberland and once at New Creek, Virginia, plus he had sent a man with consumption (advanced tuberculosis of the lungs) back to his regiment. In the second trial it was charged that he had sent two Ohio privates to their homes without their final discharge papers. The witnesses called presented testimony of remarkable inconsistency.

Robert R. McCandliss, Assistant Surgeon of the 110th Ohio, had met with Dr. Oliver three times. The first was at New Creek, and in regards to sobriety he recalled that "Dr. Oliver was in a condition incapable of attending to business." At their second meeting in early December, he noticed nothing unusual, and at their final meeting in mid-December, he recalled Dr. Oliver as being "very much intoxicated." In the cross-examination the defendant asked, "When you met Dr. Oliver at Cumberland, did you have any official or personal altercation with him whereby you felt yourself aggrieved?" Dr. McCandliss replied that he had indeed been aggrieved because Dr. Oliver would not release some recovered men from the hospital, and although it was 10:00 P.M., their knapsacks and their descriptive lists were not ready. As to intoxication, the witness remembered that Dr. Oliver "spoke with a thick tongue and could not walk straight."

The next witness was Dr. George Perry, who stated that he had been a practicing physician for thirty-nine years. He had been present at the "thick tongue" episode. "It is true that Dr. Oliver was excited, but it was because Dr. McCandliss wanted sick soldiers out of their beds in the middle of the night to get ready for a train that was not leaving until the next morning. To spend the night getting ready for their discharge would mean no sleep for the nurses, the stewards or the patients."

Capt. Nathan Smith of the 110th Ohio recalled, "I saw Dr. Oliver at Cumberland Hospital around 9:00 P.M. He was at least partially intoxicated." Capt. William R. Moore of the same regiment remembered having met Dr. Oliver at the Cumberland Depot. "After transacting our business, around 8:00 p.m., and while waiting for the train, we were invited into the saloon. I drank wine. The doctor drank three times. I thought he was under the influence of liquor. However, he seemed able to give directions for the disposition of the sick." Walter S. Walsh, Surgeon of the 15th West Virginia, told the court: "I have seen Dr. Oliver night and day for months. I have a very high opinion of him as a surgeon, both as to ability and to faithfulness. He has never been unfit for duty by reasons of intoxication." The same positive thoughts were voiced by Maurice Townsend, Acting Assistant Surgeon, U.S. Army, who had been in practice for sixteen years. "I never saw Dr. Oliver drunk. He has had spells of incapacity, caused by rheumatism and neuralgia so severe that turning over in bed produced intense pain. He could walk only with a cane, leaning on my arm. His rheumatism causes an unsteadiness of gait. I have seen him on active duty day after day, when in such a condition that if it had been me, I would not have left my bed. As an administrative physician, I have never seen him surpassed."

John W. Moss, Surgeon with the 14th Virginia, was of two minds about the defendant. "Dr. Oliver was not intoxicated, but he did find fault with the manner in which I had sent the sick to the hospital. He wanted a written statement with each patient and spoke to me rather harshly." The court weighed all these opinions and found Oliver not guilty on all of the charges but added, "The Court is, however, of the opinion that there is some informality attached to the matter of not forwarding the proper papers to the proper headquarters."

Whatever the merits of his directorship at Cumberland, it was time for a change. His wife had died a few months before the court-martial, and his rheumatism was bothering him. Two months after his acquittal, he moved to Baltimore, where he was put to work examining recruits. This tour of duty lasted until September 1863. The damp of a harbor city did nothing to improve his joint problems, and his superior, George Buckley, Medical Director of the Defenses of Baltimore, wrote the following recommendation: "Dr. Oliver suffers severely from rheumatism and would be better off in the interior, places such as Utah, New Mexico and Arizona. He is an able, efficient and excellent medical officer. He has experience in the Russian service in the Crimea." Whether Buckley was genuinely sympathetic or just happy to be rid of Oliver is unknown. Either way, the effort was successful.

Halfway between today's Albuquerque and Las Cruces, New Mexico, is a long stretch of trail called La Jornada del Muerto (Journey of Death). There, in the middle of godforsaken desert, high on a desiccated bluff buffeted by the hot winds roaring up out of the Sonoran Desert, are a few crumbling adobe walls, the ruins of Fort Craig. In November 1863, when Dr. Oliver arrived at his new army home, the fort was a busy outpost. It had been the scene of the 1862 battle of Valverde during the Confederate invasion of the Southwest and was still an active way-station for men pursuing Apache Indians and a safe haven for travelers along the Rio Grande.

The dry air may have eased his rheumatism, but Oliver was still not a happy man. Late in 1863 he "caught a cold from immersion in the Rio Grande," with symptoms, he insisted, that were still present fifteen years later. In June 1864 he requested a medical leave of absence for treatment of trichiasis (ingrown eyelashes), and a few weeks later he requested a transfer to Franklin (now El Paso), Texas, citing the high winds at Fort Craig as the cause of his most recent debility.

He was still at Fort Craig when he received a brief letter from Brig. Gen. James H. Carleton, commanding the Department of New Mexico. "You should know that you are facing court-martial. You know if the charges are provable. If they are, it might be better to resign than to face disgrace and scandal." In October 1864 the commanding officer at Fort Craig wrote to General Carleton, "Surgeon Oliver has become so addicted to intemperance that I consider his reformation hopeless. I recommend that his resignation be accepted." In January 1865 Oliver's resignation was, indeed, accepted.

The postwar army in the Southwest must have had difficulty attracting doctors because six months later, we find Oliver employed as a contract surgeon with the Department of New Mexico, and in 1866 he held the same position at Fort Bliss, Texas, just east of El Paso. In 1868 he was still employed in Texas, now at Camp Concordia, when the surgeon in chief at Austin, Texas, wrote, "The commanding officer at Concordia states that Dr. Oliver is not a proper person to receive another contract."

In 1869, he applied to be appointed pension examiner in El Paso but was disappointed in this request. He apparently settled in Mesilla, New Mexico, and practiced there for the next eleven years. In 1876 he applied for another military position. His request was endorsed by both the sheriff and the district attorney at Mesilla, who wrote to their territorial delegate in Congress that Dr. Oliver bore "high character as a gentleman and during his years in Mesilla has established a well-deserved reputation for ability in his profession." On the jacket of Dr. Oliver's medical-officer file in Washington, D.C., is a bright purple stamp that reads BLACK LIST. This may explain why Oliver did not return to military life.

The following year he remarried, this time to a woman named Petra from the Spanish-speaking culture of his adopted hometown. He and his wife were united in a church ceremony that was recorded entirely in Spanish. Four years later, Oliver died of "chronic bronchitis, rheumatism, chronic diarrhea, kidney disease, neuralgia and palpitations."

His widow applied for a pension, and the usual flurry of affidavits fills the records, saying, in essence, that his service in the war caused the conditions that killed him. After an initial rejection, his widow was awarded a pension on the basis of poverty and blindness; thereafter, she received a monthly check until her death in 1904. The final note in the pension record is a sad coda to a turbulent life: "1931 . . . an old man claiming to be Dr. Oliver's son seems to think he has something coming from the government." Whatever it was, he did not receive it.

><+>•○•<+><

COMMENT: In the study of history, absolute truth is a rare commodity. Two governors, a Sanitary Commission official, a commanding general, and two post commanders all thought Oliver was a drunk—and probably brutal, as well. However, some of his colleagues said he was a fine physician and a splendid administrator, who persisted in his work in spite of crippling physical pain. His two court-martials could only find fault with his paperwork and the leading politicians in his adopted hometown spoke highly of him. Our readers must draw their own conclusions.

Oliver's story reminds us, too, of how well traveled many people were a century and a half ago. He served with the Russian army, which suggests that he spoke some Russian and French, and certainly after the Civil War he spoke Spanish. Perhaps this facility with languages merely enabled him to be ill-tempered in four languages, but it does reflect a wider scope of cultural adaptation than is seen with many Americans today.

Finally, the documents related to the hospital at Cumberland tell us, once again, of the crushing burden of sick and wounded—and how ill-prepared both the North and South were for such a task.

Chapter Seven

James H. Hereford

When the future Dr. Hereford was born, George Washington, Benjamin Franklin, and Thomas Jefferson were all still alive. Could age have played a role in the doctor's shortcomings?

He was surgeon for the 39th Kentucky Infantry, and during his nine months with the regiment, they had skirmishes at Piketown, Louisa, Coal Run, Clark's Neck, and Marrowbone Creek, all in the southeast corner of the Bluegrass State. With all the wounded, plus the victims of malaria and diarrhea, a surgeon would seem to have enough to occupy his mind. But not so. After only four months in service, he was the object of an investigation, and two months after that he was under arrest, awaiting a court-martial.[1]

The investigative report, prepared by J. G. Hatchett, "Medical Director," concluded that Dr. Hereford was "incompetent, with not enough energy to attend to his duties. The regimental hospital is invariably filthy and he had failed to manifest interest in the sanitary conditions of his command. His conduct is tyrannical and supercilious to such a degree that the sick dislike being placed under his treatment. In the treatment of disease, he shows a want of skill." This report was not enough to end his services, however, and the next event was his court-martial, held in October 1863.

The first charge was conduct unbecoming an officer and a gentleman, in which it was alleged that on September 14, 1863, he had "insulted, without provocation, Assistant Surgeon William E. Phillips (of Hereford's regiment), by publicly accusing him of incapacity as a medical officer, and on the same occasion drew a pistol and threatened to use it upon the person of Surgeon W. E. Phillips." He was also charged with drunkenness on duty at Louisa, Kentucky, and with neglect of duty for refusing to admit to the hospital three men considered sick by other doctors.

Dr. Phillips was the first witness.

Dr. Hereford undertook to examine me, asking me if I had ever studied medicine and if I knew the number of bones composing a man's arm. I asked him if he intended to insult me. He replied that he wished me to answer these questions and if I did not, he would report me. I told him that I had been before a Medical Board and had been examined. He then asked me if I felt I could fill the place of an assistant surgeon. My reply was that I thought so or I would not have accepted the position. He then said that I was not qualified and had brought no recommendations. I then called him a liar and I went across the street. When I came out at the door a few minutes later, Dr. Hereford had his pistol in his hand; his hand was at his side with the pistol pointed in the direction where I was standing.

The questioning now turned to different subjects. The court asked Phillips about the charge of being drunk on duty.

I have never seen him take a drink, but I have seen him at times when I thought he was under the influence of liquor. At those times, I think he was [still] capable of attending to his medical duties. There were times when I think he neglected his patients; some men should have been admitted to the hospital. I was a member of a board appointed to investigate several cases in this regiment and the board made a written report to Colonel [George] Gallup of the 14th Kentucky. One case was a man who had the chills and fever [probably malaria] and was returned to duty; he was laying in his tent. Another was a case of diarrhea.

Dr. Hereford cross-examined the witness: "How could you tell the seriousness of the condition of the patient with diarrhea?" Phillips replied, "By the condition of his tongue and by the signs of debility." Hereford continued, "What evidence do you have that I rejected his admission to the hospital?" Phillips responded, "I was there. I saw you refuse him. The patient said you didn't know your business and then you threatened to get your pistol and blow the top of his head off."

The defendant continued his cross-examination, speaking of himself in the third person. "Do you think Dr. Hereford was under the influence of strong drink?" Phillips answered, also using the third person: "I think he was under the influence of some unnatural stimulants. His irritable manner and disposition toward me made me think so. The second patient mentioned in the investigation also needed to be in the hospital. I could see he had the chills and fever; such patients need to be in the hospital."

Benjamin Stubbins, First Assistant Surgeon of the 14th Kentucky, was called next. "I did not see Dr. Hereford insult Dr. Phillips, but I did see each go into a house and procure a pistol. Each of them came out and stood there looking at each other." The court asked Stubbins about his service on a board appointed to investigate the cases that were rejected for hospital admission by Dr. Hereford. Stubbins answered, "I found three or four cases; one of them had a very high fever. You can tell when a patient with chills and fever is very sick, even when the chill or fever isn't upon him; you can tell by the coated tongue and general derangement of the system. The case that had diarrhea was very weak and should have been in the hospital." The court then asked about doctors carrying pistols. Stubbins replied, "It is not the custom for medical officers to carry arms, but I have seen Dr. Hereford carry a pistol before this incident and also afterwards."

Lt. Joseph D. Powers of the 39th Kentucky had never seen Dr. Hereford drunk. "As to medical problems, one man in my company was sent to the hospital with shaking chills, was refused admission, and returned still with shaking chills." Capt. Martin Thornsberry of the same regiment said, "I sent several men to the hospital and Private [Lorenzo] Porter was rejected. I don't like Dr. Hereford very well because I do not think he treats my men right." (It was unusual for line officers to make decisions about hospitalization. Were Powers and Thornsberry out of line, or did they have so little faith in Hereford that they tried to go around him?)

Private Porter himself testified next. "I was sent to the hospital and Dr. Hereford refused to admit me. I told him he couldn't tell if a man was sick and he said, 'Shut up, you damned son-of-a-bitch, or I'll blow the top of your head off.' I stepped out of the door, went to my tent and had another chill. Later, a doctor from a different regiment came to see me." Sergeant William Weddington confirmed Porter's story.

Two medical witnesses followed. Second Assistant Surgeon James N. Draper, also of the 39th Kentucky, recalled patients named Porter, Rogers, and Austin, all of whom, in Draper's opinion, should have been admitted to the hospital. Surgeon Strother Yates of the 14th Kentucky said he had been asked to look at sick men rejected for hospitalization and recalled "two or three cases."

All witnesses were asked about Hereford and alcohol. None had seen him actually drunk, but many men thought he might have been "under the influence" at some time.

Hereford called seven defense witnesses, all from his own regiment. Capt. Jefferson Sowards had never seen Hereford drunk and knew nothing of medical care. Lt. Lindsey Layne had never seen Hereford drunk, but conceded that he could be "irritable and short-spoken." Capt. William Ford said Hereford was "kind to his patients, never abusive." He did concede that there were some problems with the hospital smelling bad, the dead left around one or two days, and the need to burn tar to cover the odors. Capt. Lewis Sowards (three different Sowards served as officers in this regiment) said that Hereford was never drunk, and "the boys report they are well taken care of."

Hospital Steward Isaac Rice conceded that he, himself, had no medical education at all and was "never acquainted with the business before I came in the army." Rice told the court that the hospital was in bad condition, that Hereford had bought some medicines out of his own pocket, and that it was necessary to rent a house to provide shelter for the patients. Privates Hargus Bowe and Jonathan Webb confirmed the earlier stories about the pistol-toting quarrel between the two doctors.

The court weighed the evidence, found Hereford guilty, and dismissed him from the service. Their decision was approved by Brig. Gen. Jeremiah T. Boyle (himself a controversial figure, a slave-owning Unionist, hated by half the people in Kentucky).

In 1870, Dr. Hereford, then age seventy-three, applied for a pension, based on a scrotal hernia received when his horse fell on July 1863, and he was struck by the pommel. "Since then, I cannot ride a horse, have had to abandon my profession as a physician, and cannot do manual labor." Dr. Draper contributed an affidavit, stating that he had seen Hereford's horse fall. The Pension Bureau rejected the claim, noting that Hereford had been (dishonorably) dismissed and that there were no records showing the hernia problem. He appealed, and an investigator was appointed. Life in Kentucky in 1870 is reflected in the statement of James Hatcher, Hereford's son-in-law: "My wife's brother said he would kill me if I testified and the claim is rejected, and others, if the claim is accepted, would accuse me of false swearing." Eventually, the claim was accepted. Reexamination by a Dr. Atkinson in 1880 noted that Hereford was age 83, weighed 145 pounds, stood 5' 10", and had a readily reducible hernia "about the size of a hen's egg."

In 1885 he developed what was diagnosed as a strangulated hernia. After several days of suffering, Hereford was dead. His widow's application for pension—stating that they were married in Piketown, Kentucky, in 1840, and that she was now age sixty-nine—was rejected, but her 1887 letter to President Grover Cleveland reopened the case. Meriba Ratliff Hereford was awarded a pension, which she continued to receive until her own death in 1903. In 1918 their seventy-six-year-old daughter enlisted the aid of her congressman to collect "arrears of pension," but this last grasp at the federal treasury came to naught.

>—+—4>—+—O—+—4>—+—<

COMMENT: Dr. Hereford appears to have been an early advocate of "managed care" and "cost containment," sending seriously ill men off to sweat and shiver in their miserable little tents, without even the offer of a dose of quinine and whiskey to quiet the plasmodia spawning by the billions in the victim's bloodstream. The threat to blow the patient's head off may be the Civil War equivalent of an HMO's "claim denied." Then as now, even the lay public was able to distinguish reasonably competent and compassionate care from its opposite. Of equal interest is the apparent advent of peer review, in which a board of doctors was asked to review and comment upon the quality of another doctor's judgment.

Dr. Hereford served his country less than nine months, not entirely satisfactorily, and received the equivalent of a dishonorable discharge. Whether this entitled him and his family to thirty-three years of government support is a moral question, not a medical one.

Chapter Eight

Lyman Allen

The trajectory of Lyman Allen's life arced from the bloody battlefields of Chaffin's Farm on the shell-torn Peninsula to the peaceful vineyards of Napa and Sonoma Counties in Northern California's rolling hills and fertile valleys.[1]

Becoming a regimental surgeon in 1863 was different from the requirements for today's Army Medical Corps. Allen had been a medical student from 1859 to 1861 and although he does not give the name of his school, he had attended a "full course of medical lectures" as well as a "course of practical anatomy." When the war came, he soon enlisted as a private in the 41st Ohio Infantry and rose to the rank of quartermaster sergeant. After two years of soldiering, he decided to try for a billet as an assistant surgeon with the U.S. Colored Troops. On August 14, 1863, at Manchester, Tennessee, he sat for the examination for the position of "assistant surgeon in colored troops." He was twenty-six years old. Allen was apparently successful because he was not only appointed to that position with the 5th U.S. Colored Troops, but in May 1864 he was promoted from assistant surgeon to surgeon. It was at this rank that he was court-martialed.

Throughout October 1864, a major battle and a number of bloody skirmishes took place at Chaffin's Farm as General Grant probed the outlying defenses of Richmond, Virginia. The charges against Allen were that on October 23, 1864, at Chaffin's Farm, he was guilty of 1. gross neglect of duty, 2. disobedience of orders, and 3. gross inhumanity. A wounded Union soldier, whose name is not given, had been carried into the camp of the 5th U.S.C.T., with part of his foot cut off by a shell. Allen "refused to attend the wounded man" when called upon by Capt. E. C. Ford. The disobedience charge arose when the commander of Allen's regiment, Maj. J. C. Terry, gave a direct order to Surgeon Allen that he go and attend the wounded man. The charge of inhumanity stemmed from his "failure to attend the wound of an enlisted man who was suffering the most severe pain." As in most litigation, there were differences of opinion.

J. C. Terry, now the lieutenant colonel of the 22nd U.S. Colored Troops, recalled that a sergeant first spoke to Allen about the wounded man but received no satisfaction. Five minutes later, Captain Ford addressed the doctor, with the same results. Ford then went to Colonel Terry's tent and said there was "a wounded man in great agony." When Terry spoke to the doctor, the reply was, "I am very busy doing sick call for members of my own regiment." On cross-examination by Allen, Terry admitted that the doctor had always been obedient in the past and that he had recently complained of being sick, although he was continuing to do his medical duties.

Captain Ford recalled: "The wounded man was sitting with a twisted leg and seemed to be suffering considerably. He was located about 100 yards away from Surgeon Allen, who said that he was busy with sick call." On cross-examination, Allen asked, "Did you not say that the man was very composed?" Ford replied, "No, I said he appeared as well as could be expected." He was then asked by Allen, "How soon did I go to see the wounded man?" Ford answered, "My estimate is that it was 20 or 30 minutes before you went to see the man."

Captain E. T. Grabill, 5th U.S.C.T., confirmed the stories already told and added that the doctor had complained for some time of being sick. Sgt. John Moorley of another regiment recalled that he had helped the injured soldier through the camps of three regiments without being able to find a doctor. Cpl. Jordan Brisentine told the Court, "Two different people told the doctor that the wounded man was not bleeding very much." As was customary in court-martials at that time, the defendant made a statement that summarized his position. Allen had this to say:

> Gentlemen, I wish to enumerate the facts in this case. The commanding officer and the captains say that I have always performed my duties. Here we have a single instance in which I am charged with neglect of duty. I had been sick that week and was not fit to attend to duty, but I was doing so anyway. When the sergeant told me there was a wounded man I asked where he was and where was the surgeon who was supposed to take care of him. He had no good answer. I suggested that the sergeant get an ambulance and take him to the hospital, but I was told that there was no ambulance and the sergeant did not know where to find one. I asked the sergeant if the man was suffering and was told no. I told them to bring the man out of the road area and near my quarters and that I would attend to him as soon as sick call was over. I had similar conversations with the two captains. I felt that staying at sick call until I was finished best served the needs of my regiment after which I would attend to the wounded man. If I did neglect my duty in this case it could only be an error in judgment. As to being ordered to go and attend the man, leaving my sick call, I did not understand that it was a direct order. From the information given to me he did not seem to be suffering or bleeding severely. Further, he had not been carried through the camp of my regiment but through the camps of other regiments. I never refused to treat him; I only said

I would do it as soon as I could. I have served for over three years and passed the examinations of two army boards of examination and have done my best to serve this regiment.

The members of the court-martial found him guilty of inhumanity, but not of "gross inhumanity," and of refusing to attend the wounded man. He was sentenced to forfeit one month's pay and allowances and to be reprimanded in general orders.

The case was reviewed by Brig. Gen. Charles J. Paine, a Harvard graduate, Boston lawyer, and future director of three different railroads. His review burns with indignation, expressed with the supercilious elegance that one might expect from a graduate of the Boston Latin School.

> The Court having found that Surgeon Allen was guilty of neglect of duty, but not guilty of gross inhumanity, it can only be inferred that their opinion is that the neglect was caused by professional ignorance. This opinion must be shared by everyone who knows that a part of the defense was, that a man with part of his foot cut off by a piece of shell was not suffering much pain. While the brigadier general commanding regrets extremely that a medical officer in this division should be found so ignorant of his profession as to set up such a defense, he much prefers it to be so than to think any officer could be so grossly inhuman as to leave a wounded man to suffer.

Allen continued to serve with his regiment and was honorably discharged April 22, 1865. In 1897 he was living in Los Angeles and applied for a pension because of problems with rheumatism and mitral valve regurgitation. When examined, he was 5'4" in height, weighed 115 pounds, and was age fifty-nine. He continued to receive a pension and lived in Berkeley, California, from 1908 until 1913. He spent the last six years of his life in the California State Veterans Home at Yountville, built upon an oak-studded hillside looking out over miles of vineyards. He passed away in April 1919 as the newly green grapevines spread along the trellises.

>––•›–•–O–•‹•–•–‹

COMMENT: This seems a case of the line officers second-guessing the surgeon. At this point in the war, the surgeon's primary responsibility was to the men of his own regiment. The wounded man had been unable to obtain treatment in his own regiment or in any of the others he had passed through. Nor did his bearers bring him to the doctor; they dropped him a hundred yards from the doctor's tent, and then summoned Allen. Having come that far, why not complete the journey? Allen seems to have done his best to accommodate the conflicting demands put upon him.

Chapter Nine

Henry A. Armstrong

"His attacks usually take place at the *full moon!*" wrote the wife of Dr. Henry A. Armstrong. This surgeon not only had trouble diagnosing his own patients but is a diagnostic puzzle himself, who was evaluated in 1887 by America's most famous physician. The venue of his Civil War problems was Fort Corcoran, today the site of Wilson School in Rosslyn, Virginia.[1]

Little is known of Henry Armstrong before the war. He enters the records in December 1861 as surgeon of the 2nd New York Heavy Artillery. In June 1863 he was court-martialed for a series of incidents during the spring of that year—incidents that read like the devil's own shopping list. In a paraphrase of the formal structure of court-martial language, his transgressions ranged from the trivial to the carnal to the fatal.

The first charge was disobedience of orders. His commander, Lt. Col. Jeremiah Palmer, ordered that hay and oats be removed from the hospital buildings. Armstrong refused to cooperate and gave countermanding orders to the privates and teamsters. Palmer ordered that the regimental ambulance should be used only for the sick. Armstrong used the ambulance (and, of course, the horse and driver) to take a woman to the theater in Washington, D.C. Twice.

"Neglect of duty" focused on his professional work. He failed to properly diagnose Cpl. Washington Pierce, who had smallpox. The result was that Pierce died, and the other men in his tent contracted the disease.

Conduct unbecoming an officer and a gentleman, if proved, means automatic discharge from the army. Armstrong had a young woman, not his wife, living in his tent for three months, and fed her from rations intended for the patients. It was well-known that he had an actual wife at home. In another "unbecoming" activity, he visited Grover's Theatre in Washington, D.C., in his uniform, escorting a well-known prostitute, Lucy Hart, who kept a house of ill fame at 27 Pennsylvania Avenue in the capital. To compound the mischief, in the parlor of Miss Hart, he slapped Lt. Isaac Richmond across the face. In another transgression, he slammed his fists together in the presence of enlisted men and said to Colonel Palmer, "You have no right to interfere with my business. I will prefer charges against you." A parade of witnesses gave their evidence.

Pvt. Oliver Fountain described how Pierce first complained of aches and pains, then had a red rash on his back. Within twenty-four hours Pierce was too sick to stand. Dr. James Howe, another surgeon with the 2nd New York Heavy Artillery, visited the tent and prescribed "powders." The next day both Howe and Armstrong came to the sick man's quarters. "There were eruptions all over his body . . . blotches were red with a little yellow speck in the center. . . . Pierce asked if he had the measles and Surgeon Armstrong laughed and said that many people have the measles two or three times. The next two days no doctors came to see Pierce. On February 5th both doctors visited, pronounced the case to be smallpox, and transferred Pierce to Kalorama Hospital, where he died. Now Private Ham in our tent has smallpox. The men I have seen with smallpox have all died."

Dr. Robert Thomas, who had been in charge of the Kalorama Heights Hospital for Eruptive Diseases for two years and had treated over 2,000 cases of smallpox, gave his testimony: "When Pierce was admitted his smallpox was confluent. He had great debility and typhoid-type symptoms. The disease was diagnosable three days before he was transferred, and should have diagnosed. Measles eruptions blanch with finger pressure and smallpox lesions do not." In cross-examination, Armstrong asked, "Don't you think that these typhoid-like symptoms could have been caused by Pierce being transported in the cold air, away from his warm tent?" Dr. Thomas did not think any such thing.

Sgt. Eliakim Howell seemed an observant man: "I know Pierce had the measles already the previous winter. What he had now looked like smallpox and I went and told Dr. Howe that Pierce had the smallpox." Howell's testimony was followed by a long quibble over which doctor was actually treating Pierce, Howe or Armstrong.

Colonel Palmer gave his evidence, in tedious and painful detail, about the storage of hay and oats, then proceeded to recall that Armstrong's actual wife had visited the camp several times in 1861 and 1862 and that the other woman arrived in late 1862. Ephraim Smith, the hospital cook at Fort Corcoran, testified that Armstrong and his female friend ate from the hospital supply. Smith was not aware of any reimbursement to the hospital fund by Armstrong. Maj. William McRay, the next witness, said that his tent was ten feet from Armstrong's, that the surgeon referred to the young woman as his niece, and that he had seen no inappropriate behavior. Lt. James Lawrence told the court that he frequently took his meals with the doctor and the doctor's niece, Miss Faussett. "I saw no bad behavior."

Pvt. Andrew Rising, who kept the regimental books, appeared for the defense: "The doctor paid for himself and for the female when they boarded at the hospital." Pvt. William Cole took care of Armstrong's horse and slept in the doctor's tent. "The doctor slept on a lounge and the lady slept six feet away on a cot. He slept with his drawers on; I don't know what she wore to bed. I never saw any impropriety."

The court then called Miss Faussett, who gave her first name as Maria. She stated that Armstrong was her uncle; that after the death of her mother, her father in Ireland had sent her to live in the United States with Dr. and Mrs. Armstrong; and that she and Mrs. Armstrong "did not get along." Maria was unsure of her own age but guessed that she was sixteen.

Dr. Armstrong's written defense statement runs for dozens of pages and denies each and every charge. The court found him guilty on three of the many specifications: disobeying the order to move the hay and oats, of having a female in his tent (but attaches no criminality thereto), and of telling the colonel that he had "no right to interfere." Armstrong was acquitted of neglecting his patient. The sentence: suspension from rank and pay for two months, a penalty approved by Brig. Gen. Gustavus DeRussy. Judge Advocate General Joseph Holt thought that Armstrong should have been dismissed.

His military history thereafter was that of a drifter. He was a contract surgeon at Carver Hospital in Washington, D.C., for three months; at Emory General Hospital for one month; and equally brief stints at Alexandria, Camp Bailey, and Forts Strong and Whipple in Virginia. His contract was annulled in January 1866.

It is unclear what became of the first Mrs. Armstrong, but seventeen years after the war, while traveling in England, he met and quickly married Sarah Attfield, a hospital nurse. After the marriage they crossed the Atlantic and settled in New Jersey. Three years later she had him committed to the Insane Asylum at Morris Plains, New Jersey, where he remained most of the time from 1885 until his death, at age seventy-five, in 1894. His insanity, or lack of it, was the subject of unending debate and litigation.

Taking his wife's side were Dr. E. C. Booth, Director of the Asylum, who said that Armstrong had "chronic mania of a probably incurable nature," with his principal symptoms showing "fury toward his wife, accusing her of actions which are highly improbable, and boasts of his extraordinary powers, and claims intimacy with distinguished men, who disclaim any knowledge of him; he repeats the same stories day after day." Dr. Booth cited "acts of sexual bestiality and brutality" claimed by Mrs. Armstrong.

William Hammond, former Surgeon General of the U.S. Army and in the late 1800s, the country's most famous (and high-priced) specialist in nervous and mental diseases, examined Armstrong. In a three-page letter, he described the patient as "markedly deranged in his mental processes. He has various fixed delusions, has lost his original sense of decency to such an extent that he conversed freely with strangers and servants in regard to alleged obscene acts with his wife. . . . [H]e does not hesitate to declare that, should the occasion offer, he will do her personal violence."

Dr. P. F. Hyatt, a surgeon who had served in the army had "found the said Armstrong running through the halls of the hospital at night clothed only in his nightshirt, with a big knife in his hand, threatening vengeance on some imaginary person."

On the other hand, the family doctor, who had known the Armstrongs for years, "had never seen any evidence of insanity." A government pension examiner noted that when Mrs. Armstrong was "pressed on the witness stand by counsel in cross-examination, she refused to tell her movements prior to the marriage and her sister refused to tell where she [sic] was born and raised." Another government examiner, in November 1886, saw no signs of insanity and noted that Armstrong's shoulder had been dislocated by the nursing staff at the asylum. Judge Suydam of Plainfield, New Jersey, called Mrs. Armstrong an "adventuress" and thought Armstrong quite sane.

The husband himself had this to say about Sarah Armstrong: "I was never so deceived. Instead of getting a good, true, young Christian lady as she tried and did make me believe she was, I got a sly, sneaking, treacherous piece of furniture." He went on to say that she had stolen his pension checks and run him into debt.

The Washington, D.C., *National Free Press* on October 31, 1886, ran a 2,000-word article headed "A Doctor's Wicked Wife—Dr. Armstrong Locked Up as Insane and then Robbed." The thrust of the text is contained in this sentence: "The investigations show that the doctor's confinement as being insane is nothing more nor less than an ingeniously planned and skillfully executed conspiracy."

In a parallel development, Congressman John H. Bagley submitted a Special Bill, passed in July 1884, awarding Armstrong a pension on the basis of service-connected hernia and blindness of the left eye. He received this pension until his death in 1894, and his wife received a widow's pension until her death in 1915.

>–+–‹›–•O•–‹+–+–‹

COMMENT: In regards to Dr. Armstrong's professional skill, he seemed less able to diagnose smallpox than did his own sergeant. On another occasion, described by Dr. Hyatt, Armstrong killed a patient while treating a dislocated left shoulder, apparently through an overdose of chloroform anesthetic. Civil War deaths from chloroform anesthesia were rare: one in 10,000 operations. The word "incompetent" comes to mind.

As to his social discretion, escorting a known prostitute to the theater certainly violated the spirit of the officer's code. As a brief excursion into the murky waters of psychohistory, we might speculate that his apparent mood shifts and hypersexuality were premonitions of his developing what is now called bipolar disorder, or manic-depressive illness.

Chapter Ten

Augustus M. Clark

Uncontrollable diarrhea or intentional fouling of his own bed? These were key questions in the trial of Dr. A. M. Clark, surgeon of U.S. Volunteers, in charge of the hospital of the 2nd Division of the V Army Corps at Falmouth, Virginia, in April 1863. Clark was charged with neglect of duty.[1]

The specification reads, "In this, that [he] did return or cause to be returned to the 17th Regiment of Infantry [regular army] Private Melvin Wade, a patient in the divisional hospital, the said Private Wade being so diseased at the time that he died within six days after being returned to his regiment, the said surgeon A. M. Clark giving as a reason for his conduct that the said Private Melvin Wade caused trouble and inconvenience in the division hospital by his filth." In his plea, Dr. Clark agreed that he had returned Wade and that Wade had died, but he denied any neglect or malpractice.

The first witness for the prosecution was Surgeon H. M. Hall of the 17th Infantry:

> I saw Melvin Wade on the morning of 7th April, the day after his return to the regiment. He attended sick call; I excused him from duty. I found him suffering from chronic diarrhea and general debility, but not such an extent as to convince me that he was dangerously ill at that time. I prescribed tincture of iron plus quinine, and returned him to his quarters as convalescing. [Iron was considered a general tonic; quinine was seen as helpful in most fevers.]
>
> On the morning of the 8th, he again appeared at sick call in about the same condition. He received the same treatment. On the morning of the 9th, he did not appear at sick call. I inquired for him and found him in camp. I gave him no medicine but prescribed rest in quarters. On the 10th, he appeared again at sick call. I prescribed more iron and quinine. On the 11th, he came again to sick call and I had considerable conversation with him. I thought him no worse, but on the contrary, better.

I had learned on the 9th that no quarters had been prepared for him [i.e., Wade was sleeping on the bare ground.] and I sent word to his company commander to furnish him quarters. I ascertained on the 10th that nothing had been done in reference to quarters, and I referred the case to Dr. Colton [probably the regimental surgeon] and sent orders for a second time to his company commander. On the morning of the 11th, I ascertained that Wade had been furnished with two pieces of shelter tent, but with no blanket. At this point, I left to go out on picket with the regiment. The regiment did have a hospital tent.

The court asked why Wade had not been put in the regimental hospital. Hall replied, "We had accommodations but I considered him a case for quarters and not the hospital—I had several cases equally bad and returned them to quarters." The court then asked about policies regarding transferring men from division hospital to regimental hospital and received this reply: "I do not know the custom or official orders, but I know that men were returned who, in my judgment, were in as bad or in a worse condition than the man Wade when returned." The court's final question to Hall was the cause of death. "I don't know; there was no autopsy."

Now Hall was cross-examined by Dr. Clark, the defendant. "Could not Wade have been returned to the division hospital?" Hall replied, "Yes, we never had any difficulty in sending patients to division hospital." Clark continued his questions: "After Wade returned to your regiment, was an examination made to ascertain whether he was a proper subject for discharge [from the army]?" Hall seemed unsure. "I think an examination was made by Dr. Colton or maybe by Dr. Ramsey." Clark pressed on: "If the surgeons, when they had examined Wade for discharge, had considered him a proper subject for hospital treatment, would they not have returned him to division hospital?" Again, Hall was unsure: "I cannot state, but the custom would have been either to return him to division or regimental hospital."

At this point, Hall stepped down, and the court heard from W. R. Ramsey, Medical Director of the 2nd Division until "April 12 past." He said, "There were verbal orders that patients should be returned to their regiment when *fit for duty* [authors' emphasis]." The court queried Ramsey further on this point: "Was it customary to return men to their regiments if they were not ready for duty?" Ramsey answered, "It was not."

Ramsey went on to say that convalescent men not ready for duty would be returned to their regiments only if the hospital was overcrowded or about to be "broken up" when the division was preparing to move. Why the exception in Wade's case? "Wade occasioned considerable trouble by befouling his bed and it seemed to be the doctor's opinion . . . that it was done unnecessarily, either through carelessness or from a desire to make himself disagreeable."

Now the court moved closer to the heart of the matter: "Do you think there was any impropriety in sending Wade back to his regiment?" Ramsey replied, "Yes, I think there was impropriety; he could have been cared for better at the division hospital, but I do not think that sending him back occasioned his death, nor do I think there was neglect of duty." Ramsey was familiar with Wade's case. "He'd had chronic diarrhea for two months; he'd recovered from the fever, and he was having only four to six evacuations a day. His pulse was soft and quiet and he was able to walk about with perfect ease. I concluded that it was a case of debility and relaxation of the bowels, and that the man should be discharged. I had the papers ready." The court acquitted Dr. Clark of the charge of neglect of duty.

><+>-O-<+><

COMMENT: Chronic diarrhea can be very hard to treat, even today. In 1863, what with total ignorance of bacteria, viruses, and parasites and in the absence of specific treatments, diarrhea could mean death. Since Wade's discharge papers had already been made out, it is clear that he was considered incurable. One wonders whether had he reached home, with a roof over his head and a diet more nutritious, he might have survived.

However, in Wade's case his treatment seems substandard. It is obvious that he was discharged from the division hospital because he soiled his bed. It would be idle to speculate on Wade's motives or lack of motives for soiling. On return to his regiment, his "quarters" (what an inappropriately elegant term) consisted of lying on the ground. Only after the passage of six days, and after a repeated direct order by the surgeon, did his captain provide a tent for Wade—and still no blanket. The unclear boundaries between medical and administrative responsibility played a part in Wade's death.

It is true that most treatments for diarrhea were useless, his condition was no worse than many men in the camp, and even the best medical care might not have saved him. But he was denied even the minor comforts of a tent and a blanket. Was he so disagreeable, so undesirable, that he was left like a beast in the field, exposed to the sun and to the rain? Wade's is not a pleasant story and it does not have a happy ending.

Chapter Eleven

Bernard J. Bettleheim

The 106th Regiment of Illinois Infantry, camped at Little Rock, Arkansas, seemed to have seethed with ill will. One of the storm centers was Surgeon Bernard J. Bettleheim. At his court-martial in 1864, he was charged with neglect of duty, conduct prejudicial to good order and military discipline, and with conduct unbecoming an officer and a gentleman.[1]

His neglect of duty was a medical issue: He insisted that a man was not sick; within three days, the man was dead. As to the second charge, Bettleheim had ordered one of the hospital nurses to go to the river and fish for him, and the surgeon had also eaten some of the rations provided for the hospital patients. Regarding the "officer and a gentleman" charge, Bettleheim had announced several times that his commander and most of the officers of the regiment were drunkards. At his trial, he raised a number of objections at the outset, all of which were overruled.

The first witness for the prosecution was 2nd Lt. H. C. Northington, who said, "Private J. C. Lindy was left sick at Devall's Bluff, Arkansas. When we came to Little Rock, he joined us as a convalescent. On the evening of October 7th, he was taken sick with vomiting. In the morning, I saw Major Bettleheim and told him about the man. As I understood the major, he said there was nothing wrong with Lindy. That morning about 10:00 o'clock, Lindy was dead." (In the written trial record, the time sequences are often unclear.)

Pvt. James Whitley was one of the men who dispensed medicine at the hospital, following the doctor's orders. Unfortunately, when he testified, he could not recall what had been prescribed for Lindy, and the hospital records appeared to be scarce or nonexistent. As to the dying patient's condition, to one set of questions Whitely responded, "Private Lindy did not appear too sick," but earlier he had told the court that Lindy was "in a swoon" and that Bettleheim had bled the patient, bathed his feet, and rubbed him all over with alcohol. (As late as 1892, William Osler recommended bleeding for early pneumonia, arteriosclerosis, and cerebral hemorrhage.) "Before he went into a swoon, he appeared about right and asked for a chew of tobacco."

The hospital steward, Fred Barker, knew nothing about Lindy being refused admission to the hospital. Barker seemed most informed on the subject of fishing for the doctor. "Dr. Bettleheim and I had seen some good fish caught in the Arkansas River and he told Private Bennett, the man who drove the medical wagon, to go fish for him. The driver refused, saying he did not enlist to go fishing. The doctor replied that if it were a direct order, then the man must fish, whether for a few hours or for all day." (Later, Bettleheim mused, "Can a foreigner understand the customs of this country?" This, and his name, suggest a Germanic origin—and an imperfect grasp of the more egalitarian and inchoate culture of frontier America.)

Pvt. D. B. Minsker, a nurse in the hospital, recalled the arrival of the patient. "Lindy was brought by stretcher and put in front of the tent. Dr. Bettleheim told Lindy to get up and walk in, but Lindy said he was too sick. The doctor replied, 'What does that mean, that he can't walk? He ain't dead.' Then the sergeant and the boys carried Lindy in. The doctor said that Lindy wasn't sick. The sergeant disagreed with the doctor, but he replied, 'He is not sick. I can tell when a man is sick.' The doctor felt Lindy's pulse but did not prescribe. The next morning I called the doctor because I thought Lindy was dying. Lindy got up, took a drink from the tin cup, lay down and died." This is as much as the trial record reveals as to clinical observation, diagnosis, and treatment. Of course, there was no lab work or autopsy. The former did not exist, and the latter would have been most unusual.

The often-present issue of doctors' rations seemed to occupy the court as much as did the death of Private Lindy. Hospital Steward Barker recalled that Dr. Bettleheim ate hospital food through September and October of 1863, supplemented by duck and chicken from the local countryside, and that the doctor's mess included Dr. Bettleheim, Dr. P. Harvey Ellsworth, and the convalescent attendants. "As far as I know, Dr. Bettleheim never paid for the hospital patients rations that he ate." When asked directly by the court, Barker admitted to ill feeling between himself and Dr. Bettleheim. Dr. Ellsworth told the court that he himself contributed local produce and poultry to the mess, but he had not seen Dr. Bettleheim pay for anything.

Dr. M. Stockloff, senior surgeon of the 2nd Brigade, described army policy for the messing of regimental surgeons: "Surgeons mess with the assistant surgeon and the hospital steward. They buy their own food, but have it cooked by the same man who cooks for the hospital. The custom is that the surgeons buy their own provisions and throw them in with the hospital steward's rations or with the rations of the hospital in general." (This seems a recipe for administrative confusion.)

The final subject of the court-martial was Bettleheim's numerous public assertions that the officers of his regiment were drunkards. Nearly every witness had heard the doctor describe his attempts to resign—which had been rejected, and his plans to resubmit his resignation, giving as his reason that only a drunkard could be happy in the 106th Illinois. Bettleheim's concerns were not entirely without merit. One witness had seen Lt. Col. Henry Yates drunk, the other officers made repeated and fraudulent attempts to obtain medicinal alcohol from the hospital, and a keg of hospital whiskey had been stolen from under the head of Private Whitley as he slept.

At the end of the trial, the defendant submitted a fourteen-page defense. He made light of the fishing story, claiming that he had furnished his share in the mess, and then made a strong defense of his medical work. Viewed in today's perspective, his arguments sound fairly reasonable. The court thought otherwise. He was acquitted of neglecting his patient but convicted of eating the patient's food and of disrespect to his superiors by his accusations of intemperance. He was sentenced to be dismissed from the service.

Parallel with these proceedings, he was ordered to appear before an Army Medical Examining Board. They found him to be unqualified, and he was discharged December 28, 1863, by Special Order No. 575 of the Adjutant General's Office. The next month, according to the record, he resigned.

The following February the governor of Illinois wrote to the army, stating that Bettleheim had passed an examination required by his state for commissioning of medical officers in Illinois regiments. The governor strongly suggested that if Bettleheim was good enough for the state of Illinois, he ought to be good enough for the Federal government. Nothing came of this correspondence. Bettleheim died February 9, 1870, at Brookfield, Missouri, without ever reentering the Army.

>-+-+>-0-<+-+-<

COMMENT: The trial neglects the role of the doctor who sent Private Lindy back to his regiment; whatever Bettelheim's flaws, he seems to have inherited a moribund patient. We also see the jurisdictional problems when a doctor was approved and appointed by a state government but judged by the Federal government. The Federal medical examiners overrode the state medical examiners. Who was to set the standards? These are no longer issues in the United States Army, but the appointment of officers by governors in the state-run, federally funded National Guard units continues to be a source of difficulty.

Chapter Twelve

John D. Johnson

Abraham Lincoln, no less, rescued John Johnson's career from disgrace. His was a life that ranged from West Africa to New York, from Baltimore to New Orleans. He was investigated for drinking the patients' whiskey, for saying (at a later date) "treasonable" things about Pres. Andrew Johnson, and for being an "opium-eater." In a war filled with forceful personalities, Johnson was in the front ranks.[1]

He was born somewhere around 1820 and served between 1843–1845 as a hospital steward aboard a U.S. Navy ship stationed along the west coast of Africa. A year after his return to the United States, he graduated from the medical department of Pennsylvania College in Philadelphia. His whereabouts for the next fifteen years are unclear, but in 1862 he was examining recruits in Baltimore and for the first seven months of 1863 was assigned to hospitals in the same city.

In July 1863 he arrived in Chattanooga, Tennessee, as a surgeon of U.S. Volunteers, and four months later he was court-martialed for drinking whiskey prescribed for the patients. The chief prosecution witness was a Private Doty, who swore that Dr. Johnson had drunk whiskey intended for his use and thereby delayed or prevented his recuperation. Johnson, testifying on his own behalf, stated that he needed some whiskey "to correct the sick stomach created by the effluvia arising from the discharge, which was extremely offensive." In other words, the foul stench of dozens of infected wounds made the doctor sick to his stomach. Testimony by Johnson's colleagues described him as a man of "good character," and other witnesses established that the total amount of whiskey consumed by Johnson was less than half a pint.

He was convicted of "conduct prejudicial to good order and military discipline" and sentenced to be dismissed. But the story wasn't over. After the conviction, Doty made a deathbed confession that he had always received enough whiskey for his needs and that he had testified falsely; his motivation does not appear in the records. A testimonial filed in his record shortly after the conviction states, "Dr. Johnson has invented the best splint for fracture of the forearm and elbow that has ever been brought to the notice of the profession." The sentence was reviewed by Maj. Gen. George Thomas (the "Rock of Chickamauga"), who suspended the sentence and passed the case onward "to await the pleasure of the President," with a strong recommendation that the dismissal be commuted to a reprimand in general orders.

On March 4, 1864, Judge Advocate General Joseph Holt issued his report. Noting Thomas's recommendation, the deathbed recantation, and the small quantity of whiskey involved, he concluded, "The conduct of the accused was reprehensible, but it is not believed that the interest of the service will be promoted by the dismissal of this officer." This phase of Johnson's career was brought to a conclusion by the following note in the President's own hand: "Recom. of Gen. Thomas approved and ordered. A. Lincoln April 26, 1864." Dr. Johnson's army career was saved—for the moment.

Other than his invention of a new splint, Johnson's activities in the six months between his trial and Lincoln's decision are unknown. Nor does he appear in the records again until he was hospitalized for cystitis in January 1865. Three months after that, the man who spared him was assassinated at Ford's Theatre. Lincoln's successor, Andrew Johnson, apparently did not make a favorable impression upon Surgeon Johnson, who was arrested in May 1865 for "treasonable language" against the new president. It seems that nothing came of this charge since the doctor was "honorably mustered out as a U.S. Volunteer surgeon in July 1865." He then served two months as a surgeon with the 20th U.S. Colored Troops until they, too, were mustered out. From there, he went to the 81st USCT, a Louisiana-based unit, until that regiment, as well, completed its term of service in January 1866 and Dr. Johnson with it.

Late that same year, he was at work as a contract surgeon in New Orleans; we next hear of him in August 1867, an eventful month. He met with a Medical Board of Examiners, which queried him on the newest medical knowledge. As part of the application for that examination, he certified that, "I have never been connected with homeopathy." Later that same month, he suffered an injury that had many consequences. His letter of November 16, 1867, written at Willard's Hotel in Washington, D.C., tells us much of medical practice in 1867, of the growing concern over narcotics addiction and of the relative rapidity and convenience of transport in the years just after the war. The letter is addressed to John S. Billings, Brevet Lieutenant Colonel (and future Deputy Surgeon General of the U.S. Army) and one of the great names in late-Victorian American medicine.

"I respectfully ask to submit the following to your consideration, viz—on the 20th August past, you gave me a contract as Acting Assistant Surgeon, USA, of same date, with orders to report for duty to General [Thomas] McParlin, Medical Director, 5th Depot at New Orleans, Louisiana, and transportation by sea from New York City. On the Friday evening ensuing [two days later], I was attacked with strangury [slow and painful urination] as the result of contusion of the perineum from a fall across the top of my trunk while assisting at getting it downstairs, which delayed my departure from New York until the sailing of the steamer following the one originally fixed upon. The severity and persistence of the disease demanded very active treatment, including bleeding from both arms to forty ounces in amount.

I left New York weak from the loss and the pain of the attack, continued sick during the passage and was so unwell on arriving at the New Orleans Quarantine Station that its medical officer, Dr. [Henry] Heilner, late Acting Assistant Surgeon, USA, refused my passage up to the city in its then-unhealthy condition [probably the usual epidemics of cholera and yellow fever] and detained me five days at the Station, at the end of which period I reported to General McParlin (on a Saturday), and on Monday was assigned to duty at Jackson Barracks under . . . Surgeon [Charles B.] White, he being in charge pro tem, from the fact of Surgeon [Bennett?] Clement's sickness from yellow fever.

The garrison was 900, the sick list 200, and the average mortality [was] six in 24 hours. I was placed in charge of Wards A and B, numbering about 100 sick, all, or nearly all, diagnosed as yellow fever. On the evening of the third day of my assignment to the post, I was desired by Dr. White to call upon him at his quarters at 10:00 p.m. I did so. He ordered me to go to my room and to no longer visit Wards A and B, or in any way attempt henceforth to treat any of the garrison, [stating] that I uncovered, or permitted to continue uncovered, the sick of my charges, that my prescriptions on the dispensary file were professionally improper, that one of my patients, then just dead, should not have died, that he believed I used opium as a habit, and that he should make a written statement of the case to the medical director in the morning. I asked him in what consisted the impropriety of my prescriptions, what part of my treatment it was that caused the death of a patient, and what [were] his grounds for the charge of opium eating? His answers were: The impropriety consisted in having ordered so large a quantity of laudanum at a time as two ounces, that my malpractice in the case of the patient was uncovering him and bathing the perineum and parts around the anus with cold water, as well as giving a suppository of opium and coconut butter, and the opinion, of opium eating, rested upon my having taken at the counter of the dispensary two fluid drams of paregoric, on the first day of my arrival and 30 drops of tincture of opium on the second day.

In answer to this, I respectfully submit that the two ounces of laudanum was prescribed for general use in Wards A and B in the preparation of the starch and laudanum injection, diarrhea being one of the complications of yellow fever. And I was not aware of violating any rule of Dr. White's, in having the quantity of two ounces in the wards at a time. The paregoric was taken by me, combined with Tincture of Capsicum [a cayenne pepper derivative] half a fluid dram, and brandy, six fluid drams, for prostration with some diarrhea, and the 30 drops of tincture of opium the following day for the same purpose. [These dosages are handwritten in apothecary abbreviations, and difficult to read.]

The suppository had been ordered for the patient by the medical director, in the presence of Dr. White, at the bedside, the same morning, which, with the bathing with water of the excoriated parts were the only changes made in the treatment from that laid down by Dr. White himself.

In all this, I acquit Dr. White of intentional wrong to me. I made a bad impression on my arrival at the post, from my sickly appearance, which perhaps, to some eyes, simulated the results of debauch. I was not very efficient, being still weak, and with diarrhea. While the use of preparations of opium for two days might lay me open to the suspicion of its habitual use, I have reason to know that one of the female nurses, whom I have reproved for a slight negligence, reported the matter of uncovering the men untruthfully to him in a spirit of revenge. Independently of all this, I recollect suffering, for a season, from cystitis while at Sedgwick Hospital, a year since, and using sulfate of morphine for the time more or less, and Dr. White was a member of our mess at the time.

I would submit that my record of near-five years service in the department has, up to this unfortunate matter, been fair. That I am endorsed by Surgeon [first name unknown] Perrin, late Medical Director, Department of the Cumberland, and also Surgeon [illegible], late Medical Director, Department of Ohio, both of which are in the office of the Surgeon General, in a way commendatory of my status as a medical officer, and I respectfully ask, should it meet the approval of the department, that I may be given a contract as Acting Assistant Surgeon, USA. My contract was annulled at the end of the first month on the grounds that my services were no longer required. I have the honor to be, most respectfully, your obedient servant, John D. Johnson, M.D.

Two days later, Billings referred the letter on to General McParlin "for investigation and report. Dr. Johnson's record and his testimonials on file in this office are good. By order of the Surgeon General." There the record stops, except for a brief note that Dr. Johnson had died "of natural causes" in 1874.

>━┼━◆>━◦━<◆┼━<

COMMENT: Tincture of opium and paregoric (an opium derivative) are still used today to treat diarrhea. They are ancient and honorable remedies. The brief observations in the record are not enough to establish whether Johnson was overusing them. The medical theories of the Civil War era explain the use of cayenne. On the premise that his system was indolent and plethoric, an irritant like red pepper would seem reasonable. Brandy, like whiskey and wine, was widely used as a medicine and as a carrier for alcohol-soluble medications.

Johnson was also criticized for "exposing" his patient and washing the perineum. Since the patient's perianal region was excoriated from severe diarrhea, washing away the acidic fecal matter and letting the skin dry seems like excellent nursing care. It is unclear why Dr. White objected to this procedure.

As to Johnson's drinking hospital whiskey at Chattanooga, that, too, seems to have little substance. The complainant told the court that he'd fabricated the story. The total amount consumed over several days was less than half a pint. Assuming a four-day period, that yields a daily intake of two ounces of whiskey—two weak drinks at an honest bar. The Surgeon General noted a good record and positive testimonials. Perhaps all Johnson's problems were a tempest in a teapot.

Chapter Thirteen

William Soule

Seven days after the bloody repulse at Fredericksburg, the 21st Connecticut camped in the bitter cold along the north bank of the Rappahannock. There, just three days before Christmas, 1862, they court-martialed their surgeon. None of the misdeeds alleged were connected with the battle.[1]

The regiment had begun their service with three months at Arlington Heights, in the Defenses of Washington, D.C. In early December they started south, but by a circuitous route, which took them through the village of Lovettsville, in the little bulge of northern Virginia that lies just below Frederick, Maryland. At Lovettsville, "Surgeon Soule . . . neglected to examine and prescribe for Private Francis Cosgrove of Company A . . . who was then lying upon the ground, coughing violently and raising blood."

There were three other parts to the charge of "neglect of duty: At Wheatland, Virginia, Soule refused to examine Pvt. William McClellan, a man with a broken collarbone; on December 10th, at Fredericksburg, Dr. Soule failed to examine Cpl. Henry B. Luce, who was "helpless in his tent with fever"; the same week he failed to visit Sgt. A. L. Prentice, who was in a "dying condition." The eleven witnesses summoned told eleven different stories. All those who testified were from the 21st Connecticut, except for two surgeons.

Capt. Joseph Jordan recalled:

> While at camp near Lovettsville, I was called to look at Francis Cosgrove, who was lying by the side of the campfire, coughing and raising blood. I ordered that the surgeon be called. I went with the messenger, it being on my way to regimental headquarters, and stopped to hear what reply the surgeon made. He told the sergeant that they were 'all abed' and he could do nothing for him that night. After the surgeon refused to prescribe for Cosgrove, I reported the fact to the colonel of the regiment, who sent for the hospital steward to prescribe for him. As to Private McClellan, he came to me while we

were near Wheatland, Virginia, and said that he had hurt his arm. I went with him to the surgeon's quarters. Dr. Soule said that he could do nothing for McClellan that night. I heard him say that myself; I then directed McClellan to Surgeon [Abner] Warner of the 16th Connecticut, who bandaged the shoulder and put the arm in a sling.

Jordan also had some information about the treatment of Corporal Luce. "Luce was unable to answer the hospital call. He remained in his tent, and was examined later that day only when I called the attention of the three surgeons to him. Surgeon Smith and Dr. Soule looked at him, but did not prescribe any treatment."

The defendant then cross-examined Captain Jordan. "Exactly what time did you see Private Cosgrove lying on the ground, did you personally see what was wrong with him, and how did you know it was from the lungs and not from vomiting?" Captain Jordan, who had made no claims to being a doctor, said he did not know the exact time, but it was clearly "after candlelight"; he had personally seen blood coming from Cosgrove's mouth; and he had no way of telling what organ it came from. He added, "Cosgrove has been troubled badly with a cough ever since he joined my company, and although he is now on duty, he is about as unfit for duty as any man who is up and around." Soule then insisted that he was not the regimental doctor assigned to Jordan's company. The captain replied, "I have never been officially notified of who our surgeon is. At various times, Drs. Soule, [Lewis] Dixon, and [Hamilton] Lee have prescribed for men in my company."

Lt. George P. Edwards recalled that at Lovettsville, after the march from Pleasant Valley, Maryland, Cosgrove was taken with violent coughing and raised blood. The surgeon did not come to see him, but later the hospital steward did, and he prescribed salt and water. Sgt. H. F. Roberts had sat next to Cosgrove and saw "blood coming from his mouth, almost a stream. Cosgrove lay down on the ground, and said he was too weak to sit up." Roberts confirmed the story of Soule, saying that he had gone to bed, but added that he called out of the tent, suggesting the use of salt water.

Surgeon Wagner of the 16th Connecticut recalled, "At camp near Wheatland, a man came to me and said he had hurt his shoulder. He was sent to me since his own surgeon would not attend to him. I examined him and found a simple fracture of the collarbone. I put his arm in a sling, and put a pack in the axilla and told him to see his own surgeon in the morning. I do not remember his name. I don't think any injury would have come by delaying the treatment until the morning."

Capt. Jeremiah Shepard stated that Prentice was his orderly sergeant and had died at 4:00 in the morning on the 9th of December. He visited Prentice at the hospital two days before the death and found him unconscious. "Dr. Soule made no prescription for him whatever, although the man was evidently dying. I also noticed on several visits that Prentice was not clean and that the bedding and ventilation were poor. Dr. Lee ordered that Prentice should have stimulants and warm bricks be placed to him, but Dr. Soule did nothing about that." Soule's first cross-examination question was, "What would you have prescribed for a dying man?" Shepard's answer, not surprisingly, was, "I don't know; I am not a doctor!" He then went on to add that he was concerned for Prentice's comfort, as there was no hay or straw for a bed.

The next witness was the man who had been coughing up blood. "At the time we marched from Pleasant Valley, I had a cold and was taken with coughing and raising blood. Dr. Soule did not come to see me, but the hospital steward did. The spitting of blood stopped about an hour after the salt water [maybe it does work!], but not the coughing. The next day, I was strong enough to march, but without a knapsack."

Soule's first defense witness was Dr. Dixon, who stated that he had been a practicing physician for eleven years. "The usual prescription I would give for spitting up blood would be salt and water. It is a favorite prescription with old-school physicians, and I think it would be good judgment to use it. The man with the injured shoulder came to Dr. Soule, who told him to bathe his shoulder in cold water and said that there were no medicines, since they were still behind with the transport. There was no neglect on the part of Dr. Soule to prescribe. With reference to the case of Luce, Dr. Soule went up with a committee to visit the tents, and when he came back, he told me to attend to Corporal Luce, which I did." The witness also spoke to the problem with Prentice's bedding, saying that neither hay nor straw was available, and Prentice was kept as clean as possible under the circumstances. His final statement explains some of the conflict in the regiment. "I have heard Captain Jordan make threats against Dr. Soule, and has shown ill will against him. The problem has been about which men were too sick to march. Soule thought men should march who Captain Jordan thought were too sick for the march."

William Smith, a surgeon with the 103rd New York, had been in practice since 1846. He also endorsed the use of salt and water for spitting blood and described it as "a good astringent and a domestic remedy." He thought the hospital under the charge of Dr. Soule was in good condition and the patients well cared for. As to the dying Prentice, "If a man is insensible [unconscious], and apparently suffering no pain, there is no need for treatment." He also spoke to the relatively benign aspects of fractured clavicle but admitted that a compound fracture could be a very dangerous injury.

Lt. Hiram Richmond, the regimental quartermaster, stated that for six days it was impossible to get any straw for the hospital beds, and he, too, had heard Captain Jordan make threats about Dr. Soule. Pvt. Aaron Eldridge had been a nurse at the hospital and confirmed that Prentice had been unconscious for the twenty-four hours before his death. "The night before he died, Prentice had an involuntary discharge. His drawers were then taken off and he was kept as clean as he could be. I fed him gruel three times a day. The last day, both Dr. Lee and Dr. Soule made an examination, and said that he would die." Pvt. John Simmons, another hospital nurse, confirmed that Prentice was washed every day and seen by the doctor every day. The hospital steward, James S. Barber, recalled that Dr. Soule had paid so much attention to the dying Prentice that Barber thought that Soule might "be acquainted with him."

The penultimate witness was Dr. Warner, who was called back to testify again. He also spoke of the benefits of salt water but said it was for hemorrhage of the lungs, not for hemorrhage of the stomach. The court asked him, "Would it not be in your opinion neglect to prescribe in a case of vomiting blood without examining the patient?" Warner sidestepped the question deftly: "I think he should have made such an examination, unless he had a previous knowledge of the case." Closing out the witness parade was the hospital steward, James S. Barber, who spoke of the man with the broken collarbone: "That night, Dr. Soule asked the man if he had broken anything. In the morning, he set the bone and excused the man from duty."

The court rendered their verdict: not guilty. This conclusion was approved by the much-wounded Maj. Gen. John Sedgwick, best known for his last words: "They couldn't hit an elephant at this distance."

Two months after his court-martial, Soule resigned. On the back of his letter, someone has written, "Surgeon's Soule's usefulness is much impaired by reason of difficulties with the officers of the regiment. A change in his department would be highly beneficial to the service."

>─┼─◆>─○─<◆─┼─<

COMMENT: In many ways, Soule's treatment ideas met the standard of practice. Salt and water for coughing up blood was a well-accepted (if utterly useless by today's standards) remedy. Uncomplicated fracture of the clavicle is still treated with the simplest of bandages. Poor Sergeant Prentice, unconscious and dying, was apparently not in pain, so no specific treatment seemed indicated.

The defect in Soule's behavior seemed to be a lack of initiative, bordering on callous indifference. Cosgrove's comrades, facing a great battle, might well have wondered, "Will the doctor exert himself for *me* if I am wounded or sick?"

Whatever technical advances occur, a physician has a duty to reassure. The ancient joke about the two factors needed for a successful practice (gray hair for a look of dignity; hemorrhoids for a look of concern) has more than a little truth to it. Surely, Soule's professors at Yale had told him that. Every real doctor has had night duty and knows that "being abed" will not do as an excuse.

In 1890 he applied for a pension, saying that he had been sick with chills and fever (probably malaria) since 1862, was ruptured, and was totally deaf in one ear. In 1900 he died in a carriage accident at Jewett City, Connecticut. Four years later his widow, Martha, applied for a pension, but she was turned down, because she had an income in excess of $250 a year.

Chapter Fourteen

Edward L. Feehan

Col. Florence Cornyn was soaked through and through by the night air and the cold February rain. At 3:00 in the morning he reached his camp, found that the doctor and the quartermaster had eaten most of the food, and, by feeling under the canvas fly of a tent, determined that his surgeon "was sleeping very comfortably." This, and the fact that the surgeon had failed to report an officer's plot to murder the colonel, led to some ill feeling and a court-martial of Edward L. Feehan, surgeon of the 10th Missouri Cavalry.[1]

The charge of "neglect of duty," contained these particulars: On the night of February 25, 1863, the regiment was on the march from Tuscumbia, Alabama, to Corinth, Mississippi. Its ambulances, containing patients, were at the bottom of a hill. Dr. Feehan was a mile away on top of the hill, sleeping on a dry cot, while most of the other men were cold and wet.

Feehan's other act of neglect was his failure to examine Capt. Patrick Lanagan, who claimed to be too sick for duty. As to the mutiny charge, the court papers stated that on the night of March 18, 1863, Dr. Feehan was present at a meeting of Maj. Thomas Hynes, Capt. Duncan McNicol, and Captain Lanagan, where Hynes said, "I am only waiting my time when I can kill Colonel Cornyn." Feehan failed to report this threat.

The first witness was the regimental sutler, Michael Kearby, who was at the meeting briefly, felt that some remark was directed against him personally, and left. "I was hurt by what the doctor said about me. Later that night, standing in the dark, Dr. Feehan said, It was not about you. I was speaking of Colonel Cornyn. He goes about at night listening to what is said in the tents. One of these nights, he is going to have his head shot off.'"

Another witness told a somewhat confusing story about Dr. Feehan, Captain Lanagan, Major Hynes, Captain McNicol, Lt. Michael Ravolds, and Lt. Charles Barton all being sent to Corinth under arrest for the crime of conspiracy. It appears from the record that all were soon back on duty.

W. L. Tolman, Assistant Surgeon of the 10th Missouri, told his story. "Colonel Cornyn ordered me and Dr. Feehan to examine Captain Lanagan. I think the colonel said, 'If your report does not please me, I will make a report that will not please you.' At Captain Lanagan's tent, Dr. Feehan asked a few questions, but did not make an examination, then he left. I did not examine the captain because I was only the assistant surgeon and Dr. Feehan did not ask me to make an examination." In response to a question by the court, he added, "Yes, it is unusual to make a report on a patient's condition based solely on the patient's report."

Lt. Jeremiah Young was called to testify: "That night in the rain there were about a thousand men under Colonel Cornyn's command. I was busy with my duties and only saw Dr. Feehan a few times. Later in the evening, I saw him asleep on a cot at headquarters, under a fly. The headquarters was on the top of a hill. The sick were in ambulances at the bottom of the hill."

Surgeon Joseph Pogue of the 66th Illinois was present on the expedition to Tuscumbia. He recalled his authority as very vague, the situation as chaotic, and the weather as dreadful. He simply treated anyone who came to him, regardless of their regiment. Pogue did not believe that the patients suffered by Feehan's absence.

John D. Riedy, Feehan's hospital steward, added his recollections:

> We had about seven men who were very sick on the Tuscumbia expedition. There were more sick men than we had transportation for. Dr. Pogue prescribed for them. Dr. Feehan was not there and had not told me that he would be away that night. It took us four days to get back to Corinth from Tuscumbia. One of the sick men died in the hotel at Jacinto [Mississippi]. The man who died had been carried in the negro ambulance. Dr. Feehan did not want to leave any of the sick behind, because a Rebel prisoner had been shot trying to escape and the doctor thought the Rebels would kill any sick men left behind."

Colonel Cornyn, a central figure in this drama, had much to say:

> Our headquarters were on top of the mountain about five miles west of Tuscumbia, on the road to Corinth. The rain and bad roads caused us a lot of trouble. About 3:00 in the morning, having accomplished putting the train up the mountain, except for the ambulances, I came to my headquarters on the summit. I found my negro servant cowering over the coals of a fire. He told me that Dr. Feehan and the acting quartermaster had eaten their supper and gone to sleep. The negroes had eaten what was left. It was too dark to see under the fly, but I could feel the doctor sleeping comfortably on a cot. There were many men under the canvas, so I took my chair and sat in the rain. I had no sleep or food.

In the morning, I roused the camp. When the doctor was dressed, I asked him where his sick were. He said he thought they were down the mountain. I told him his place was with the sick and he should have stayed with them. I ordered him to go to the ambulances and told him he'd been grossly neglectful. The doctor muttered some surly reply and left.

The court-martial concluded on June 26, 1863. Dr. Feehan was found not guilty on all charges and specifications. The commanding general disagreed and asked that they reconsider their findings. This they did, and they found Feehan guilty of neglecting the sick on the night of February 25, 1863. He was sentenced to be publicly reprimanded by Colonel Cornyn.

On November 20, 1863, Dr. Feehan deserted his regiment and went to Ireland. The following April, he was dismissed from the army by War Department Special Order No. 134. After the war he returned to America, practiced as an allopath, and died in St. Louis, Missouri, on May 8, 1902.

>—+—◦—+—<

COMMENT: From the record, it looks like Colonel Cornyn was correct: Feehan was negligent. He was snug and dry on top of the hill while his commander sat in the rain, and the sick and wounded remained on a muddy road a mile away. The ambulance train was at the tail end of the column, vulnerable to capture and possible execution by the Confederates. Dr. Pogue generously said that Feehan's absence caused no harm, but he did add that in Feehan's absence, the entire medical burden fell upon him. If a doctor's duty is to his patients, Feehan failed the test.

PART TWO

Stranger Than Fiction

Chapter Fifteen

George G. Potts

After his head was reattached, Pvt. Benjamin Anderson was buried, 1,100 yards east of Fort Harrison, Virginia.[1]

Today, thousands of visitors pass the site of the fort each year, in Richmond's eastern suburbs. Anderson's unmarked bones are no doubt scattered, as the area where he was buried is now a gravel quarry; he belonged to Company C, 23rd Regiment of U.S. Colored Troops, and his story is inextricably entwined with that of George Potts, the regimental surgeon.[2]

The 23rd USCT was formed in the spring of 1864 and served in the siege of Richmond and Petersburg. The month after Lee's surrender, the regiment was placed on the transport ship *Richmond* and sent to its new duty post, Brazos Santiago—a low, humid, sandy island at the mouth of the Rio Grande. There they stayed until November 1865, when the regiment was mustered out. Dr. Potts was with the regiment nearly the entire twenty months of its life—except when he was twice being court-martialed.

The charges of his first trial sound like the bill of fare at a horror show. There were eleven separate specifications. The first of these, in its original wording, reads: "The said Potts, under the pretense of holding a post mortem examination of the body of Benjamin Anderson, deceased . . . proceeded to cut down to the femoral artery, open the sheath, and place around it a ligature, for the purpose of practice, this . . . near the camp of the 23rd, near Fort Bunkingham, Virginia, on or about the 21st day of March 1865, in the presence of enlisted men."

The other items charged against Dr. Potts, put into more succinct modern phraseology, were as follows: Potts attempted to ligate the subclavian artery, and in the attempt he cut the jugular vein for the purpose of practice. After Assistant Surgeon B. N. Bethel requested that he wished to examine the heart of Pvt. Anderson, Potts cut the heart out in its entirety, without ligating any of the blood vessels, causing blood to flow profusely and rendering the dispensary "perfectly horrible." Using the pretense of not having enough time, Potts refused to examine the removed heart. Potts then decapitated Private Anderson "for the purpose of practice" and put the head under the bunk in the dispensary. "On the pretense of holding a post mortem examination," Dr. Potts removed one kidney and the stomach, and, and along with the heart, he put them in a sack and threw them under the bunk, as well, where they remained overnight, until ordered by the commanding officer to replace the organs into the body. After mutilating the body of Anderson, Dr. Potts offered Pvt. Leonard Gant a dollar to sleep with the body until the morning. Dr. Potts took the head of Private Anderson to his quarters and when ordered to bring it back, he returned it "entirely flayed and did enclose it in a blanket and left it for burial without sewing it to the body." During those proceedings, Potts said to his assistant, Dr. Bethel, that nothing would please him more than being dismissed from the service. Further, Potts, when ordered by the colonel of the regiment to return the skin of Private Anderson's head, denied having such. In addition, Potts removed Anderson's head and substituted a bottle for it.

Dr. Potts's defense of his actions took the form of his description of the autopsy (in which he gives medical and anatomical details that are rare in court-martial records):

Acting Assistant Surgeon B. N. Bethel of the 23rd Regiment of USCT informed me that a private soldier by the name of Benjamin Anderson had dropped down dead suddenly when leaving his quarters on the afternoon of the 21st of March and Dr. Bethel desired to know whether a post mortem examination should be made.

I was detached from my regiment and at brigade headquarters, by order of Brigadier General [Henry] Thomas, and acting as brigade surgeon. I immediately instituted inquiries in reference to the case. I found that Acting Assistant Surgeon Copeland, late of the 23rd Regiment, had treated this soldier for 'neuralgia scorbutus and dysentery,' frequently changing treatment. The patient passed under the care of Dr. Bethel, who treated the case as for catarrh and first registered the man for treatment on the 17th of March, evidently considering that the case was not of sufficient importance to call my attention to it or to send the man to hospital. During the following week, he continued to treat the case by exhibiting the cough mixture, but on the 21st of March, found a change in treatment necessary and exhibited gentian and whisky, from which time he paid no further attention to the patient and when he next saw him, the man was dead. I immediately repaired to company quarters, examined the body and developed the foregoing facts. The fact that several cases of sudden death had occurred in this regiment, and from unknown causes, decided me on making a post mortem examination, and I accordingly ordered the body to be removed from company quarters to the dispensary, a [tent] about 200 yards to the rear, for convenience, to perform the necessary examination. I directed the hospital steward to remove the clothes carefully and to arrange the body for this purpose. This was around 3:00 P.M. I was not ready to proceed before 7:30 P.M., at which time it was falling dark. The body was perfectly cold and partially stiffened.

Candles were placed at convenient distances around the body, and only one man was permitted to remain in the tent. I ordered Dr. Bethel to make the examination, and having procured paper and pencil, I would take down the several stages of the autopsy and give what directions might be considered necessary. Dr. Bethel begged to be excused, alleging that he had never made a post mortem examination, nor had ever seen one made, although he had seen bodies after they had been opened. I was consequently under the necessity of proceeding with the examination myself.

I observed a considerable enlargement in the right femoral region, and apprehending that it might be an aneurysm of the iliac or upper portion of the femoral arteries that had burst, I determined to cut down upon the swelling. I commenced the incision close to Poupart's ligament and cut downwards to the fascia. I discovered that the swelling observed arose from the enlarged glands, several of which being divided in the incision. I exposed the femoral artery and then passed a ligature around it. I examined it upwards to its origin with the iliac. The deep profundus was given off three-quarters of an inch below the origin of the femoral, a singular and uncommon occurrence. I closed the incision by sutures and proceeded to the next step. I made an incision from the top of the sternum to the pubis, dissected back the pectoral muscles, separated the sternum at the costal cartilage, from the ribs, and first examined the organs of the chest. I found the heart hypertrophied. There was no serum in the pericardium. The lungs had suffered extensive disorganization, especially the upper lobe of the left lung, which was atrophied and adherent extensively to the intercostal pleura. The left lung was considerably hepatized.

I examined the aorta and its branches and took special pains to note the position of the right subclavian artery, which in this case, passed deep behind the scalenus anticus muscle, the curve lying well under the clavicle. I separated the sternal cartilage of the clavicle and drew it upwards to observe the position of the artery. It is not true, as was stated by Dr. Bethel, that the vessel was punctured or wounded, or that any flow of blood took place in the operation. [It would appear that Dr. Bethel had given the regimental commander a much different picture.]

I next examined the abdominal viscera and found the kidneys enormously enlarged, being at least four times their normal size, and I estimated their height of from ten to sixteen centimeters. [Note that

Dr. Potts uses the metric system here.] They presented the appearance characteristic of Bright's disease, having a marbled look and being very friable. The cortical substances were thickened, indurated and brittle, readily breaking into square and angular pieces on pressure. The malpighian bodies were very distinct.

The spleen was very large, being seven or eight inches long, and over two inches thick. It resembled a clot of blood. When cut into, it presented a spongy, congested, and very peculiar appearance. The malpighian bodies of the spleen were distinct. The stomach was then removed, the cardiac and pyloric ends having been previously secured. I stated to Dr. Bethel my opinion regarding these organs, and told him I thought they were perfect curiosities and it was my intention to send them to the Surgeon General for microscopic examination and for the medical museum in Washington, D.C. I asked Dr. Bethel whether he had any whisky [to act as a preservative] in which I could place these for transportation.

My opinion was that notwithstanding the abnormal state of the important organs, the sudden death of the subject was hardly warranted, and I remarked upon the necessity of making an autopsy of the brain. By now, I needed rest. It was near midnight and raining, and the floor of the tent was flooded and slippery. Dr. Bethel, under my instructions, removed the small intestines. While he was engaged at this, I noticed the bladder distended and directed a specimen of urine to be obtained. A bottle was placed in contact with the origin of the urethra, and about three ounces of highly albuminous urine, opaque, and of a ropy, mucilaginous consistency, was obtained. After resting a little while, I was obliged to sew up the body myself, as Bethel stated that he could not do so, not knowing how to replace the parts. At this time, I determined to decapitate the body. The lateness of the hour, the state of the tent, and my own bad condition precluded any prospect of being able to make the autopsy of such an important part of the body as the brain. Accordingly, I made an incision through the integument, an inch below the occipital protuberance, along the side of the head, and continued it along the borders of the lower maxillary, dissecting the integument downward to the clavicles. This was done for the purpose of obtaining covering to lap over the cavity that would be left after the removal of the head. I then removed the head, and adjusted the parts carefully by sutures, and finished the sewing up.

This completes the technical description of the autopsy, and the rest of his narrative can be paraphrased as follows: Since the body would present an unusual appearance without a head, Dr. Potts found a quart bottle, wrapped it in cloth, and then sewed the body (and bottle) up in a blanket, creating the appearance of an intact person. He placed the head, heart, stomach, spleen, and left kidney in a small box, covered them with a piece of canvas, and placed them under the bed. By then, it was 2:00 in the morning. Potts returned to his quarters, but worried that one of the many dogs around the camp might enter the dispensary tent and make off with the body parts, since no one remained with the body. He returned to the tent alone and moved the body parts to his quarters. He considered it one of the most important cases he had ever done an autopsy on, and he felt strongly that the viscera should be preserved and sent to the Surgeon General's medical museum.

Back at his own quarters, Potts, unable to sleep because of his curiosity as to the condition of the brain, peeled back the scalp in preparation for sawing open the skull, a usual procedure in postmortems. However, at this point, the regimental commander intervened and demanded the return of all of Private Anderson's various parts. Potts noted that the colonel was very excited and turned the specimens over to him, feeling that argument would be useless, because his commander had no understanding of the importance of these specimens.

In conclusion, Dr. Potts wrote that he had a good record with the regiment, that the line officers wished him to resign rather than fight the charges, and that he preferred to be moved to a different regiment. He also noted that disease in his right ear had almost entirely deprived him of his hearing, and he had received no treatment for this. Finally, as to the charges that he had done the autopsy "in the presence of enlisted men," the only witnesses were himself, Dr. Bethel, and one enlisted man who was an assistant to the hospital steward and had witnessed two previous postmortems. Finally, the postmortem was conducted in a tent 200 yards away from the camp, at night—hardly a public exhibition. Dr. Potts cited his own credentials, which included working as a coroner for several years, practice as a surgeon for twelve years, and being present at more than 100 autopsies. The regimental commander, Lt. Col. Marshall Dempsey, referred the matter to William A. Conover, Medical Director of the 25th Army Corps, adding, "Actions such as these being known to the enlisted men, if permitted to pass unnoticed, will demoralize troops and destroy all confidence and discipline, is beyond a doubt; especially among men of such superstitious cast of mind as the colored men." (It is worth noting that Colonel Dempsey had been invited to the autopsy but never appeared.)

In Dr. Conover's lengthy review, he begins with the statement, "Post mortem examinations are justifiable and often absolutely necessary in those cases of sudden death, where the disease has been developed in obscurity, there being no other means of ascertaining its nature." He noted that Private Anderson had died suddenly, attributing this to "[t]he colored soldiers having been enlisted without regard to their physical condition, old and young. Men afflicted with organic disease of the heart and kidneys are liable to die at any moment." As to regulations regarding post mortem examinations, "No orders have been issued as regards postmortem examinations, it being considered that the good sense of the medical officers and their professional knowledge would not lead them to abuse the privilege and bring disgrace upon all connected with it." In his review of Potts's examination of Anderson, Conover concluded that it was not a dissection but rather a mutilation. He seems to have accepted Bethel's view of the matter when he refers to the autopsy being conducted in "a place exposed to view" and carrying the man's head "through the camp to brigade headquarters." He concluded that Dr. Potts "should be dismissed [from] the service, which I recommend without any hesitation."

Potts's defense did him no good, and the version provided by Drs. Bethel and Conover prevailed. Special Order No. 178, dated April 21, 1865, notes that "By direction of the President, Dr. Potts is hereby dishonorably dismissed . . . for unjustifiably mutilating the body of a dead soldier, in the presence of the enlisted men of the command." The next day Potts submitted his resignation, and it was accepted, giving him an honorable discharge. The same week, he was also given a dishonorable discharge, and the week after that, Potts, "having filed with the Secretary of War satisfactory evidence of his innocence," was restored to duty.

Unfortunately, he was restored to duty with the same regiment whose colonel considered him to be a madman and a mutilator. It is not difficult to predict further trouble.

A few days after Potts returned to his new/old regiment, they all left City Point, Virginia, on the transport ship *Richmond*. As in centuries before—but inexcusable in 1865—the regiment arrived in Texas racked with scurvy. (At harvest time, in a victorious nation, there seemed little excuse for sending men to sea without a supply of fruits and vegetables.)

The regiment had only been in Texas a few weeks when Potts wrote to the adjutant general in Washington, D.C., that there were at least 120 cases of scurvy in his regiment, and both his assistant surgeons had been detailed for work elsewhere. A week later Potts made the same plea to the same office, and the following day he wrote to Dr. Joseph K. Barnes, then Surgeon General of the Army, that the medical conditions at his post were "a disgrace." By now his regiment had 200 cases of scurvy in the hospital, they had been without medical supplies for six weeks, they had no access to "anti-scorbutics," and, in Potts opinion, the medical director for the corps showed no concern over these problems. Potts concluded with this accurate prediction: "I am aware that such a sweeping accusation exposes me to the vengeance of all concerned. I would solicit your protection while I fearlessly discharge this painful duty." He concluded with a dramatic description of the suffering of the soldiers in his regiment and praised their bravery and fortitude.

Potts's increasing sense of isolation and suspicion is shown by his sending *two* copies of his monthly report for July to Dr. Barnes, one via Adams Express (a private company) and the other through official channels. "I believe my communications have been interrupted and opened by interested parties."

In his August report he noted that action had finally been taken to stop the scurvy epidemic, by collecting and distributing of a plant called "Aqua Montana," not at the instigation of any medical director but at the command of Maj. Gen. Philip Sheridan. The hero of Cedar Creek and the scourge of the Shenandoah Valley seemed much more concerned with the soldiers' welfare than did the higher medical authorities of the corps, who were deaf to Potts's pleas for vegetables.

Meanwhile, Potts himself was becoming literally deaf. Beginning in mid-1864, a progressive infection, with drainage from both ears, had troubled him severely, and his reports are punctuated with requests for a medical leave of absence to see an ear specialist—a request that was never honored.

On September 22, 1865, Potts's second court-martial began. It revived all the previous charges from Petersburg as well as accusing Potts of being drunk on two occasions in Texas and refusing to appear before a medical board. (He said that the board would be stacked with his enemies.) Potts objected to several of the charges, pointing out that he was not in the service at the time they occurred, but this objection was overruled. Potts offered no defense and simply asked the court to treat him fairly. He was convicted of every charge and specification, then cashiered. A year later, his appeal to Pres. Andrew Johnson was rejected.

Dr. Potts moved to Canada, and in 1891 he applied for a pension, based upon deafness. His request was rejected because there was "no evidence of deafness or ear disease while in the service," which is hardly accurate. He died on April 22, 1915, in Clinton, Ontario, Canada.

>⊶⊷⊶O⊷⊶⊷⊰

COMMENT: The key to this case may be Dr. Bethel. Private Anderson died under Bethel's care. Bethel had never performed an autopsy and knew so little of anatomy that he declared himself unable to replace organs in their correct position. He saw Potts's dissection of the enlarged inguinal nodes as some sort of practice in artery ligation. He seems to have gone directly from the autopsy table to the colonel's tent with wild tales of spurting blood and ghoulish procedures.

Contrary to the refrigerated body storage, preservative-filled specimen jars, bright lights, trained technicians, and legal backing that today's coroners enjoy, George Potts worked in a flooded tent, by candlelight, with an assistant not only ignorant and incompetent but actively hostile. Was Bethel so upset by the unpleasant sights of a postmortem that he misinterpreted events, or was he a fabricator of wild tales, hoping to become the chief surgeon for the regiment by engineering Potts's dismissal? All of these speculations are based upon Potts's own version of events. Our tendency is to believe Potts because he showed his willingness to take political risks on behalf of his scurvy-stricken men at Brazos Santiago. Other factors in Potts's favor are his competence in anatomy and pathology—as demonstrated in his autopsy report—and his having been, in June 1864, "assigned as operating surgeon to the division, second table at the hospital." While others may see it differently, we think Potts was not a decapitating ghoul but instead a man struggling to advance medical knowledge while providing the best care for his men—men that he genuinely admired.

A 1998 review of these records, by an experienced autopsy pathologist, yielded these observations:

> Anderson did not die of cerebral hemorrhage or infarction, because death from these causes is not instantaneous: victims do not drop dead. Sudden death is almost always cardiac: cardiac hypertrophy was, at the time, known to cause sudden death. Anderson had been sick at least a week with catarrh. The left lung was hepatized [solidified with loss of air spaces], suggesting lobar pneumonia of between three and six days standing. Patients with lobar pneumonia can drop dead, and all hypertrophied hearts have deficient coronary arterial oxygenation: the hypoxia of pneumonia could easily have precipitated fatal arrhythmia in this hypertrophied heart. Enlarged right inguinal lymph nodes could have led to deep vein thrombosis with death from massive pulmonary thromboembolism, but there is no evidence for this diagnosis. [Here the reviewer considers, but rejects, the possibility of malignant lymphoma.] The evidence, in my opinion, suggests death from lobar pneumonia."[3]

Since most Civil War doctors routinely used neither stethoscopes nor thermometers, much less X-ray machines, a diagnosis of pneumonia in a living patient was not easy.

As a final reminder of the difficulty of finding conclusive answers, even with primary sources, Private Anderson's own service records list three different causes of death: heart disease, kidney disease, and gunshot wounds from combat.

Chapter Sixteen

Charles E. Briggs

The movie *Glory* showed the trials, tribulations, and triumphs of the 54th Massachusetts Infantry (colored), an inspiring story of the bravery and dedication of a pioneering regiment of African American troops. Not all the drama of that regiment was encompassed in the cinematic version—and certainly not the charges of cruelty and malpractice filed against Surgeon Briggs.[1]

He was a graduate of Harvard and received his medical degree in 1856. His first war service was with the 24th Massachusetts, seeing action in the Carolinas as an assistant surgeon. He was promoted and appointed surgeon of the 54th Massachusetts on November 24, 1863.[2]

Almost exactly one year later, an event occurred that seems unparalleled in Civil War records. It began with the court-martial of seventeen-year-old Pvt. James Riley of Company H, 54th Massachusetts (colored).[3] Riley was charged with bestiality, that he "did on the fifth day of November 1864 between the hours of 8:00 and 9:00 o'clock P.M. proceed to the stable of the horses of the Field and Staff of the 54th Massachusetts Volunteers and then and there hold sexual connexion with a mare. All this at Morris Island, South Carolina."

The first to testify was Pvt. John Brown. "I heard a fuss over at the stables and went over. Riley was about a pace from the mare, right behind her. He said he was getting hay, but the mare's head was tied down close to the manger, Riley's pants were unbuttoned, the mare's private parts were wet, and there were horse hairs on Riley's coat. He ran, but we caught him and took him to the doctor. It was after dark."

Dr. Briggs told the court that he went immediately thereafter to the stables.

A candle was brought and I examined [the] prisoner's clothes. I found one short hair from the coat of a horse on the right breast of Riley's coat toward his waist. I found no other horse hair about him. His clothes were not wet. Several buttons [were] presumed to be wanting in the front of his trousers. His trousers gaped in front so that

When Col. Robert Gould Shaw asked Harvard-trained Dr. Charles E. Briggs why he had mutilated a soldier's penis with a scalpel and hot iron, Briggs refused to answer. MASSACHUSETTS COMMANDERY, MILITARY ORDER OF THE LOYAL LEGION, USAMHI

his private parts were visible. His private parts were dry. I found no horse hair on his body. His penis was slightly swollen, the prepuce drawn back. I am uncertain whether he pulled the prepuce back to show me the organ or not.

I had the mare brought into the stable. The mare is naturally skittish, but showed unusual irritability, snapping and biting at him, more than is customary with me. Riley had been thrust with considerable violence into the stable striking the mare, and perhaps that irritated her. The mare's private parts were dry. On the right flank about eight inches from the anus horizontally was a small glutinous mass, partially rubbed into the mare's hair. If it was semen, the odor was overpowered by the natural odor of the mare. The mare's head was drawn downward to the manger by the halter. I sent the man to the guard house. My assumptions are based on the words of the men who captured Private Riley. My examination did not conclusively prove that Riley had intercourse with the mare. The effects of masturbation would appear to be the same as those of intercourse."

In other testimony, Riley's captain described him as being "of good character," while Pvt. John Davis, who had known Riley since age three, also spoke well of him. After the testimony was concluded, the Court deliberated and gave their verdict: not guilty.

The trial was held on Sunday, November 9, 1863. At 10:00 that night, Briggs "without the knowledge or consent of his regimental commander or of the regimental Officer of the Day sent to the regimental guard house for two sentinels and did place them as a guard over his own tent." Briggs then "caused Private James Riley . . . to be taken under a double guard to his own private tent and did cause him to be partially stripped, gagged, and bound down upon a bed and did then and there inflict upon him the act of circumcision as a punishment . . . and to make the punishment more painful and severe did scar the cut parts with a hot iron, without the administration of anesthetics." Briggs then returned Riley to the regimental guardhouse (it is unclear why he was still in the guardhouse, having been acquitted) "and did neglect to take measures to alleviate the pain."

That same night, the commander of the 54th Massachusetts, Col. Robert G. Shaw, demanded a written report from Briggs concerning Riley's circumcision. No reply. The following day, the commander repeated his order for the production of a report, again receiving no reply. When confronted, Briggs said, "I do not recognize that you have the right to demand such a report."

What followed next seems a mystery. Briggs was not court-martialed. A thorough search of the court-martial index, as well as scrutiny of his medical officer file, compiled service record and pension file, enhanced by Archivist Michael P. Musick's search of record group 94 (Letters Received, Colored Troops) and Briggs's record with the 24th Massachusetts, shows only the charges and specifications but no actual court-martial. What is most likely is that the case was dropped. But why? Thus far, the record is silent.

Dr. Briggs was mustered out of the service August 20, 1865. In 1869 he married Rebecca Whitaker in St. Louis, Missouri. In 1871 he signed a memorandum, in which he gave his rank as "Acting Assistant Surgeon," USA. Later that same year, his contract was terminated. He died in Boston in June 1894 at the age of sixty-one, from cancer of the gall bladder, and was buried at Pembroke, Massachusetts, the place of his birth.

Even less is known of the fate of Private Riley. He was wounded in battle July 16, 1863, at James Island, South Carolina; the nature of his wound is not recorded. There is no application for pension; there is no further record of his life.

>-!-◆>-O-<◆-!-◁

COMMENT: From a medical-legal point of view, Briggs's actions seem to be clear malpractice, combined with assault and battery. This case, in the absence of further facts, could give rise to the wildest flights of speculation. Briggs's testimony was very helpful to Riley and seems the basis for Riley's acquittal. Why would Briggs then turn on Riley? Did Briggs secretly feel that Riley was guilty, even when the objective medical evidence did not support a finding of guilt? Did Briggs feel that he was to be the agent of a justice higher than a mere mortal tribunal, a sort of "Vengeance is mine, saith the Lord"? (Carnal connection with other species is one of the oldest Judeo-Christian "abominations.") Did

Briggs feel that Riley's *possible* transgression reflected ill upon the regiment—or upon the concept of African American men in uniform? Or perhaps, deep in his heart, Briggs, like the Southern plantation owners, feared that the "darkness of Africa" lay just beneath the surface, ready to break out in bestiality and lust, an outbreak to be nipped in the bud (so to speak) by the symbolic double castration of circumcision and the hot iron? And what of the African American troops who were Briggs's accomplices in this act? Did they assist out of fear of white authority or out of a repugnance for Riley's (possible) intercourse with the mare?

A whole other realm of speculation rests upon the old boy network. Briggs was a Harvard man; this was a Massachusetts regiment. The 54th was supposed to reflect the patriotism and reliability of Negro troops, and their officers were to reflect the white, liberal, Republican, and abolitionists' highest hopes for an oppressed race. The public disgrace that would attach to the publicity of a trial, with the sensationalist newspapers in a feeding frenzy over (hypothetical) black bestiality and (almost certain) white sadism, would be a great setback for the cause of the North. But, once again, these are flights of fancy. The record allows us to present what is known. Other researchers may find the answers to what remains unknown, to pierce the veil of mystery, to relive and exorcise our vision of the doctor with his knife and glowing iron, menacing the bound and gagged Riley, struggling on the cot, wide-eyed with terror.

Chapter Seventeen

Edward Donnelly

"An act of inhuman vandalism . . ." was how a chaplain described Surgeon Edward Donnelly's picking over the bones of the dead at the battlefield of Bull Run.[1]

On the evening of April 15, 1862, at Manassas Junction, Virginia, the Reverend W. H. D. Hatton, chaplain of the 1st Pennsylvania Rifles, wrote in a flowing, calligraphic hand, to Maj. Gen. George A. McCall:

> Impelled by a sense of humanity, as well as a feeling of respect for the quiet repose of the sacred remains of the Patriot Dead, I deem it my duty to lay before you a statement of facts, which, I trust, will not be passed over; if for no other purpose than the vindication of the character of the Pennsylvania Reserve Volunteer Corps, for which, I am, in part, responsible.
>
> I make a simple statement and leave the matter in your hands. On yesterday about 4:00 P.M. as I was riding over a portion of the battleground at Manassas or Bull Run, I suddenly came upon a party of six or eight men (of the reserve corps) standing around what I immediately discovered to be the grave of one of our soldiers, slain in that battle. In the center of the party was one of the surgeons of the Fifth Regiment of your corps (with a piece of rail or stick in one hand and a bag in the other) in a stooping position, rooting out the remains of one of those unfortunate men, who fell there and which was merely covered by the Rebels in the place where found.
>
> He (the doctor) had the leg joints in the bag and was in the act of pulling up the stockings that had contained the ankle and feet bones, which he picked out of the flesh with his fingers (I shudder at the thought!), leaving the shirt, pants and stockings and portions of the body and bones (which he did not consider of value) lying around on the surface of the ground.

I remonstrated with him, saying that 'Such an act of inhuman vandalism was a disgrace to our army and nation,' and that he was enacting a second addition of the Rebel atrocities on the remains of our dead, to which he replied, that "Every man had his peculiar taste in such matters,"—I remarked that "Such taste does not appear to me very refined in a Christian land in the 19th Century." To which he answered, that the chaplains ought to be more efficient in teaching their regiments a better civilization. I told him, "I expected a different state of refined civilization from a man of his profession and an officer in our army," to which he coolly replied (blushing) that he could not be better employed than providing a novelty for the New York Museum (I presume he meant [P. T.] Barnum's). I then asked him to which of the regiments he belonged, to which he replied he "was one of the surgeons of the Fifth Regiment of Pennsylvania Reserves." He then tied the bag after putting in the two hip bones, tied it behind his saddle and rode off.

General, if such acts are to be perpetrated (as I learn they are every day by such men) unnoticed and unpunished in our Federal army, I think we need say no more about Rebel barbarism.

McCall passed the matter on to the brigade commander, John F. Reynolds, who noted, "I do not think the chaplain has characterized the act in terms at all too strong. I would in fact fairly suggest that the case may be reported to the Secretary of War with the recommendation that the surgeon be dismissed from the service as an example, or he be brought before a military board on improper conduct."

Donnelly himself requested a court of inquiry, which assembled at Falmouth, Virginia, May 14, 1862. The court members included Brig. Gen. George G. Meade, Col. Thomas L. Kane, and others. (A court of inquiry reviewed a situation and made recommendations. It could neither convict or acquit.) The first witness was the Reverend Hatton, whose testimony added little or nothing to what he had already written. The defense presented two witnesses. Surgeon Samuel G. Lane of the 5th Pennsylvania Reserves had heard of others collecting battlefield bones. He observed that Donnelly's bones were bleached from long exposure on the surface and did not think they looked dug up. He recalled Donnelly's "profound sorrow" when he became the object of official displeasure. Lane confirmed that bones were scattered on the surface throughout the Bull Run battlefield and that the government and commanding general had taken no steps to have them buried. As to Donnelly's collector credentials, Lane had seen Donnelly's reports on the natural history of Brazil, published in the bulletin of the Philadelphia College of Pharmacy and in other journals. "The doctor has more extraordinary fondness for scientific research than any man I know of. He has a fondness for relics which is unaccountable to me."

Pvt. James Wetzel of the 5th Pennsylvania Reserves was at the site of the alleged offense and confirmed that the bones were lying on the surface and that there had been no digging. Here, testimony closed, and Dr. Donnelly submitted his written statement.

"I will not criticize Mr. Hatton's letter, which has by a singular perversion of language magnified the simple act of my picking up a few bones into a great crime." Donnelly absolutely denied having ever said that he planned to put the bones in P. T. Barnum's Popular Museum:

> [i]t would have been contrary to the characteristic reverence my countrymen have for the remains of the dead; it would have been contrary to the teachings of my Holy Church! My own father is buried on a battlefield. If I had been advised that it was against orders to take the bones, I would have been the last man to disobey such an order. I hope you will not blast the hopes of a man, who in a life of 40 years, has never knowingly committed a crime and that you will pardon what is deemed a serious offense, leaving me thanking God for the escape from a dread which has already fearfully chastened me.

The Court of Inquiry recommended a court-martial. A week later, such a court assembled. After a brief recess to find the transcript of the Court of Inquiry, which had been lost in the intervening week, the trial began. Surgeon Lane and Private Wetzel both testified again, adding nothing new to their previous statements. Donnelly pled guilty to collecting bones "for purposes other than interment." Of the specifications, he was found "guilty but attach no criminality thereto" and of the charge, "not guilty." He returned to active duty.

Two months later he was captured at Charles City Cross Roads, Virginia, having stayed behind with the Union wounded.[2] After two months in Libby Prison at Richmond, Virginia, he was exchanged and then captured again at the second battle of Bull Run, having once again elected to stay with the wounded. He was paroled and returned to duty, only to be captured a third time at the Wilderness in Virginia. His later service included time with the 31st Pennsylvania, the 196th Pennsylvania, and the 2nd Pennsylvania Cavalry, which served near Petersburg, Virginia. Surgeon in Chief E. J. Marsh, writing on the Richmond Campaign, described Donnelly as "energetic and untiring in attention to the wounded." Altogether, he was present at twenty battles.[3]

Who was this naturalist, pharmacist, physician, and collector of pickled snakes and soldier's bones? Donnelly was a native of County Londonderry, Ireland. When he was three, his father, a captain in the East India Company, was killed in Bengal. Young Donnelly, an only child, came to America with his mother; he graduated from the Philadelphia College of Pharmacy in 1843 and spent several years on a U.S. Navy ship commanded by Passed Midshipman

Isaac Strain, U.S.N., making voyages of exploration and discovery in the West Indies, South America, and Africa. The records of the Philadelphia Academy of Natural Sciences show that on April 7, 1846, they received a donation of "a large collection of reptilia, in spirits, from Brazil, presented by Mr. Edward Donnelly." (His obituary states that he became a friend of Dom Pedro, Emperor of Brazil.) After years at sea, Donnelly returned to the States, and in 1854 he graduated from the Philadelphia College of Medicine.

Following the Civil War, he practiced medicine at 139 Grant Street, in Pittsburgh, Pennsylvania until 1879, when he moved to the San Francisco Bay area in California. There, he had a medical office at 832 Howard Street, was active in veteran's organizations and as a medical examiner for pension claims. He died of a stroke in 1891 in Piedmont, California, a quiet, wooded town in the hills above Oakland. In 1896 his widow Florence claimed destitution in her pension application. After an initial rejection because she owned two lots near the beach in San Francisco, an investigator was appointed. He described her holdings as "just billows of sand . . . nothing crosses them but the winds, the birds, and an occasional chipmunk or jackrabbit. . . . [T]hey may possibly be of value in fifty or a hundred years." Florence received her pension. The two lots today would be worth more than $100,000 each.

➤━◆〉━○━〈◆━━◄

COMMENT: It might first be noted that because of the mass casualties in the Civil War and the shortage of labor to bury the corpses properly, the remains of the dead protruded from thousands of shallow graves. The men who had been covered were often reexposed by erosion and the predations of wild animals. Photographs and contemporary writings confirm this observation. The Reverend Hatton appears to have overdramatized the doctor's actions.

Every medical school anatomy lab today has dozens of skeletons and hundreds of boxes of loose bones. The student is responsible for knowing the function and geometry of each of the 206 bones of the human frame. (The great novelist C. S. Forester became a writer after failing his medical school examination in "Bones.") Where do the schools obtain their bones today? At one author's school, the answer was "India"—without further clarification. In Donnelly's day, the origin of bones for study was even more obscure. The conflict seen here between the physician and the cleric is one that, in all its varied aspects, reaches back centuries and persists today. Two hundred years ago dissection was considered immoral; today ethical issues include cloning and artificial fertilization. As to Donnelly's transgression, the reader is free to choose his own interpretation. A positive view is that he was a forerunner of the formation of medical museums in America (they were well-known in Europe); the Civil War saw the beginning of the Armed Forces Institute of Pathology, today one of the world's great repositories of medical knowledge.

Chapter Eighteen

Jotham Donnell

"Jotham Donnell . . . did handle the penis of Private William Steward . . . sick of gonorrhea, verulenta and chancre, and did immediately . . . examine with his fingers the throat of . . . another private."[1]

The 15th Maine was famous for other intramural excitement, as well. Its colonel, John McCluskey, had thrown the regimental flag into the ocean off Florida, and on the same sea voyage, there was a near riot between "American" and "Irish" soldiers.

In his March 1863 court-martial, Dr. Jotham Donnell, of the 15th Maine, faced two charges and a total of nine specifications. The regiment had traveled from Maine to Ship Island, Mississippi on the *Great Republic.* Under the heading of "neglect of duty," the papers filed accused Donnell of failing to erect tents for the sick until the third day at Ship Island. When the regiment moved from Ship Island to New Orleans on the *Tamerlane,* Donnell failed to inspect the vessel or to note the unsanitary conditions aboard that transport. At Camp Parapet, Louisiana, Donnell failed to regulate the sanitary conditions of the camp. For six months he failed to keep the regimental prescription book, case book, and quarterly sick reports (in violation of Army Regulation No. 1254), failed to attend a private who died of diphtheria, and failed for two days to visit a sergeant under his care, who also died.

Under the heading of "conduct unbecoming an officer and a gentleman," he was charged with handling the gonorrheal and chancred penis of Private Steward, and then inspecting the throat of another private on April 15, 1862, and with a similar transgression involving the infected private parts of Pvt. Thomas Maloney (Company F), and then the throat of Private Gordon Perkins. It seemed understood that neither an officer nor a gentleman would handle private parts in such a public manner.

As always, the testimony showed the stories to be open to different interpretations. Lorenzo Dodge, Acting Assistant Surgeon, was one of the three medical men attached to the regiment. Dodge said that on arrival at Ship

Island, Donnell had failed to order cooked food for the patients the first two days on shore, and the sick men were fed moldy hardtack and sugar. Dodge also confirmed that Donnell failed to inspect the *Tamerlane* which was "filthy and unfit." Dodge verified Donnell's failure to keep a prescription book plus his not visiting the two men who died.

The plot thickened on cross-examination when the defendant asked Dodge if he had ever called Donnell an "old fart," an "old rake," or an "old hypocrite." Dodge hedged his reply: "I don't know that I have—when others have been talking I may have given assent." Dodge was clearly a hostile witness and became more so when asked if he possessed a medical diploma, a question that he refused to answer. His objection to clarifying his medical credential status was sustained by the court. Further questioning showed that Dodge was a student and close friend of Dr. Kimball, the assistant surgeon; that both Kimball and Dodge stood to be promoted if Donnell was dismissed; and that the regimental colonel, who had hurled their flag into the sea, had appointed Dodge as hospital steward, not as acting assistant surgeon.

On the subject of pitching a hospital tent at Ship Island, Dodge asserted that the only barrier to the quick erection of the tent was Donnell's lack of initiative, while Donnell reminded Dodge that when they had departed Augusta, Maine, the tent pins were frozen into the ground, making it necessary to cut the tent ropes and abandon the pins. Further, the main tent pole had been broken during the ocean passage to Ship Island. After further intensive cross-examination, Dodge conceded that some of the sick had been sheltered in tents elsewhere until the hospital tent was erected and that jelly and farina were available to the sick as well as the moldy hardtack and sugar described earlier. (The tent pin and moldy hardtack event had happened a year before this court-martial. It was unusual in Civil War trials to wait so long before pressing charges; in fact, military custom frowned on "stale" charges.)

Other witnesses gave their views. Pvt. H. S. Owen agreed with Dodge that sufficient tent supplies had arrived on the *Great Republic* and that bread and molasses could have been drawn the first two days at Ship Island. Maj. Franklin Drew recalled that the *Tamerlane* was too small for the number of men, was indeed filthy, and had not been inspected by Donnell. When the defendant asked when the regiment had learned that they were to board the *Tamerlane,* the judge advocate objected to the question, and the court sustained the objection. (It is shown later in the trial that there was only a few hours' notice.)

Hospital attendant C. P. Stover seemed to give damaging evidence. He stated that he had seen Dr. Donnell examine Maloney's infected penis and then Perkins's throat without washing his hands in between. However, Stover was not clearly able to identify Maloney. Dr. J. H. Kimball's testimony exactly mirrored the charges: Donnell had neglected to put up tents, did not draw provisions for the sick, failed to keep records, failed to follow his diphtheritic patient, and examined a penis and throat in the manner described before.

To make matters more complex, Capt. John Wilson had been assigned as surgeon during Donnell's brief illness. No explanation appears in the records as to Wilson's medical background or the whereabouts of Dodge or Kimball. Wilson recalled that the private with diphtheria had been neglected.

The defense witnesses presented a very different story. The quartermaster of the 15th Maine, Lt. W. S. Locke, recalled the Ship Island tent incident: "Dr. Donnell came to me so many times about the tents that I finally told him not to come to me anymore, that we would get them up as quick as we could." Sgt. James Tilton said, "Dr. Donnell came to me continuously about putting up the tents." Tilton also recalled the *Tamerlane* as filthy but not overcrowded and certainly little different from most transports of that time.

Pvt. Gordon Perkins was a night nurse and stayed with the sick "in a hospital tent" the first night ashore at Ship Island. This was the same Perkins whose throat was allegedly probed by Donnell after examining Maloney's afflicted member. Perkins had no recall of having had a sore throat in November 1862, nor did he recall any examination of his throat at that time.

The sergeant who had allegedly died at Pensacola, Florida, from neglect by Donnell was Giles Straw. Sgt. Robert Seaberm testified: "Giles and I were both sick in the same room at the hospital. The doctor came to see us twice a day. I never saw any neglect." Quartermaster Locke returned to the witness chair and refuted Kimball's story of having drawn provisions for the sick the first two days at Ship Island.

Five different witnesses said that they had never seen the doctor handle the penis of any patient. Dr. Enoch Blanchard of the 7th Vermont (whose own trial revealed a beneficient concern for his regiment) testified for Donnell. "When there are many patients and few doctors, it is very difficult to keep records in the precise form required by the regulations. As to the examination for gonorrhea, it is neither necessary nor customary to handle the penis; further, I have never known the throat of a person to become impregnated with the gonorrhea virus. I should not believe it is possible."

The court also considered several documents offered in evidence. The quarterly reports showed no diagnosis of gonorrhea, chancre, or syphilis in either April or November 1862, the months in which Donnell's unwashed hands allegedly endangered patients. The court found him not guilty.

He may have been acquitted, but it was not the end of his troubles. In July and August 1862 he was off duty sick, and in September he turned in his resignation. "I am worn out in the effort for the last few months to perform the duties of my office, with little assistance, and have failed to do so to my own satisfaction."

Later in September, Lt. Col. Isaac Dyer, commanding the 15th Maine, forwarded the resignation with a note saying that Donnell was "unfit, the service will get along better without him." In November, his file shows a most unusual entry: "He is hereby suspended from duty. He will be allowed all the liberties of an officer on duty but will not visit the hospital of his regiment officially." Whatever the reason for this suspension, it lasted for four months, until his return to duty in April 1863. He continued to serve until January 1865, at which time he was discharged "by expiration of service." After the war, he did not apply for a pension. We do know that he received his M.D. from Bowdoin in 1839 and was age forty-seven when the war began. He died in 1889.

>+◆>+O+‹+‹

COMMENT: The tenor of the trial, the frequent sustained objections, and the very dubious testimony suggest that the court was biased, convened with the goal of getting rid of Donnell. The trial brought out the manifold and unreasonable expectations placed on surgeons: They were to examine patients, prescribe medications, make and file many reports, find tent pins, produce food and inspect ships—all of this with little or no clerical help. Certainly Donnell kept some records because they played a prominent part in his defense against the gonorrhea and throat accusations. A further factor may have been fatigue. Donnell was almost fifty when this trial began; active service was hard on men not in the blush of youth.

Whatever the merits of the Donnell-Kimball-Dodge feud, it was certainly not helped by the example of the regimental commander, Colonel McCluskey, who was court-martialed as soon as the *Great Republic* reached Ship Island, or the generally fratricidal atmosphere that seemed to pervade the 15th Maine. And as for Dr. Blanchard's views that the throat cannot be infected with gonorrhea, time has shown that, sadly, he was wrong.

PART THREE

Misuse of Food & Money

Chapter Nineteen

Perkins Gordon

"An enlisted man is the social equal of a commissioned officer!" This was the basis of Dr. Perkins Gordon's spirited defense of his actions with the 35th Ohio Infantry.[1]

The regiment had served first at Somerset, Kentucky, then saw action at Mill Springs, Kentucky, in January 1862; three months later they fought at Corinth, Mississippi, and in October the regiment was back in Kentucky for the battle of Perryville. They spent the early months of 1863 guarding Nashville from the gray peril, where two of the officers in Dr. Gordon's regiment filed the following charges against him.

First was "conduct prejudicial to good order and military discipline, in that he ate the rations of the hospital steward and also messed with and ate the rations of Charles Fisher, Joshua Davis, John Leach, and Samuel Dennis, privates of said regiment, used as servants and assistants," during the period of January 1862 to March 1863 and "whilst the regiment was on the march through the states of Kentucky, Tennessee, Mississippi, and Alabama." (Experienced military legal authorities frowned on such "stale" charges. If someone has been doing something wrong for fourteen months, it should have been acted upon much sooner.)

The second charge was misapplication of hospital stores. His accuser alleged that Gordon "did about January 20, 1863, use for his own and his servant's mess the greater part of a barrel of potatoes which had been received by him . . . for the use of the sick and convalescent men of the regiment, this near Nashville." Further, it was alleged that for the previous fourteen months, he had used the hospital cooking utensils in preparing his own food and, in September 1863, at Crescent Church, Tennessee, had used some of the whiskey and sugar reserved for the sick.

The third charge related to his using the ambulance, after the battle of Perryville, to carry his own bedclothes and provisions, and that at Nashville, he had "habitually used the ambulances provided for the sick for the purpose of carrying his own baggage and provisions." From these charges, Dr. Gordon would appear to be a rather selfish fellow. Once again, it was the testimony that shed a clearer light on such matters.

Charles O. Wright, the Regimental Assistant Surgeon, had worked with Gordon for five months.

> The doctors have a mess and the hospital attendants mess with us. They put in their rations and add to what we furnish. We buy whatever we can, wherever we are. In January, Dr. Gordon got a barrel of potatoes off the Sanitary [Commission] boat. We used part, we fed part to the sick, and part went to [Lieutenant] Colonel [Charles L.] Long's cook. It is true that we used a medical department mess chest to cook our meals, but many of the utensils in the chest were furnished by Dr. Gordon. The only time I saw him use an ambulance was when we were on a scout and had no other wagon.

The questioning turned to the subject of whiskey and sugar, and here the Judge Advocate of the Court objected to the introduction of testimony about sugar. His objection was overruled. Dr. Wright testified, "At Concord Church, Tennessee, Colonel Long and Colonel [Ferdinand] Van Derveer and other officers were in the tent drinking rum punches and the white sugar was used to mix these punches."

Dr. Wright confirmed that Gordon had indeed eaten some of the hospital supply of vegetables, but it had been to treat his own scurvy. Furthermore, Gordon bought vegetables for the sick out of his own pocket, and when they resumed the march, there was no transport space for vegetables, so they needed to be either eaten or thrown away. Wright also recalled that Dr. Gordon had shared his canteen of whiskey with the sick men and had heard him admonish the ambulance men to carry nothing but the sick and wounded.

Hospital Steward Cleaver (first name unknown) said their mess consisted of himself, Dr. Gordon, Dr. Wright, and Privates Fisher, Leach, Davis and Dennis. "In January, at Nashville, we received Sanitary [Commission] stores, a barrel each of onions, potatoes, and dried apples, also a keg of pickles. About one-sixth was eaten by the sick. As to hospital mess gear, I only know that Dr. Gordon bought an oven." Cleaver recalled that the doctor had bought canned fruit, flour, sugar, coffee, "poultry of every sort," hams, and oysters for the hospital mess, and he had fed several sick patients at his own table—some for months—when he felt the usual rations would slow the patient's recovery. "Food for the sick was prepared before the food for the hospital mess, and Dr. Gordon never refused whisky when it was necessary for the sick."

Hospital Steward Cleaver's final recollections were that the hospital attendants had no objection to messing with the doctor, that Gordon had bought medicine for the sick out of his own pocket, and he had bought ale for the patients at Paris,

Kentucky. The court asked the witness, "Were the purchases from Dr. Gordon's own funds, or from the hospital funds?" The answer tells much about army life: "From Dr. Gordon's funds. We never had any hospital funds."

Pvt. Charles Fisher, Dispensing Clerk at the hospital, recalled that Gordon always gave more than he took and never refused any patient. Pvt. William Graham, an ambulance driver who had held this post for the previous seven months, had never carried any of Dr. Gordon's baggage or provisions.

Defense witness Surgeon Jason Arter of the 31st Ohio added his views on the subject of food and doctors. "So far as my own practice and observation goes, I have carried my own mess arrangements in the medical department chest, using promiscuously some of the articles belonging to the chest and having mine, in turn, used by the department." With this description of kettle mingling, the testimony ended.

Dr. Gordon's written defense, which occupied three single-spaced handwritten pages, contained these observations:

> By the drift of the testimony and proper understanding of the charges, I infer it is sought to make the Court find me guilty of conduct prejudicial to good order and military discipline, for messing with hospital attendants. This may be the case in the regular army, but I very much doubt if [it applies] in the Volunteer Service, where the privates are not only the commissioned officer's equal in point of talent, but whose condition . . . socially is nearly always equal to that of the commissioned officers at home. Is it against good order and military discipline for an officer to eat with his equals, men equal in every respect except military rank? I trust not. I believe my conduct has not resulted in any disobedience or disorder."

He closed with an appeal to common sense regarding vegetables: "If a doctor with scurvy eats vegetables, it is not an abuse of a privilege, but is a medical necessity and a treatment." The court was unmoved. He was found guilty of the first charge and sentenced to forfeit one month's pay.

This outcome appears to have cooled Dr. Gordon's affection for his old regiment as three months later he applied for permission to appear before a Board of Medical Examiners to become a Surgeon of U.S. Volunteers. In his application, he gave his age as forty-one and his medical degree as originating from Western Reserve Medical College in Ohio. While in Ohio, he had practiced ten years in Cleveland and one year in Mansfield.

The full text of his examination appears in his file. A few questions may show that such a test was not to be taken lightly. "Give the chemical history of sulphur, enumerate some of its compounds, give the mode of obtaining the sulphuric acid of commerce and the rationale of its chemical production." There were similar questions regarding oxygen, arsenic, chlorine, and "vegetable acids," such as the acetic acid of vinegar.

Questions about quinine included the manufacture of quinine sulphate from raw cinchona bark and the relationship of Jesuit's powder and Peruvian bark. There were complex questions about mercury compounds, chloroform and diaphoretics (medicines that induce sweating).

The prospective surgeon had further challenges: "What makes a man unfit for military service? How do you tell if a water source is healthful? How do you prevent sore feet on the march? How do you select a suitable campground? How do you diagnose and treat peritonitis, pneumonia, pleurisy, bronchitis, typhoid and tuberculous meningitis?" (As to the latter, there being no treatment, the candidate was to describe the stages leading to death.) There were questions on intestinal parasites and the structure of the spinal cord. One set of questions seems strange for a military surgeon—"Describe the appearance and origin of spermatozoa?"— but it was no more irrelevant than the five-question section on obstetrics.

Directly related to battlefield surgery were very detailed questions about how and where to ligate (tie off) the carotid, subclavian, and femoral arteries as well as the indications for amputation. Dr. Gordon seems to have passed the examination, but a severe sunstroke that summer ended his participation in the War Between the States. He was discharged on November 22, 1863.

He died in 1892, in Milan, Ohio, after receiving a pension for twenty-nine years. Over those three decades his own doctor filed many reports, describing dizziness and partial blindness, both attributed to the sunstroke, as well as progressive inflammatory rheumatism. His wife, Frances, survived him.

⋙—⊶•O•⊷—⋘

COMMENT: Again, we see an issue of food. Officers were to dine separately from enlisted men, but much of the army was on a four-year camping trip. The regimental surgeon and his small staff worked together every day in tending the sick and wounded. The camaraderie so often established by shared burdens, and the impracticality of sorting out "his" pots and pans from "their" pots and pans—while marching across four states—make it not surprising that shared food and utensils would be commonplace.

Further, in this trial, it was never shown that the sick were harmed by these arrangements but rather seem to have benefited by them. The authors, who share military medicine experience, cannot but wonder if spite and animosity, not concern for military efficiency, were the bases for these charges. This suspicion is enhanced by the attempt of the judge advocate to suppress testimony regarding the regimental white sugar, which was going into the rum punches served by the colonel.

The details of Dr. Gordon's examination for promotion for Surgeon of U.S. Volunteers reveal a medical world far more complex than the stereotypical drunken army surgeon sawing off arms and legs. Many of the questions would challenge a medical student today, and it would be a rare cardiologist, dermatologist, or family doctor who, at the millennium, would consider doing an amputation, much less a dozen in a day.

As a final note, Dr. Gordon's appeal to the social equality of enlisted men and officers raises again the dilemma of rank and authority in a citizen army. During the war, the 35th Ohio had 80 men killed and 128 die of disease. Death, the Great Leveler, would be present in the mind of any thinking doctor. It is said that after the chess game is over, the kings and the pawns go back into the same box. Dr. Gordon may have well thought, "What's a few shared meals when we may soon all be dead?"

Chapter Twenty

N. S. Drake

"I cannot make an honorable organization of this regiment. Its officers are beyond redemption." Thus wrote one of the commanders of the 16th New York Cavalry as he resigned. Another colonel was dismissed for sexual advances to both men and women. A major of the same regiment, while being court-martialed for one offense, was dismissed by direct order of the President for a prior offense. In a regiment where fifteen officers were dismissed, twelve were discharged before their term of service was finished, and another eleven officers resigned, Assistant Surgeon N. S. Drake was not exceptional for being court-martialed.[1]

Long before his November 1863 trial for conduct unbecoming an officer and a gentleman and neglect of duty, Drake found himself in legal difficulty. His credentials for becoming a surgeon were better than many of his contemporaries (an M.D. from both Woodstock College in Vermont and the College of Physicians and Surgeons in New York), but that did not prevent him from being reported for being drunk on duty in early November 1862.

The occasion seemed to be celebrating his escape from a perilous situation. He had been appointed as surgeon aboard the transport *Daniel Webster*, carrying over 400 sick and wounded soldiers. It was not a happy voyage.

> I had passed through three days of the most intense nervous excitement without sleep and without food, suffering a combination of apprehension and anxiety such as I never have been called to pass through before. At sea, in one of the most appalling storms that had ever been witnessed on our coast, on board an old vessel in which none had full confidence, masses of sea dashing over us constantly, the prospect of a fearful death imminent, having the responsibility of nearly 450 helpless sick and wounded soldiers in my charge and last, but not least, my poor young wife, whose destruction with me must leave my boy a lone orphan in the world.

When the *Daniel Webster* staggered into port, Drake had "two or three glasses of Madeira wine" to steady his nerves, being "excited and cold," and in this condition greeted a Dr. McDougal of the New York Harbor Medical Directors Office. McDougal wrote to William Hammond, Surgeon General of the Army, that Drake was drunk. Drake wrote in response, saying he was not. A week later, McDougal wrote again to the Surgeon General: "I feel satisfied, from the promises given, that he will hereafter abstain from all intoxicating drinks." A few more weeks passed, and Drake was now an assistant surgeon with the 16th New York Cavalry. A year later he was in trouble for "messing [eating] with enlisted men," drinking with the hospital steward, and with treating a private without reporting him on the sick list.

Drake's first line of defense was technical:

> It is alleged that I performed certain acts on or about September 20 to November 12, 1863. Now, what does that mean? Does it mean on or about September 20th or on or about November 12th or at some time in between these dates? If it means the latter, see how unjust for the accused, for if the specific time is not stated, the prisoner is cut off from proving that he was not at said time in the place mentioned, and consequently could not have been guilty of the alleged offense. I cannot think that this Court will force me to trial upon a defective specification and thereby jeopardize my character as an officer and citizen.

Drake thought wrongly. His objections were overruled, and the trial proceeded.

The central issue was that of an enlisted man's mess, as distinguished from an officer's mess, with all the issues deriving from that distinction: Did a single meal, taken together, constitute a "habit" of messing together? What were the sources of the food before preparation? Was the food purchased by the officer, or was it from the regimental or hospital rations? Was the food prepared by the same cook, and were the foods of different sources mingled together during the preparation? Who owned the utensils with which the food was prepared and served? (The rules appear at least as complex as those of an Orthodox kosher kitchen.) Did the surgeon sit at the same table as did the hospital steward? (Hospital stewards were enlisted men.) And what of the case of A. Winthrop, one of the hospital stewards of the 16th New York Cavalry, who was not commissioned as a surgeon but was told by Maj. Morris Hazard to buy and wear a surgeon's uniform—was he a steward and therefore an enlisted man, or a surgeon and therefore a commissioned officer? Many witnesses were summoned to shed light upon these perplexing issues.

One witness, 1st Lt. H. M. Taylor, recalled visiting the hospital tent once at breakfast time and found around the table the surgeon, two assistant surgeons and, possibly, two hospital stewards. "I think they were all eating the same food from the same table."

A hospital steward with the elegant name of Alcide Froidevaux told the court that he was "in the habit of eating in the hospital tent" and that he, the cook, and Hospital Steward Winthrop all drew their rations from the commissary. Froidevaux recalled that Drs. James Horniston and S. P. Vondersmith ate with them occasionally and Dr. Drake "many, many times." When asked if this constituted a mess, Froidevaux replied, "I did not understand what it was, a mess, but I have asked some friends and I know now that a mess is a regular association of men to eat together." The court pursued Froidevaux doggedly on these questions, and he added, "I didn't feel I belonged in a mess with the doctors; we ate sometimes together, but there was no regular association."

The situation of the next witness, Hospital Steward Winthrop, had even more inconsistencies and mysteries. "When Dr. Drake came to the regiment, I told him what my duties had been and he knew I had no commission and was no surgeon, but I had been appointed to act as a surgeon, the colonel promised me I'd be paid as a surgeon, and Major Hazard ordered me to wear a surgeon's uniform." (Since Winthrop claimed to be a graduate of the College of Physicians and Surgeons in New York City, it remains quite unclear why he had not been commissioned as a surgeon.)

Winthrop testified that his messing with Dr. Drake did not follow a consistent pattern. They had sat at the same table at Vienna, Virginia, but not when the regiment moved on to Centreville and Fairfax Court House, both in Virginia. "At Vienna, I ate with the doctor, but not in the sense that I consider a mess." The Judge Advocate asked, "What do you consider a mess?" And Winthrop responded, "A mess is when two or more persons club together to procure food for their own use or their servant's use. I don't know if I have eaten with Dr. Drake enough times to consider it a habit, but I have sat down with him at the same table a number of times."

The dining facility described by Winthrop was hardly some posh officers' club. At one location, the medical staff ate in the blacksmith shop. There was a "division" in the shop; surgeons ate on one side and hospital attendants ate on the other. Winthrop went further in clarifying this complex amalgam of military custom and victual accounting. "The same cook cooked for me and for Dr. Drake. I bought my food, Drake bought his, and the cook drew some from the commissary. The food was placed on the table together. Froidevaux and I took the liberty of sitting at that table and no one ever objected."

Thus, Drake's "conduct unbecoming an officer and a gentleman" consisted of eating at the same table, an ill-defined number of times, with a hospital steward who was not quite a surgeon (though he dressed as one) and a second steward who was clearly not a surgeon. The venue of these misdeeds was principally a blacksmith's shop. Since this was a cavalry regiment, it is reasonable to presume that it was in active use and contained the expected melange of farriers, forges, clanging anvils, and drifts of horse manure.

Dr. Drake's "neglect of duty" centered around his failure to report or document his treatment of Pvt. Charles D. Aylesworth. This issue is even more perplexing than that of what constitutes a mess. Although Drake belonged to the 16th New York Cavalry, Aylesworth was a member of the 5th New York Infantry. Aylesworth was "sick all the time," and Drake arranged for him to travel in the ambulance of the 16th New York Cavalry. Further, Aylesworth stayed as a "guest" of Dr. Drake, often dressed in civilian clothes, and took some of his meals with Dr. Drake. One witness saw Aylesworth drinking whiskey with Drake, Maj. John Nicholson, and Brig. Gen. Rufus King.

(King is best remembered for his skedaddling at the second battle of Bull Run, thus forcing James B. Ricketts' division to pull back, opening a gap that allowed James Longstreet's corps to unite with that of Stonewall Jackson, paving the way to Union defeat.)

Another witness recalled that Aylesworth, Drake, an unnamed hospital steward, and the hospital cook all shared the same quarters: the same blacksmith's shop used as a dining room. Aylesworth had previously been chief clerk in the "Provost Marshal's Office" (location not specified); the record does not clarify the reason for this sickly private living with a different regiment than his own.

Drake produced no witnesses for the defense and simply presented a written statement in which he reviewed the evidence already described and concluded, "I must say that when Brigadier General Rufus King, and so many other officers who were military officers and my superiors, set me the example, I had not the remotest idea that I was committing a crime."

The court found him guilty, ordered his dismissal, and then recommended mitigation. Six months later the Adjutant General's Office reviewed the case and agreed that Drake had "been misled." This office recommended mitigation, which was endorsed by Joseph Holt, the Judge Advocate General. On June 24, 1864, the War Department sent to the governor of New York a form letter stating, "By direction of the President of the United States . . . [Drake's] . . . disability is hereby removed and he may be re-commissioned should your Excellency so desire."

By the time of this decision, Drake had taken and passed the examination for Assistant Surgeon of U.S. Volunteers and had received his new commission. He served at City Point, Virginia, and was honorably mustered out in late 1865. The following year he was honored with the bars of a brevet captain's rank.

Drake died in Brooklyn, New York, in May 1880 of "edema of the lungs." His widow, Luella, applied for a pension in 1904 and was initially rejected because of her husband's sentence of dismissal. After further investigation, her pension was finally granted. She died in 1911.

>-+<>-+O-+<>+-<

COMMENT: The military legal system devoted many hours to the "crime" of officers and enlisted men eating at the same table. Drake's case is yet another variation on this theme. At least two factors were at work: the traditions of a (partially) egalitarian society and the army regulations themselves. As to the first, there were regional variations. On the East Coast, the patricians, aristocracy and cavaliers of the South, as well as the gentlemen of the Yankee regions, all considered themselves above the artisans and merchants of the middle class, while in the more recently settled states any man of enterprise might be well regarded. In a volunteer army, whose regiments were raised locally, the soldiers remembered their officers as neighbors rather than as august figures. In a hospital especially, shared duties lead to shared tables.

As to the regulations, these lent little guidance and seemed more designed for fixed garrisons with distinct mess halls for officers and men. In such an established post, the officers' mess might be decorated with regimental memorabilia and encrusted with the patina of age and tradition. A dozen men sitting on a log in the wilderness has a leveling effect and is less conducive to social stratification.

Chapter Twenty-One

Edmund Boemer

The trial of Dr. Edmund Boemer (also spelled Bömer) gives a special insight into hospital nutrition during the Civil War. One witness described the "bill of fare," a rather elegant term for what was actually being offered to the patients. Taking his words directly from the transcript, we see the following.[1]

"Breakfast—coffee, bread and the quarter-ration men, water soup. Dinner—beef and beef soup, and the quarter-ration men, water soup. Supper—tea or coffee, bread and molasses, sometimes butter, and the quarter-ration men, water soup again."

However, the court-martial of Dr. Boemer—surgeon of the 4th Regiment of Missouri Infantry, camped near the town of Pacific City in Franklin County, Missouri, just west of St. Louis—had nothing to do with vitamins or a balanced diet. The charge was "misapplication of stores and money."

The specifications with which he was charged were "1. Edmund Boemer boarded himself on hospital stores and provisions, drawn and purchased for the use of the sick of said regiment, from and after the fifth day of June, 1862 up to the present time [November 1862], 2. Edmund Boemer received money for board from officers of said regiment, sick at the hospital, to the amount of $30.00 or $35.00, of which, although it belonged to the hospital fund of said regiment, he has not rendered an account." The third specification brought the issue down to the personal level: "Dr. Boemer took Conrad Klinge of Company B, while he was sick in the regimental hospital, to his own table, and boarded him, for which extra attention, although the doctor's table was entirely supplied from stores and purchases belonging to the hospital, he received of said Klinge $6.00 of which he has not rendered an account."

In reading these records today, at least two points stand out. First, this is clearly a German regiment, and all the members seem to have been friends—or at least neighbors—before the war. Second, the financial issues that concerned this trial are tiny in scope. Today, with $2,000-a-day intensive-care units, $5,000 come-and-go surgeries, and tens of millions of dollars of overbilling by health maintenence organizations, it is easy to forget that the country was poor in 1862, that a dollar went a long ways and that the doctor's small-scale avarice was probably a very sore point with his comrades.

Klinge, the man cited in the specifications, told the court, "I was in the hospital six weeks. I paid a dollar a week for my food. I needed extra food because I was very weak from having homeopathic treatments." When questioned, Klinge had no idea where the $6 went. Lt. Henry German had been in the hospital for six days and was billed 30¢ for each day, which he paid to the hospital steward. Lt. Louis Miller was in the hospital nine weeks and paid $18 for his food.

John Lellweger, a hospital nurse at Boemer's establishment, told the Court that the written instructions he had received were not useful because he could read only German and the instructions were in English. He seemed clear on one point: "Dr. Boemer had chicken and eggs more than the rest of the men." Pvt. Joseph Huter, another nurse, who had provided the court with the "bill of fare," added, "Sometimes we had eggs but we never had chicken. There were never delicacies for the nurses or the patients." However, he did think that the doctor "was doing the best he could."

Pvt. Louis Dauth, a hospital cook, told the court that the patients had eggs every day in the soup, and that the patients might have been unaware of the eggs presented in that form. (It is unclear whether the eggs were in the beef soup or the water soup.) Regarding the more refined cuisine, Dauth explained: "Sick officers sometimes got chicken, and if the doctor prescribed it, a sick soldier might receive fruit. The doctor never paid for his own food, but he once asked me to make out his bill. I never did make such a bill, because I cannot write."

During his six weeks in the hospital, 2nd Lt. Frank Emger was joined by his wife and two children. "I know that I should pay and I asked the doctor to make out a bill and he did. The bill was for $15.00 and I paid it." Hospital Steward Herman Dietzel told the court that the doctor was away about two days in every week, but Dietzel was unsure about where or why. Like all the other witnesses, he had no idea what became of any money collected from the patients.

The man most likely to have such information was Lt. George Husman, the regimental quartermaster. He was quite definite when he explained to the court that the doctor had not accounted for any moneys received from the patients. Husman attempted to enlighten the court with an explanation of how the fiscal system worked: "The hospital fund is formed as follows. The hospital rations are commuted at 13 cents and the difference between the 13 cents, and the 30 cents regularly allowed, forms the hospital fund."

If this explanation clarified matters for the court, it was not so recorded. It certainly did not pacify them. Although the defendant submitted crowded pages of explanation, rebutting every point of the testimony, the court found him guilty and sentenced him to be dismissed.

><-I-<>-•-O-•-<>-I-<

COMMENT: To an observer from a different place and time, it appears that the process of trying to raise, fund, and organize an enormous volunteer army might be as much at fault as the narrow and penurious transgressions of the doctor. The court was not so forgiving; they saw Boemer as very clearly in the wrong. He certainly succeeded in annoying his companions in the regiment. Unlike some other surgeons tried over issues of food, Boemer seemed to have had more greed than compassion. He was not tried on any medical grounds, but judging from the bill of fare, his patients seemed more likely to suffer from scurvy, pellagra, and beri beri (all vitamin deficiency diseases) than make a hearty recovery.

There were further difficulties in the system. Men who could not read or write were asked to prepare bills. Men who read only German were given instructions in English. Billing the patients for food provided by the government seems to have been the final straw in a chaotic situation.

Chapter Twenty-Two

Enoch Blanchard

Many New Englanders go to Florida for the winter; so did the 7th Vermont Infantry. In the late fall of 1862, at Pensacola, Florida, their surgeon, Dr. Enoch Blanchard, got crossways with the army system.[1] It was not from lack of patients—403 enlisted men in this regiment died of disease. His problems derived largely from the perennial problem of paying for the doctor's food.

The first charge reads: "The said Enoch Blanchard appropriated to his own use or to the use of his private mess, potatoes or other vegetables and provisions, belonging to and bought for the said hospital with money from funds of said hospital." He was also charged with "conduct unbecoming" for striking Pvt. James O. Dodge and for abusing other patients "in a shameful manner." The final charge, neglect of duty, asserted that Blanchard failed to visit the hospital for seventy-two hours.

The first witness, Jacob E. Dodge, one of the regimental cooks, agreed that Dr. Blanchard had taken some food from the private's hospital to the officer's hospital; however, he also testified that the doctor had paid for the provisions: "Dr. Blanchard had a fund for boarding [feeding] officers. We have never had so many provisions as when Dr. Blanchard was in charge. I don't think there was any dishonesty. I don't think the doctor profited. His cook and I cooked together in the same room and take provisions off the same table. I do know that Dr. Blanchard bought extra provisions for the hospital, from the quartermaster."

Pvt. William Ward, the hospital wardmaster, said that the doctors were billed 50¢ a day (close to $20 in today's money) when they boarded at the private's hospital. Some of the confusion about food and money are seen in Ward's attempt to clarify the subject: "What provisions were drawn for the hospital were taken to the hospital and those drawn for his mess or purchased for his mess were taken to his room and he said whenever we wanted any of them to come and get them."

The rest of Ward's testimony was even more favorable to the doctor: "The money from the officer's board bills was used for purchasing extras. Dr. Blanchard said that whenever we needed anything he would purchase it for us.

Since Dr. Blanchard has had charge there has been a vast difference. Before, we lived on salt junk. If we wanted extras we had to purchase them ourselves. Now we have potatoes, onions, butter, and milk nearly all the time. I saw no evidence of dishonesty. The hospital actually made a profit by boarding the doctors." (And the patients received vitamins A, C, and D.)

The next witness, Pvt. Jessee Grover, was also questioned closely on the subject of potatoes. He recalled that the items in question were sweet potatoes, purchased from New Orleans with hospital funds. "Potatoes were carried from the hospital to the doctor's quarters by Lieutenant [Allen] Spaulding's darkie. The patients had enough to eat most of the time—12 quarts of milk a day, eggs, onions and butter almost constantly." Grover had no clear idea how these foods were financed.

Pvt. George Wardwell, another cook at the hospital of the 7th Vermont, gave testimony in which he seemed to contradict himself. "What we drew from the doctor's quarters was not enough to pay for what he drew from the hospital cook room. Dr. Blanchard took money out of his own pocket and gave it to me to buy extras for the sick. The patients fared much better after Dr. Blanchard took over." Pvt. Henry Filmore, another hospital cook, recalled that the doctor had given him money to buy whatever he wanted and that he had purchased dried apples and oysters for the patients. "While we were at Carrolton [Louisiana], we lived better than any other time." These gustatory memories seem to exhaust the subject of food, and the court moved on to the doctor's slapping of Private Dodge.

Sgt. Myron Owen told the court that Dodge had a reputation as a shirker. Dodge had come to sick call, where Blanchard told Dodge that he was not sick and must do duty. Dodge muttered that the doctor was "damned petty," and Blanchard slapped him across the face once. Owen also said that the doctor was abusive and unsympathetic to other patients in the hospital. On cross-examination, it turned out that Owen himself was the only man who felt abused. Pvt. Enos Fletcher was also present at the slapping. He recalled, "Dodge said he was weak. Blanchard replied that Dodge had been 'playing off' for two months and was not sick. Dodge cursed the doctor, who then slapped him once."

The final witness was Col. William Holbrook. "Dr. Blanchard presented a plan for charging the doctors to eat at the hospital and I approved it. I visited the hospital several times a week and heard no complaints from either the officers or the patients. For two months, Dr. Blanchard was the only surgeon for the regiment and he was very busy." As to paying for food, the colonel had never seen any accounting, but he recalled that there was almost always money in the hospital fund, and the patients ate well.

When it came time for a verdict, the court hedged a bit. On the subject of food they concluded: "Assistant Surgeon Enoch Blanchard is not guilty, yet it is also our opinion that he is censurable for taking provisions from the Soldier's Hospital and especially for not keeping an accurate account of same." As to slapping Private Dodge, Blanchard was "not guilty, but censurable for striking with sufficient cause." In regards to not visiting the hospital, testimony had shown that the previous surgeon had left and that no clear orders had been issued assigning medical responsibility. The verdict on that was also not guilty. In brief, he was acquitted of all charges.

Blanchard's record shows that he was on duty with the 7th Vermont until at least February 1865. After the war he practiced medicine in the tiny town of Minonk, Illinois, forty miles northeast of Peoria, even though he qualified for a pension based on service-connected rheumatism and "malarial cachexia." He died suddenly in 1891, probably of artereosclerotic heart disease. His wife, Susan, outlived him.

>-·-◆>-·-O-·-◆>-·-◁

COMMENT: If Dr. Blanchard was a native of Vermont, his malaria was almost certainly picked up in Louisiana and/or Florida, since the regiment went by ship directly from New England to Ship Island, in the Gulf of Mexico. The frequent bouts of chills and fever, and the strain of often working alone, may have been factors in his impatience with Private Dodge. Blanchard's enlightened concern for his patients' nutrition puts him above many of his colleagues. He appears to have been a victim of the vagueness and impracticality of the rules governing the food for officers and men, doctors, and patients. In retrospect, this trial was a waste of time and effort.

Chapter Twenty-Three

Alfred L. Castleman

The court-martial of Dr. Castleman seems to illustrate several points: Credentials for doctors were far different 130 years ago, the guidelines for new army doctors were close to nonexistent, doctors were as likely to be crippled by disease as their patients, and the concept of honor played a larger role in public life back then.[1]

Castleman was a surgeon with the 5th Wisconsin. In July 1861 he applied for this post, and his credentials were examined by a board of three surgeons. The high points of their report show:

> He has an honorary degree of Doctor of Medicine conferred upon him by the Board of Regents of the University of Wisconsin, July 2, 1857. He also has a license (considered worthless by this board) to practice medicine at Vincennes, Indiana, issued by the President of the Board of Physicians for the First Medical District of the State of Indiana. On this license, the name is partially obliterated by blots and scratches and the name Alfred D. Castleman is written in one place and Alfred S. Castleman in another, in both instances written over other writing and indistinct. There are also several letters signed by physicians, and one by a clergyman, stating that they have seen a diploma in the possession of the said Castleman, and that in 1849, he was elected a member of the Wisconsin State Medical Society. In conclusion, none of the documents presented for our consideration seem to meet the requirements of the mustering office.

A note in a different hand says, "At the urgent solicitation of the Governor of Wisconsin, I mustered A. L. Castleman . . . he did not have any papers whereby I could call him a surgeon or physician."

In January 1862, only five months after he joined his regiment, he was court-martialed on charges of embezzlement, conduct unbecoming an officer and a gentleman, and "tyrannical and capricious conduct." It was alleged that he used hay designated for the ambulance horse to feed his own horse; he used hay, intended for the beds of the sick, to feed his horse; he used hospital supplies of sugar, rice, tea, wine, bread, beef, and chicken to feed himself, his servant, and the brigade surgeon; he used wine and "desiccated milk" supplied for the patients by Miss [Dorothea] Dix; he forbade Frank Johnson (the acting apothecary) and John Roberts (hospital steward) to give medicines prescribed by the other surgeons of the regiment; he accepted money from four privates for getting them extra pay as hospital cooks and nurses; he accepted money from two privates for getting them discharged; and, finally, he ordered Assistant Surgeon George D. Miller to cease performing medical duties. All of this happened at Camp Griffin, near Washington, D.C.

Like today's tabloid headlines, these charges, on close examination, promised more than they produced. The first issue was that of stolen hay. Lt. John Clark, the regimental quartermaster, testified that he had ordered 500 pounds of straw for the beds of the sick, but hay was delivered instead of straw. The hospital steward swore that Castleman had fed some of the hay to his horse. On cross-examination the steward had to concede an important point: After all the bed ticks (mattress sacks) had been filled with hay, about a bale was left over. As there was no place to store it, Castleman asked the steward to charge him for it, then used the leftover hay to feed his own horse. Pvt. William Schoonmaker of Company H testified that he had heard the doctor say to the steward, "Charge this hay to my account." Pvt. George Foote, the hospital cook, testified, "I would not believe the steward even under oath," while Pvt. Francis Johnson called the steward "a man who would not hesitate to tell an untruth."

As to the issue of restricting the steward and the apothecary in their filling of prescriptions, Dr. Castleman was concerned that the doses of mercurial compounds ordered by the assistant surgeon were twice what they ought to be and might endanger the health of the patients. (He was not alone in this; Surgeon General William Hammond, who forbade the use of mercurials in the army, lost his post in part because of traditional doctors who used mercury in large quantities.) Castleman also put restrictions on handing out the whiskey and quinine compound, feeling it was not the appropriate medication for the conditions for which it was prescribed. (This could be seen as an early and primitive form of peer review and medical-quality assessment.)

The alleged bribe for obtaining extra pay for the hospital workers also took on a different light in cross-examination. William Bennedict was a nurse at the hospital of the 5th Wisconsin. He recalled: "As nurses, we were supposed to get extra pay. Dr. Castleman said he had made out the payroll three different times, putting the nurses and hospital cooks down for their extra pay, but extra pay had never been disbursed. He said that he would make a trip into Washington D.C. to get us paid properly, but he would need something for his expenses. Captain [Richard] Emmerson suggested that we make up a fund for the doctor for his trouble. Each of us gave the doctor 25 cents. I offered him a dollar, but the doctor said that was too much." Then the Dix story was confirmed by Pvt. John Riley; this witness was too sick to attend court, so the court went to his bedside, where they heard him say, "The doctor did not ask for money. He just said he would need something for his trouble. We gave him something for doing this for us." The court now turned to the issue of a bottle of wine furnished by Miss Dix and the United States Sanitary Commission. The hospital steward made this statement, implicating Castleman: "I do not know that Surgeon Castleman used wine furnished by Miss Dix, but Surgeon Castleman told me to credit him with a bottle of wine, as furnished by him to the hospital, a bottle that had come from Miss Dix." From this, it would seem that the doctor was himself receiving credit for wine donated to the regiment by Miss Dix, but the next round of questions and answers described many different bottles of wine from many different sources, and Castleman's culpability vanished.

Item by item, the sins of Dr. Castleman evaporated as the defendant and the Judge Advocate queried the witnesses. George Foote, another hospital nurse, recalled that the doctor repeatedly told the hospital steward to keep careful accounts against him for all hospital stores and provisions.

Both sides brought forth accounting sheets and lists of items. While they confirmed the testimony already given and introduced no surprises, their major value might be to illuminate how far a dollar went in 1862: thirty pounds of sugar, $2.75; ten pounds of butter, $2.50; one dozen chickens, $3.50.

The last witness was the Brigade Surgeon, Dr. I. Owen, who said, "I have served in four different brigades and I have seen none which were as well managed, or as good for the patients welfare, as the 5th Wisconsin under Dr. Castleman."

The final documents submitted by Dr. Castleman were two memoranda and a defense summation. In the first memo, sent to the Surgeon General of the army, Castleman described his efforts to obtain food for the sick, his struggles with the quartermaster, the necessity of funding patient needs out of his own pocket, and his attempts to function within the bureaucracy and the convolutions of army regulations. He ended the memo with this plea for help: "If I am acting in this manner contrary to the intentions of the regulations, will the department please instruct me as to my duty under the circumstances." His second memo noted that he had received no reply to the first memo, and the new missive concluded, somewhat plaintively, "It is greatly to be regretted by volunteers that there is nowhere to be found, in one body, full directions on this subject."

In his summation, Castleman began, "This, gentlemen, is not only a court of law, but a court . . . of higher and mightier significance—a court of honor." He went on to speak of his rise from being a poverty-stricken young man, isolated in the back woods of the Far West, to a man of fifty-three years, a man who "would not lightly throw away honor, sincerity and integrity." He pointed out that due to the lack of response from the Surgeon General's Office, he had bought additions to the patients' diet from his own funds for nearly half a year. The remainder of his summation was a rebuttal to every point of the charges and specifications, utilizing the testimony of the defense witnesses.

Although the court acquitted him on every charge, his army days would soon be over. At Antietam, Maryland, in September 1862, he acquired "an ulcer on the left hand resulting from inoculation of poisonous matter from dressing a gangrenous wound." Three weeks later he obtained a medical leave, the certifying surgeon finding that Castleman "is laboring under general nervous excitement, nervous prostration, induced by arduous and continuous labor in the field and greatly aggravated by the effect of a dissecting wound received after the battle near Sharpsburg." Castleman never returned from his leave and submitted a letter of resignation that was accepted on Christmas Eve 1862. He died in 1877, cause unknown. His widow, Abby Hubbard Castleman, whom he married in Vermillion County, Indiana, in 1832, applied for a pension in 1892. She was living in San Jose, California, and was described as aged eighty-three and "destitute." She claimed her $8 a month for a year, then disappeared from the records.

>—1—+>—0—<+—1—<

COMMENT: Although Dr. Castleman's official documents as a surgeon were below the standards of today—and not even up to par for 1862—he seems to have functioned well and had the welfare of his patients at heart. The local medical board cited in his credentials is of interest. With slow transportation in that era, a central state authority was far removed from the country doctors. It is our understanding that regional groups such as the First Medical District of the State of Indiana were well regarded in the 1860s.

Castleman's plea for guidance is a poignant one. Since volunteer surgeons had neither instruction nor courses in their administrative duties, nor had the Surgeon General's Office prepared a manual for their use, Castleman, like most volunteers, labored as best he could in the obfuscation and miasma generated by decades of inertia in the medical department of the old regular army.

Chapter Twenty-Four

Alonza M. Eisenlord

Only eleven days after the first rebel cannonball streaked through the sky and plunged into Fort Sumter, South Carolina, New York City's Steuben Regiment was mustered. A month later they were in Newport News, Virginia, and they were still there, with a front-row seat, when the *Monitor* and the *Merrimac* (the *Virginia* may be more correct, but it fails at alliteration) hammered each other full of dents in Hampton Roads.

The Steubens, better known as the 7th New York Infantry, were largely German and seemed, for reasons unknown, to have difficulty with their surgeons: One died, one went missing, one was dismissed, and three were discharged prematurely. Among them was Alonza M. Eisenlord, who seemed to combine the morals of a petty thief with the untidy habits of a magpie. For these shortcomings, he was court-martialed twice.[1]

In the fields near Fort Monroe, Virginia, the 7th New York used as a hospital the farmhouse of a Mr. West. While going through the furniture belonging to the Wests, Eisenlord found two $1 bills in a bureau drawer. He stuffed them in his pocket without reporting them and was charged with conduct unbecoming an officer and a gentleman.

His principal defense witness was Col. John E. Bendix. Eisenlord examined his witness: "Did I not report taking the two bills from the drawer of the hospital to you, and state to you where I found them?" Unfortunately for Eisenlord, the colonel had no recall of such a conversation and had learned of the stolen bills only after their loss had been reported by others, including the private who had seen the doctor put the money into his pocket. The defendant was found guilty and dismissed from the service, a sentence approved by Maj. Gen. John Wool. Eisenlord was reinstated by Abraham Lincoln, but upon his return to the regiment in January 1862, twenty-two of the officers of his regiment signed a petition asking that he be removed from their regiment and sent elsewhere. That same month Eisenlord was tried again—for going over the head of his commander to obtain a leave of absence and for misapplying food and supplies sent by a civilian relief agency.

Many citizens at home were concerned that their boys in uniform, especially the wounded, were not receiving nourishing or attractive food. (They were right.) These good-hearted citizens shipped boxes of "delicacies" (such as canned meat, wine, and cheese) to the camps. The men of the 7th New York were the beneficiaries of luxuries shipped to them by the New York Union Defense Committee. Eisenlord was charged with keeping rice, brandy, preserved meat, and preserved birds for his personal use. The testimony tells us much about mid-Victorian techniques of food preservation, concepts of what would benefit a sick soldier, and, of course, Eisenlord's habits as a record keeper, stock clerk, and doctor. More than half a dozen witnesses testified against him.

Capt. Edward Becker had been acting quartermaster of the regiment and recalled:

> Colonel Hoffman came into my office with an invoice for preserved meat and birds, coffee, sugar, rice, and pineapple cheese. The colonel thought pineapple cheese might not be good for the sick but might be all right for the [healthy] officers. I sent some men to the wharf, but they could not find these articles. I gave Dr. Eisenlord the invoice and told him to locate these articles. Later, he told me he had found most of them in the camp of the 9th New York and brought them to his own tent. He found all the items on this list, but told me that he could not dispose of them until he had written to the colonel. Three weeks later, the food was still in the doctor's tent. [This was in July in Virginia!] About that time, I was sick. I told the doctor that I could not get food fit for a sick man. He sent me some butter crackers but said he could not give me any preserved chicken because he had not yet heard from Colonel Hoffman. I saw the boxes in the doctor's tent. They were . . . unpainted boxes, about a foot square.

On cross-examination, Eisenlord insisted that Becker had merely "thrown" the invoice into his tent. The doctor also claimed that Becker had not told him that the boxes were from the Union Defense Committee. Becker contradicted both assertions.

Capt. F. H. Gaebel said that one of his lieutenants had been sick a long time and needed wine, but none could be had. "When the doctor left the regiment, I saw bottles in his tent, as well as preserves, sugar and other things for the sick, some in a bad state of preservation."

Capt. Christopher Christman told the court that while he was provost marshal, Lt. Col. Edward Kapff had come to him, along with Eisenlord's brother, carrying a trunk and a large tea box. The latter contained small empty tea boxes and loose unroasted coffee. Christman said that he refused to open the trunk. (The record does not say why.)

Maj. Casper Keller had been appointed to examine the doctor's tent for items belonging to the regiment. "There were many boxes addressed to Dr.

Eisenlord from the United Defense Committee. They contained fruits, meats, brandy and port wine. Much of the food was spoiled and the bottle of brandy half full."

Hospital Steward A. Plaeltenen told the court that preserved meat, preserved fruit and wine were never available for the patients, even when requested.

> The doctor always told me there were none. I asked him for quinine and opium for the sick and he said there was none. I saw boxes in his tent marked SHEETS, but the doctor said there were no sheets. The only items we ever got from the doctor's stores were five pounds of sugar, five pounds of coffee, and half a barrel of crackers. These articles were damaged. I was with the committee that examined his tent. Although the doctor always told us he had no supplies, we found two syringes, a bundle of flax, two boxes of lint, four dozen bandages, two double wool blankets, four pillows, a dozen drawers, eighteen gowns, six shirts, two loaves of sugar, five pounds of tea, twenty bed ticks, twenty pillow ticks, nine bags of cocoa, one box of coffee, two bottles of pickles, two bottles of port wine, one bottle of dark brandy, one bottle of bourbon whisky, and two boxes of solidified milk.

A hospital cook, Louis Schmidt, added his evidence. "I had no preserved meat and no fruits. What I had to work with was salt pork and salt beef. When we had fresh meat, it was not through Dr. Eisenlord. When I was sick myself in the hospital, I wore my own shirt and brought my own blanket."

Henry Doell, who had been a hospital nurse under Eisenlord, said that the sick lived on "rice, coffee and crackers [probably hardtack], but a man who was very sick might receive some arrowroot. I was sent to the doctor's tent many times to get things for the sick, but he told me there were no such supplies. Once he sent to the hospital a quarter of a barrel of crackers and four pounds of ground coffee, but both were spoiled. He did send tea to the hospital once or twice a week, but never more than half an ounce."

Frederick Thibault, the regimental quartermaster, had examined the doctor's stores. "Some boxes were empty and some had been cut round with a knife. There were small boxes inside of large boxes. Some had labels on them such as peaches and apples, other boxes had rice, coffee, and sugar all mixed together. There was a loaf of sugar half eaten by rats; a loaf of cheese had not been cut, it was rotten." Two other witnesses gave almost identical evidence. Amazingly, the court found Dr. Eisenlord innocent on all charges.

Who was this doctor who lived in his tent with rat-bitten sugar, rotten cheese, and half-empty bottles of brandy? Was he senile or alcoholic or perhaps an obsessive who would rather hold on to goods than distribute them, a sort of medical miser? Or perhaps his shortcomings were merely acts of petty, mean-spirited revenge.

Although in a German regiment, he was born in New York State and attended the common schools there. He had a year of lectures at Geneva Medical College and a second year of lectures at the University of the City of New York, which issued him a medical doctor's diploma in 1844. He had been in practice sixteen years when he entered the army at age forty.

He appears too young for senility and no witness thought him drunk. Certainly he sounds peculiar. The vitamin-deficient diet common in Civil War hospitals was not aided by a surgeon who preferred to have food rot in his tent rather than feed it to the sick.

➤┄◆➤┄○┄◈➤┄◄

COMMENT: The science of nutrition was in its infancy in 1862, but the line officers of the 7th New York had no hesitation in expressing their opinion. When Eisenlord was ordered to be reinstated, he returned to his regiment and was "treated rudely" by both Col. Edward Kapff and Lt. Col. Casper Keller, as Eisenlord complained later in a letter. The quartermaster refused to issue him a living space until directly ordered to do so. Colonel Keller forbade Eisenlord to enter the hospital. This contempt and hostility may have been mutual; it seems probable that his dog-in-the-manger hoarding was an form of thumbing his nose at his peers.

His service time from February through July 1862 is not accounted for in the records today, but in August of that year he entered Chesapeake General Hospital and was soon discharged as unfit because of "bilious remittent fever," probably a form of malaria. And there his record ends.

Chapter Twenty-Five

George W. New

In Washington, D.C. today, there is the artificial limb firm of J. E. Hanger, Inc. The battle of Bull Run is often thought of as the first Civil War engagement, but before Bull Run, there was Phillippi. What is the connection between Hanger and Phillipi?

On June 3rd, 1861, Rebel and Union forces clashed at Phillippi, (West) Virginia. In this minor action, one of the few Confederate casualties was not-yet-mustered Pvt. James E. Hanger, of the Churchville Cavalry, whose foot was smashed by a cannonball. The amputation, a successful one, was done by Dr. New, surgeon of the 7th Indiana. Hanger, who invented his own replacement leg, became one of the leading designers and manufacturers of artificial limbs, and his firm—and its affiliates—lives on after him. (Like many Civil War stories, there is more than one version.)[1]

Most Civil War doctors learned to amputate the hard way: practicing on scores of mangled men until they learned skills that civilian doctoring had never taught them. But New was better prepared than most. Beginning in 1837, he had apprenticed with Dr. W. Clinton Thompson of Indianapolis, Indiana, he graduated from the Medical College of Ohio in 1840, and he opened a practice in Greenburg, Indiana, where he was the only genuine medical graduate for miles around. For almost twenty years he performed all the surgery in a several-county area. *The History of Indianapolis* (where he moved in 1860) states that during the Civil War, "no case of surgery under his charge proved fatal." So why was such a remarkably skilled practitioner court-martialed?[2]

In November 1861 his regiment was at Camp Elk Water, West Virginia, packing to leave on the march for Romney, Virginia. It was charged that during this departure, Dr. New sold hospital whiskey to soldiers of the 7th Indiana and 2nd West Virginia and kept the money. The first witness was Assistant Surgeon William Gillespie. "I cannot say that I saw any of the liquor being sold, but I did see Dr. New filling bottles and there were soldiers standing around. I supposed it was for them. There was a chest in the tent where medicines,

Dr. George W. New, who most likely performed the first amputation of the Civil War, was accused of selling the regiment's whiskey and pocketing the money. FROM HISTORY OF INDIANAPOLIS AND MARION COUNTY, BY B.R. SULGROVE, 1884, COURTESY OF NANCY ECKERMAN

books, records and instruments were kept. When Dr. New was there, he had the key, and when he left, his son [who was hospital steward] gave me the key when I wanted anything out of the box. I saw the doctor take the liquor out of this box. When Dr. New left with the regiment, there were 177 sick men left behind. About 75 of them needed stimulants." ("Stimulants" usually meant whiskey.) Now Dr. New asked the witness, "Did I not bring the box from Indianapolis, my own private property, with my own name on it?" Gillespie replied that he did not know; all the hospital boxes had Dr. New's name on them.

The next four witnesses were privates of the 7th Indiana. John Dragor said, "I saw Dr. New sell four bottles of whisky to the Virginia men, about a week ago. The liquor was kept in a box in a place between where the doctor and the colonel lived. I saw the men pay the doctor for the liquor." John Slawson of the regimental band said, "I purchased some liquor from Dr. New. I gave him $1.75 per bottle. The doctor knew I was sick, and the whisky was meant for medicine. I told him I wanted it to treat myself." Pvt. Frank Wheatly, another musician, had seen liquor purchased by men of the 2nd West Virginia. Pvt. Irving Hongh said, "I saw liquor sold. A man who bought it gave Dr. New a $2.50 gold piece and the doctor gave him $1.50 back."

The next witness was Brig. Gen. Joseph J. Reynolds. "When I first heard of Dr. New's action, I immediately inquired in my own offices and learned that no report having reference to this matter had been made. On further inquiry, I learned that Dr. New had gone on with his regiment. I then inquired of the brigade surgeon, but he was absent at Elk Water on an official visit. As soon as he returned to headquarters, I inquired of any report concerning the sales of whisky or brandy by Dr. New and he said no such report had been made." Dr. New asked him, "Should such a report have been sent to the senior medical officer of the division, or to the headquarters of the division?" The general replied, "I know of no reference whatsoever in the regulations to transactions of this nature; they are presumed never to take place at all." (This ended General Reynolds' testimony. Fifteen years later, he himself was court-martialed for leaving a wounded man behind while fighting the Sioux. The wounded man was "promptly cut limb from limb.")

Pvt. William H. Snooks (also 7th Indiana) saw Dr. New sell four bottles of "something" for which $7 was paid. Dr. New told him that he was selling the whiskey because there was no transportation to bring it with the regiment.

The first defense witness was Lt. Richard P. Johnson, the quartermaster:

> On November the 30th, the regiment moved, everybody except the sick men, the nurses and the medical officers. Dr. New called on me about two hours after the regiment had gone and stated that he had no transportation for his personal baggage, nor medicines, and asked my advice what he should do with the liquor. He told me that he had an opportunity of disposing of the liquor in a way and at a price that would save the situation and himself. He asked me what he should do with it. I was not sufficiently acquainted with his duties to be able to advise him, but I could see no reason why he might not turn it over and replace it after getting up to the regiment at some other post. There was certainly considerable difficulty in getting transportation, and I had to make arrangements with the brigade quartermaster to find a wagon. We had nothing to furnish from our regiment. Dr. New offered to turn the money over to me—but this was after he was arrested.

The final witness was Frank R. New, hospital steward and Dr. New's son:

> Dr. New and I were packing his goods. Colonel James Gavin [New's commander] asked what we were doing, and Dr. New said he was packing things to get them into as small a package as possible. The colonel then said that was right to dispose of everything because transportation would be hard to get. Dr. New sold about 20 bottles of liquor and said that he would account for the sale and the money but he did not know whether it should be to the quartermaster or to the colonel. Dr. New got a man from the 25th Ohio to take his baggage on to Beverly [Virginia]. He also gave the cook and the nurses two bottles of liquor from the hospital stores.

In his final defense statement, Dr. New withdrew his not guilty plea and pleaded guilty. His three-page defense, based on the concept of ignorance of proper procedures, concludes with the remarkable statement, "It would indicate an error of judgment in the accused, instead of a gross and criminal neglect of professional duty and dishonesty of purpose, growing out of a sickness and bad heart."

He was found guilty and sentenced to pay the proceeds of the liquor sales to the government and be dismissed from the service. This decision was endorsed by General Reynolds.

A few weeks later this case reached the desk of the President, who wrote, "I am not satisfied with the sentence of the court in this case, so far as it dismisses the accused from the service. That he sold the liquor is unquestionable, but that he did so with any improper intention, or that he ever intended to appropriate the proceeds, I think is not proven. I therefore wish to restore him to the service, if it is lawfully competent for me to do so. A. Lincoln."

A legal opinion by John F. Lee, Judge Advocate of the Army, refers to the Act of August 6, 1861, vesting such appointments in the Governor of Indiana. The President did not have the power to restore a state appointee, and Major Lee recommended that Lincoln send the sentence and the presidential opinion to the governor, then let him decide. It is clear that the governor approved this plan because three years later, Dr. New was still the surgeon of the 7th Indiana.

The records suggest that he continued to be an ornament to his profession. He was promoted to Brigade Surgeon, then to Corps Surgeon, and in late 1864 he was sent by the governor to New Orleans as Military Agent for Indiana. For the two years after the war, he served as Examiner of Drugs in the New Orleans Custom House. In 1867 he returned to Indianapolis, where he practiced almost until the time of his death in 1891, at the age of seventy-three. For many years he was active as a member of the Christian Church (Disciples of Christ), the Masons, and the Grand Army of the Republic.

Like so many officers and men, he carried the Civil War with him for the rest of his life. An attack of typhoid fever in 1864 left him with a partial paralysis of the left leg and a crippling destruction of the left knee joint. In his final weeks he required increasing doses of morphine to relieve the pain in his left leg.

⊱┄◈┄○┄◈┄⊰

COMMENT: Dr. New appears to have been one of the good doctors. If he lost not one surgical case in the years of the war, he was indeed a most remarkable surgeon. His one brush with the law seemed to follow an unwise decision about what to do with twenty bottles of whiskey for which there was no transportation. At $1.75 per bottle, it seems to have been a popular decision with the soldiers.

With Dr. New, the government got three sets of skilled hands for the cost of only two salaries. Joining the doctor and his hospital-steward son was the doctor's wife, Mrs. Adelia Carter New, who served as a nurse for three years.

Chapter Twenty-Six

James M. Hoffman

James Hoffman served only six months, then was cast out. Was he cruelly and improperly expelled from the army, a victim of a conspiracy, guilty only of providing whiskey to frozen soldiers and of eating part of a can of peaches? Or was he a war profiteer and parasite, selling government liquor, pocketing the proceeds, and dining on delicacies meant for the sick?[1]

Dr. Hoffman began his service with the 99th Pennsylvania Infantry, but he transferred into the 155th Pennsylvania as soon as it was organized, in September 1862. Three months later his new regiment saw its first combat, in the Union disaster of Fredericksburg, Virginia. A month passed, and the regiment found themselves unwilling participants in yet another of General Burnside's well-intentioned blunders, the infamous Mud March, where men who had survived Confederate bullets succumbed to pneumonia, fatigue, hypothermia, and despair.

Hoffman's court-martial was convened in March 1863, near Falmouth, Virginia. There were two charges. The first was "conduct prejudicial to good order and military discipline," wherein it was claimed that on January 27 he had sold intoxicating liquors to soldiers of his regiment, thereby causing a disturbance in the camp. The second charge, "scandalous and fraudulent embezzlement of public property," had several subdivisions. Between October 7, 1862, and February 1863, it was alleged that Hoffman had bought goods for himself, from the sutler, then billed the hospital fund for them. He had also used hospital supplies for his personal needs. Further, on February 29 he had drawn three gallons of whiskey from the brigade commissary, certified it as necessary for the patients, and had then sold two gallons of it to nonpatients. Finally, he was further charged with having sold disability certificates to officers of the regiment, thus facilitating their discharge or furlough.

Hoffman pleaded not guilty to both charges. All of the witnesses were from his own regiment. Called first was Cpl. David R. Parkhill, who told the court, "I never bought any whisky from Dr. Hoffman; I got the whisky elsewhere and paid for it myself. To the best of my knowledge, the doctor has not sold whisky to the privates of this regiment, and I certainly have never heard of any disturbance caused by the sale of whisky. I have bought whisky at the hospital, but that was through the hospital steward." Pvt. John Keefer and Cpl. Ebenezer Lowry confirmed Parkhill's testimony.

The hospital steward, Ellis C. Thorn, testified next. He recalled that Dr. Hoffman had "disposed of whisky to soldiers of the 155th Regiment and received pay for the whisky thus delivered." He went on to say, "I know of him selling liquor to several men, Handon Marshall, Harvey Mills and Corporal Parkhill, the man who was here this morning. In Parkhill's case, I was a medium; I got the whisky from Dr. Hoffman and gave it to Parkhill. Parkhill gave me the money, which I then handed to Dr. Hoffman. I did not sell the liquor myself nor have I been authorized to. As far as I know, this liquor was not drawn for hospital purposes from the commissary. We usually keep whisky at the hospital for the use of the sick. It is used for their benefit, and also in preparing medicines. I do not know where the doctor obtained the whisky that he sold."

Gilbert M. McMaster, the regimental sutler, recalled Dr. Hoffman buying a bill of goods on January the 21st. "The items ordered were all canned food such as peaches, milk, jellies, chicken, blackberries, strawberries, and tomatoes. These items were charged to the hospital fund and the bill was liquidated by Captain [Samuel] Steele, the Brigade Commissary. After the food left my storehouse, I had no way of knowing what became of it."

Brigade Commissary of Subsistence Capt. Samuel R. Steele now testified. "On a certificate signed by Dr. Hoffman, we provided on January 25th three gallons of whisky, on January 28th another three gallons of whisky and on the 30th day of the same month another gallon of whisky, all of which were said to be for medicinal purposes. On the 7th of February, on a certificate signed by Surgeon James M. Hoffman, we paid for 44 cans of assorted fruit, purchased from the sutler to an amount totaling $28.85." Captain Steele provided all the original papers to the court as verification of these purchases.

The next witness was a medical one, Assistant Surgeon William S. Wilson. He recalled the various requisitions during the month of December, food purchased from the sutler and paid for through Captain Steele's office. Dr. Wilson could not be sure as to the exact use of the entire requisition. "Some of the goods went into the hospital that I know of. As to the appropriation to himself made by Dr. Hoffman of hospital stores, I can remember one or two instances of one article, some sort of jelly and another was a can of peaches. In regards to the whisky, it was ordered either by Dr. Hoffman or by myself and the stewards and nurses attending to the patients were entrusted with the duty of distributing the whisky." As to the charge of Dr. Hoffman selling disability certificates, Dr. Wilson could give no support for such a charge: " I have never known him to receive pay for issuing such a certificate."

The court now returned to the issue of hospital stores eaten by Dr. Hoffman. "How do you know that the articles mentioned as having been consumed by Dr. Hoffman were hospital stores and not his own private stores of food?" Dr. Wilson replied, "The first article was taken from a box in which there were stores for the hospital. In regard to the first article [a can of jelly], it was consumed on our own table. [This would refer to the medical officer's mess, which usually included the doctors, the hospital steward, and some of the nurses.] The second article [the can of peaches] was consumed on the march from one camp to the battlefield of Fredericksburg, when and where we were very much exhausted. This occurred on the evening of the 12th of December, 1862. I can't say that eating the peaches was regarded as a medical necessity, but under the circumstances, it was refreshing. We had been marching two days with no rations except such as are usually carried in a haversack." The court now wanted to know about whether Hoffman had used hospital whiskey or other hospital items for his own benefit. Wilson told them, "I have known whisky that was drawn from the brigade commissary to be set on the table for friends, as is customary among medical officers." Wilson then makes wonderful use of the passive voice, saying, "I have known sugar to come into our tent and various other articles drawn for the hospital and the hospital attendants. The use of such items for the medical officer's table was frequent and habitual. It was considered a normal part of our lives. I am satisfied that the treatment of the patients was not injured by our practice of distributions of medicines and supplies."

The court now recalled Dr. Wilson and requested figures about hospital staffing and patient numbers. Refreshing his memory from the actual hospital records, Dr. Wilson told them, "For the month of January and part of February, it shows that during a 16-day period, the total number of patients was 116, making an average of seven patients entitled to hospital rations, on any given day." With Wilson's final statement, testimony closed.

Dr. Hoffman then asked for a postponement of his case because of the absence of an important witness for his defense. "My witness' evidence is material, as the party is directly implicated with the matter I intend to prove." The court recessed to consider Dr. Hoffman's request, convened again, and refused the request.

As was customary before sentencing, the defendant prepared a long statement, which was submitted to the Court. Some of the high points of his defense are as follows:

> It will be observed that I appeared before the Court without any counsel and without any witnesses for my defense. That I was unable to procure the services of a practicing attorney is made manifest by the fact that he whose services I might have obtained was, himself, a witness for the prosecution. My inability to summon witnesses for my

defense may be readily perceived when I state that I was, by order from Lieutenant Colonel [John] Cain, placed under arrest in close confinement, denied all intercourse with anyone, and without any knowledge of the character of the charges preferred against me. Nor did I learn the nature of these charges until the evening of the seventh day of my arrest. I remained on solitary confinement for a number of days; when information of my close confinement reached the general commanding the division, he issued orders returning to me the privileges of moving about the camp. My close and solitary confinement was in conflict with Article 27, Paragraphs 223 and 224, which prescribe the rules governing the arrest and confinement of medical officers. That it was in conflict is made apparent when it is remembered that I was ordered arrested and placed in close confinement when there were a great many sick in their quarters, and several dangerous cases of typhoid fever in the hospital at a time when there was no other medical officer present for duty in the regiment. Therefore, the sick were neglected from the 8th to the 10th of February.

What a deep-rooted malice and prejudice marked, step by step, the prosecutor's past conduct toward the accused, that a giant conspiracy, matured and ripened under the cloak of a secret enclave, awaited but for a pretext to put the wily machinations into active operation against me, in the form of accusations. Schemes concocted in secret, whose execution aimed at my dismissal, awaited but an opportune moment to send an arrow whizzing on its mission of my destruction and all of this may be made apparent as my defense progresses. As regards the testimony of Dr. Wilson, it is true that the can of jelly came out of the medical department box, but how can Dr. Wilson tell if that was my own private food stores in the same box? As to sharing a can of peaches with officers, that is simply not a scandal."

He concluded by stating that the hospital steward who testified against him had been promised a furlough in reward for his testimony.

The court had now received all testimony and the defendant's statement. Hoffman was found not guilty of improperly providing medical disability discharges and not guilty of requisitioning three gallons of whisky and not guilty of selling two of those gallons. He was also acquitted of having caused a disturbance in the camp by the provision of whiskey.

What remained? He was convicted of selling $2 worth of whiskey to Private Keefer (who "wasn't well"), of selling a canteen of his own whiskey to Privates Mills and Marshall, and of selling a canteen full of whiskey to Private Parkhill. Dr. Hoffman was also convicted of eating part of a can of jelly, which was shared by all of the medical officers, and of eating part of a can of peaches after the two-day march to Fredericksburg.

The sentence handed down was a peculiar mixture of lenient and harsh. He was fined $1 for his "embezzlement" of the mouthfuls of jelly and peaches, then (dishonorably) dismissed from the service with forfeiture of all pay. Having passed this sentence, the members of the court made a request for mitigation: "Feeling that the sentence passed upon Surgeon Hoffman is more severe than is demanded by the degree of guilt proven against him, and yet having no discretion as to its implication, the penalty for the crime of which he has been convicted being specifically laid down in the 36th Article of War. We feel it to be our duty to recommend to the general commanding such mitigation of the sentence as he may deem proper." The Reviewing Officer in this case was Maj. Gen. Joseph Hooker. He offered no clemency and approved the sentence. Hoffman was out.

What he did over the next eleven years is not known, but it is recorded that he practiced medicine in Reading, Pennsylvania, from 1874 to 1878, with a home at 420 Franklin Street, and he died in April 1882. Seven years later his two daughters petitioned that the forfeiture of pay be remitted and that they be awarded that sum. The acting Judge Advocate General ruled that their petitions should not be acted upon by the President since "the sentence having been carried into execution, it was beyond the reach of the pardoning power." This opinion was concurred in by the Secretary of War, who wrote, "A sentence fully executed, as in this case, cannot be reached by the pardoning power, even were the person in whose behalf pardon is sought was living." This ruling closed the books on Hoffman and his descendants.

><·<>·O·<>·<

COMMENT: No one criticized Hoffman's competence as a doctor. The issues were purely administrative. It is true that selling whiskey to enlisted men was generally forbidden, whether the whiskey was from a personal supply or from government stores. However, it might be noted that the regiment had just finished the infamous Burnside Mud March, a four-day ordeal in torrents of rain and knee-deep mud—mud that sucked the boots off the men, mud that swallowed cannons. Morale had fallen so low that Burnside himself ordered a liberal ration of whiskey issued to all ranks. Three days later, it would hardly be surprising that men, on their own initiative, might arrange an independent distribution of the same warming fluid. Hoffman might have had a better defense if he had given away the whiskey rather than selling it.

As to the jelly and peaches, they were shared by all the medical men of the regiment, but only Hoffman was prosecuted. Perhaps there was some merit to his feelings of conspiracy.

The jelly/peach issue raises a final historical note. Most narratives describe Civil War soldiers as living on hardtack, salt pork, and coffee, and that is largely true. Such items were cheap and easy to transport. They also contain almost no vitamins, and reliance upon this diet added to the ongoing epidemic of scurvy, with its attendant loose teeth, bruised bones, and slow-healing wounds. Canned food had been perfected before the Civil War; and most canned items were valuable antiscorbutics. Heavier and more expensive than the traditional fare, canned food might well have been considered a medical necessity rather than a luxury. An army attempt to combine convenience with nutrition was seen in "Portable Soup," a packaged desiccated vegetable mix. It seemed to lack taste appeal and was dubbed "desecrated vegetables."

Chapter Twenty-Seven

Samuel F. Hance

The "Railroad Regiment" was organized in Chicago, Illinois, in August 1862, and the members brought to their service a rich harvest of gonorrhea. The surgeon of the regiment (also called the 89th Illinois Volunteer Infantry) was Samuel F. Hance, who was court-martialed just five months after being mustered in.[1]

Under the heading of "conduct unbecoming an officer and a gentleman," it was charged that

> Samuel F. Hance, did on or about the 20th day of November 1862, when applied to by Private William Stanley and other enlisted men of Company F of said regiment to be treated for a disease commonly called as the Clapp, wrongly refused to furnish him or them medicine for the care of said disease and willfully and falsely informed said William Stanley and the said other enlisted men, of said Company F, that he had no medicine proper for the treatment of said disease and the government did not furnish such medicine, when in truth and in fact there then were among the medical stores in charge of the said Surgeon Hance for the treatment of the sick of the said regiment accessible to Hance, large amounts of said medicines. All this at camp near Ashville, Tennessee.

A further portion of the charge was that Hance had extracted $16 (over $600 in today's money) from Private Stanley and his friends, claiming that he would use the money for buying gonorrhea medicine, but instead he simply put the money in his own pocket.

The sponsors of the regiment had recently held a Railroad Fair and the Committee of Ladies, acting through one William Swann, had sent the regiment $100 "for obtaining such medicines and comforts as are not provided by your regulations." Dr. Hance was charged with using most of the money for "his own use and benefit" and when asked to report on his expenditures "did render a false and fraudulent account."

It is not easy to make a coherent narrative of his trial, because Hance"s lawyer, Saint-Williams H. Clark, objected to nearly every witness, nearly every statement, and nearly every document entered into evidence. Whole portions of the record are stricken, and what is left is without doubt not the whole story. Enough does remain, however, for most readers to draw their own conclusions.

Up to the witness chair came Col. Charles T. Hotchkiss, Hance's commander. Hotchkiss recalled that Hance had received two gifts, totaling $150, both from railroad charities. This sum was verbally accounted for by Hance: He bought a keg of whiskey. Hotchkiss had no objection to whiskey, saying, "Some whisky should be carried in the ambulance and dispensed to fatigued men on the march," but he was puzzled that such a large sum had produced so little, especially in a march through Kentucky, that home of the distiller's art. "At Lebanon, Kentucky, I suggested to the doctor that a portion of the money be used for a stove to heat the hospital, it being then winter. The doctor told me that the money was all gone. Later, at Bowling Green [Kentucky], Dr. Hance produced another keg of whisky, but said that was a gift from Colonel Grensel [Nicholas Grensel, 36th Illinois]. I thought that the $150.00 was to be expended for our sick as the occasion might require."

The Railroad Regiment had two doctors. The second, Assistant Surgeon Herman B. Tuttle, was called to testify. It would seem that he very much played second fiddle to Hance. "I prescribe some, but my main job is to keep the books and records, and to keep the supply of medicines up. Before we arrived at Nashville, we had been at Tyree Springs [Tennessee] for two weeks; our own supply of medicines was exhausted and I had to borrow quinine and opium from passing regiments, then several boxes belonging to our regiment caught up with us. I also made a trip into Nashville and then we had a complete supply of everything except sweet spirits of nitre [ethyl nitrite], which was not available at Nashville." (For reasons unclear, further testimony about nitre was stricken from the record.) Tuttle made it clear that he always consulted with Hance in making up the order list, and the requisitions were all signed by Hance.

The court asked Tuttle what medicines were usually used in the treatment of gonorrhea, or clap. "Balsam of Copaiba [a product of certain Brazilian trees], Cubebs [a derivative of a Javanese fruit], spirits of nitre, camphor, opium and whatever else the surgeon thinks efficacious. The nitre is not essential in the treatment of gonorrhea."

On the subject of whiskey, Dr. Tuttle shed this light: "Dr. Hance purchased for the regiment several gallons at Shelbyville [Kentucky] at a cost of $1.50 a gallon and six more gallons at Danville [Kentucky]. At Bowling Green, Kentucky, Colonel Grensel gave the doctor a keg of whisky, but the doctor said it was for him and the officers, not for the regiment." When asked about nutrition for the sick of the regiment, Tuttle explained that they received standard army rations and had no "delicacies," such as chicken, butter, dried fruit, or port wine.

The court wanted to know if the standard army "medical supply table" included all the medications needed to treat the clap, and received this reply: "The supply table is insufficient for the treatment of almost any disease, but the medications that Dr. Hance preferred for the treatment of gonorrhea were plentiful, except for the sweet spirits of nitre."

Now, the court turned to a much more personal topic. They asked him about his feelings toward Dr. Hance. Tuttle's reply was both cryptic and ominous: "They are the same which I would entertain toward a stranger whom I knew to be guilty of what I know against him. They are not unfriendly; they are friendly." Further questioning revealed that Tuttle had made a trip to Murfreesboro, Tennessee, to talk to the Adjutant General about Hance's leave of absence, which had been refused. The discussions seem to assume prior knowledge of regimental politics and makes little sense to today's reader, but appears to have been rooted in animosity between Tuttle and Hance.

Now the hospital steward, nineteen-year-old Nicholas Marshall, had his say. "The men sick in the hospital ate the usual government rations, sometimes supplemented by arrowroot and farina sent by their families. The men received no delicacies." As to the availability of medicines, "The medications commonly used by Dr. Hance for gonorrhea were scanty at the time we were at Tyree, although all other medicines were in good supply. After we arrived at our camp near the Nashville Insane Asylum, Dr. Hance gave prescriptions for [the treatment of] gonorrhea to William Stanley and the other members of Company F. All of that medicine came from the medical purveyor's office. None of it came from any other place. I do not know of Dr. Hance himself purchasing any medicine." In the cross-examination, Dr. Hance asked his hospital steward, "What are your feelings toward me?" The reply was as unusual as Tuttle's: "I can't say that I have much feeling toward you either way. I neither love nor hate you."

The private with the clap, William Stanley, was now called before the court.

When we were in camp at Nashville, near the Insane Asylum, I went to Dr. Hance for treatment. At first, he told me he did not have the proper medicine. Then he told me that men were examined when they enlisted and were supposed to be sound, and that government medicines were furnished only for the cure of such diseases as sound men were liable to have. I gave the doctor $16.00, $11.00 of W.G. money [meaning unclear] and $5.00 in a Georgia bank note. I told the doctor that the men had collected the money so that the doctor could buy medicine for the Clapp. I told Dr. Hance, "Keep the change." The doctor told me that medicine prices were very high at Nashville, and besides, he could only get 85 cents on the dollar for the Georgia money. I received only a few ounces of medicine, and I don't know what the other men received.

The final prosecution witness, Pvt. John Austin, said that he had applied for treatment of his gonorrhea several times over a period of eighteen days, and it was not until the end of this time that he received any medication.

The defense witnesses included Capt. Bruce Kidder, who had been Dr. Hance's patient back home in Aurora, Illinois. He said the doctor had a good character at home, and also had given him wine for three days during the recent campaign. Pvt. Oscar Gates recalled that Dr. Hance had sent tea, rice, soft bread, and dried fruit to two sick men. Gates seemed unaware, when questioned by the court, that the first three items were furnished by the government and were not gifts from Dr. Hance. (Both Kidder and Gates belonged to Hance's regiment.) Drs. I. M. Gray of the 39th Indiana and Jared Wheeler of the 24th Wisconsin both testified that it was not unusual to run out of medical supplies.

Several other privates recalled receiving soft bread and rice when in the hospital, and Steward Nicholas Marshall, who had been recalled as a witness, said it was true that the patients received rice and tea but that both were government issue. "The only items actually provided by Dr. Hance were some dried fruits he had brought from Aurora." Throughout the defense testimony, Hance's attorney asked a series of leading questions, implying that any "luxury" food had been provided by his client.

Three attachments appear in the record. The first is a note from the Committee of Ladies, conveying $100 for comforts for the patients. The second entry is a list of items Hance claimed he had bought with the railroad money: whiskey, port wine, brandy, white sugar, butter crackers, extract of Podophyllum (used then as a laxative), chicken, milk, fresh fruit, and cooking utensils. He also stated that he had bought out of his own pocket ipecac, potassium nitrate, quinine, and opium. The third attachment was a letter saying that Hance was not accountable to the colonel for the railroad funds. The court weighed all this evidence and found him not guilty of any of the accusations.

A few days later, Hance went home on a surgeon's certificate, describing weakness from "dysentery and ague" (malaria). The following month, he resigned for reasons of poor health. There is no pension application.

>─┼◆>─O─<◆─┼─<

COMMENT: Although he was acquitted, it is difficult to understand why. The discrepancies between his claim of expenditure and the views of the other witnesses seem considerable. Hance seemed happy to accept credit for any dietary improvements, when such "delicacies" as rice, soft bread, and tea were courtesy of Uncle Sam, not Samuel Hance. All the witnesses seemed unaware that the usual army rations lacked an antiscorbutic (which we call today Vitamin C) and that such a diet produced scurvy, which prevented wound healing. This is astonishing ignorance, considering the wide publicity given to the Royal Navy's prevention-of-scurvy program seventy years earlier. The "delicacies" such as dried fruit would be considered essentials today. In the treatment of gonorrhea, the doctor's problem seems to be attitude rather than lack of current medical knowledge. His treatment of the men seems moralistic, hostile, and extortion-ate, and he seems not to have considered either the comfort of his men or the effects of disease on their military efficiency. After all, the only function of a military doctor is to keep men ready for combat.

The questions about personal feelings are unusual in Civil War court-martials. The statements of the witnesses suggest a grim dislike: Only Captain Kidder had a kind word; the other witnesses, whether patients or peers, seem to feel that Hance was, in some way, cheating them. He was certainly not a man with a warm bedside manner.

The trial record also tells much about the standard Civil War-era treatment of gonorrhea. Whether these remedies actually killed off the bacteria responsible, or merely reduced the symptoms, is unknown. It is very likely that most of these men carried the infections home to their wives and sweethearts, with the resultant tubal infections and blind newborn babies. Medical care in the Rail-road Regiment was not a happy story for either doctor or patient.

Chapter Twenty-Eight

William A. Greenleaf

A court-martial is a trial of a member of the armed forces believed to have committed a crime. A court of inquiry is intended to discover facts, to see if a court-martial is needed. In July 1864, Dr. Greenleaf, Acting Assistant Surgeon of U.S. Volunteers, was the subject of a court of inquiry. He had been suspected of stealing the money of patients who died at his facility, General Hospital No. 3 in Beaufort, South Carolina. The court met at Hilton Head, South Carolina, fifteen miles south of Beaufort. At the time of the court of inquiry, Dr. Greenleaf had been in the army eleven months.[1]

The first witness was John F. Huber, Acting Assistant Surgeon, U.S. Volunteers.

> I have known Dr. Greenleaf about six months. At the close of May [1864], a considerable amount of money was stolen from patients. Dr. [Charles] Ingersoll informed me that money he had been keeping in his quarters, money belonging to dead soldiers, was missing. I never saw the money myself. As soon as we heard of the disappearance of the money, Dr. Greenleaf and I had a conference for the purpose of investigating the matter and, if possible, apprehending the thief, but we were unsuccessful [in catching him].
>
> We suspected Private W. M. Dixon, who was returned to his regiment a few days before the theft was discovered. Our suspicions rested upon Dixon from the fact that he was doing white-washing in the room opposite to where the money was kept. [Whitewashing walls was thought to reduce infection.] Dixon's character was said to be not very good. Soon after he did the white-washing, he applied to be returned to his regiment, frequently urging the matter. He met me at the door of the dispensary two or three times, asking to be sent to his regiment. [Men without urgent motivation would often make great exertions to stay *in* the hospital, rather than return to their regiment.]

129

Dr. Huber reported that he had no firsthand knowledge of the money, only what Greenleaf and Ingersoll had told him. He had advised them that any money should be turned over to the Paymaster. There had also been a "council of administration" about what to do with the clothes of soldiers who died in the hospital, but the decision about clothing does not appear in the record.

The next witness was Acting Assistant Surgeon Charles F. Ingersoll:

> About May 15th, Dr. Huber took charge of the hospital and I moved into the room with Dr. Greenleaf. The room had a closet containing a cigar box, said to contain the money of deceased soldiers. On May 10th, the room across the hall had been cleaned and white-washed by Private Dixon, a soldier known to be a rather light-fingered gentleman, at times, or at least he is supposed to be.
>
> About May 24th, I asked the acting hospital steward, who had possession of the key to the closet in my room, to deliver the key to me as a matter of personal convenience. A day or so after I took the key, I found my cashmere vest missing from the closet and a silk scarf missing from the bureau. These disappearances, plus several other robberies, prompted an examination of the cigar box, which we discovered to be empty. The closet had a proper key. The hospital steward had originally kept the money in his trunk and the transfer to the closet was done at Dr. Greenleaf's request. There is no safe at the hospital; the government does not furnish any means of safeguarding money in hospital.

As to who was officially responsible for the money, Ingersoll thought that it should be Dr. Huber, who was in charge of the hospital.

The third and final witness was Pvt. George M. Sull of the 52nd Pennsylvania. He had been a clerk at the hospital and when the previous acting steward had left, Sull was appointed as the new acting steward.

> The money of the deceased soldiers was in the hands of the former acting steward. After he was relieved from duty, the trunk containing the dead soldier's effects was upstairs and I was given possession of the key. When the money was put in the closet, the room opposite was cleaned and white-washed by W. M. Dixon, then a patient in the hospital. Shortly after Dixon was returned to duty, the money inside the closet was missed, and it was supposed that he was the man who took the money, as he was in somewhat of a hurry to be sent to his regiment after white-washing the room.
>
> I turned the key over to Dr. Ingersoll about two weeks after Dr. Huber took charge of the hospital. Dr. Greenleaf had kept after the previous steward, urging him to take good care of the money, and

suggesting that the trunk be locked in the closet. Dr. Greenleaf put a hasp on the door of the closet, set the trunk inside, and locked the closet. He and the steward examined the money to make sure that it was all there.

Greenleaf's written defense reviewed all the points made by the witnesses and emphasized that Dr. Huber "would not receipt for the money." The court made three conclusions. First, that the government furnished no proper means for safekeeping of funds in General Hospital No. 3. Second, that Dr. Greenleaf used all possible means for safekeeping of the money, and third, the loss of the money was not caused by any neglect or carelessness of the accused; therefore, he would not be held responsible, nor would he be court-martialed.

Dr. Greenleaf served three more months in Beaufort and another two months in Port Royal, South Carolina. During that time, he contracted malaria and diarrhea, with chills, fevers, muscular pain, and "nervous prostration." For these symptoms, he spent five weeks as a patient in his own hospital. Probably hoping that a less tropical climate would give him some relief, he arranged to annul his previous contract and signed a new one with the Department of the Northwest, then served at Camp Randall, near Madison, Wisconsin, from January 1865 to June 1866. His contract stipulated that he furnish his own amputating and trephining equipment. He was to receive $100 per month while at camp and $113.83 per month while in the field. From these amounts he was to pay all of his own expenses.

During his time at Camp Randall, he wrote many letters, trying, unsuccessfully, to obtain a commission in the regular army. He received his final discharge on June 6, 1866.

In the 1870s he began to receive a pension based on "chronic malarial diarrhea," with intermittent erysipelas. (The latter is a streptococcal infection of the skin and subcutaneous tissue, a serious and often fatal condition.) In 1879–1880, he was incapacitated with diarrhea and debility for fifteen months, unable to leave his bed for two months. He was seriously ill again in the winter of 1887–1888, and he was dropped from the pension rolls in the spring of 1894. Dr. Greenleaf was almost seventy when he died; he had not been well for thirty years.

>-+-<>-+-O-+-<>-+-<

COMMENT: There was no complaint about his medical competence. The records documented that there were neither facilities nor policies for safeguarding of the belongings of soldiers who died in the hospital. We also learned that whitewashing was believed to have a disinfectant influence on hospital rooms.

Dr. Greenleaf's postwar history shows once again that for many men the war was never over: The wounds, external, internal, and psychic, chased them, like the hounds of hell, down the long corridors of time.

PART FOUR

Wine and Women

Chapter Twenty-Nine

William H. York

"My occupation? I am a woman of easy pleasure." Thus spoke a key witness in the trial of William H. York, Assistant Surgeon, 15th Regiment of U.S. Colored Troops.[1]

His regiment had been organized in the spring of 1864 and, until it was mustered out in April 1866, performed garrison and guard duty up and down the center of Tennessee: Springfield, Nashville, Columbia, and Pulaski. York, age twenty-four, passed the examining board for "Assistant Surgeon for Colored Troops" in May 1865, and joined his regiment six weeks later. Away from home for the first time, he seems to have immediately lost himself in a blur of sex and booze, almost from his first day on active duty at Nashville. His peers must have been disappointed because the previous commander had written, plaintively, in June 1865, "The regiment has not had a surgeon for a year."

Seven months after starting with his regiment, Dr. York was court-martialed on many charges and specifications. Under "conduct unbecoming an officer and a gentleman," it was alleged that for the previous seven months he "did openly and notoriously keep and maintain and associate and cohabit with a well-known prostitute called Jennie Ward at a house of prostitution kept by one Julia Dean, and has been a constant and notorious visitor at said house . . . at all hours of the day and night . . . in his uniform . . . remaining there frequently all night, away from his quarters at his regiment." (It might be of interest that a Julia Dean kept a house of prostitution on Marble Alley in Washington, D.C., that same year.)

It was further charged that York, two days after Christmas 1865, was grossly drunk and riotous in Miss Dean's establishment and in this condition engaged in a brawl with 1st Lt. H. C. Korhammer, in the presence of the prostitutes and "diverse citizens."

He was also charged with writing prescriptions for the inmates of this Nashville bordello and with escorting Jennie Ward, dressed in soldier's clothes, to his regiment, where he bought her/him drinks at the sutler's bar. York celebrated New Year's Eve by taking Jennie, still in uniform, to Murfreesboro, Tennessee, on the Nashville and Chattanooga Railroad. He was further charged with having stolen a pair of sheets, a pair of pillowcases, a $7 chemise, and $50 in cash, all from Julia Dean. Finally, he was charged with desertion, having been absent from his regiment from January 4 to January 10, 1866.

The first witness was Julia Dean herself, who told the court, "I keep a boarding house at 17 Crawford Street in Nashville, Tennessee." She recalled that Dr. York visited one of her boarders, Jennie Ward, once or twice a week and that he would sometimes stay all night, occupying the same bed as Miss Ward.

As to the "gross drunkenness" charge, Miss Dean vigorously denied such behavior: "Dr. York was gentlemanly merry but not drunk," and there was certainly no conflict or dispute between him and Lieutenant Korhammer. As for prescribing, that was a service that York provided only for Miss Ward and not for any other of the inmates of this establishment. Miss Dean further denied that the doctor had stolen anything or had ever been drunk at her place or that Jennie Ward had ever appeared in men's attire.

The next witness was Miss M. A. Sellars, alias Ida Colinsky, another boarder at 17 Crawford Street. "As to my occupation? I am engaged in easy pleasure." Other than identifying Dr. York as one of Jennie's visitors, Miss Sellars' reply to almost every question was, "I don't know."

The sutler of the 15th U.S. Colored Troops, William Dunlap, knew nothing of a woman dressed as a soldier. The adjutant of the regiment, Lt. Frank M. Whitlaw, confirmed York's absence without leave, and the surgeon, Jefferson B. Ream, remembered that York had been under arrest at the time that he left the regiment and went to Paducah.

The final prosecution witness was the lieutenant colonel of the regiment, Alexander M. York, who was also the defendant's older brother. Colonel York had been temporarily stationed at Paducah, Kentucky, when his doctor/brother appeared there on the 5th of January. "I believe he had come to Paducah solely to consult with me. He has never been away from home before he entered the army and had never drank or kept bad company up to that time. He is impulsive and easily led by the company he is with. He had always depended on me for advise and counsel. He said to me in Paducah that he would rather have been shot than to have been kept from seeing me." Colonel York also explained the delay in his brother's return to Nashville: "The steamboat needed repairs and had to turn back, and the Nashville and Northwestern Railroad was blocked by an accident."

Maj. Henry A. Norton of the 12th U.S. Colored Troops appeared as a defense witness. He had known the defendant for over twenty years. "Before he went in the army, I never knew him to drink or associate with bad company of any kind."

The court deliberated and acquitted York of theft, gross drunkenness, and desertion, but based upon the remaining charges, it recommended that he be cashiered. Maj. Gen. George Stoneman confirmed the sentence, and on February 7, 1866, York was a civilian again. He did not apply for a pension.

>─┼─◄►─◄─O─►◄─►─┼─◄

COMMENT: Here the issues are not medical but administrative and moral, although York may well have neglected his official patients while prescribing for Miss Ward. The dramatic charge of transporting his cross-dressed paramour around the state of Tennessee evaporated in the absence of witnesses. (York was fortunate in not being additionally charged with violation of the 42nd article of war, which prohibits "lying out of camp.") His older brother's effort to shield the profligate sibling from the consequences of his own actions came to naught; as lieutenant colonel of the regiment, he should have arrested his brother and returned him to the regiment under guard. Perhaps that is asking too much of a sibling in a volunteer army.

The trial does give us a glimpse into mid-Victorian life in Nashville, site of the army's boldest and most successful attempt at legalized, supervised prostitution. But York was no part of that official effort. His relationship with the inmates of Julia Dean's "boarding house" were strictly amateur and informal, not the acts of a public health worker. Free of the constraints of home life, William York was a young man apparently without internal controls; in less than half a year he wrecked his career and his reputation.

Chapter Thirty

Henry A. Murray

". . . thereby repeatedly causing disgrace to the United States uniform." These words denoted a sad ending to a promising career.[1]

In the spring of 1863, Henry Murray, age thirty-one, entered the service as a private in Company G, 14th New York Cavalry, reporting at Riker's Island in New York Harbor. His age, maturity, and performance soon earned him a corporal's chevrons. Three months later he was captured in Port Hudson, Louisiana, and in July he was paroled in City Point, Virginia. Just before Christmas, he was promoted to quartermaster sergeant, capping an eventful and honorable first nine months in uniform.

He seems to have some talent for matters medical: In August 1864, still with the 14th New York Cavalry, he was rated as Assistant Hospital Steward and only two months later was Acting Assistant Surgeon of the regiment. The next January he took and passed the examination for "Assistant Surgeon of Colored Troops." In February, his record shows him as "acting hospital steward to be commissioned," and in March 1865, he reached the pinnacle of his career: a commission as Assistant Surgeon of the 84th Regiment of U.S. Colored Troops.

This regiment was organized at Port Hudson in the fall of 1863 as the 12th Regiment of Infantry, Corps d'Afrique. With the general reorganization of colored troops in April 1864, it was redesignated at the 84th USCT and served until March 1866. They were with the Red River Expedition and twice saw action at Morganza, Louisiana.

On February 6th, 1866, Appomattox was ten months past, and the 84th was due to be mustered out in five weeks. However, Murray did not wait to throw off the constraints of military life. In his March 1866 trial he was charged with conduct unbecoming an officer and a gentleman in that he went into a colored house of prostitution, then went into a second whorehouse after being arrested at the first establishment. Furthermore, he was "beastly drunk." Much of the story was told at the court-martial by 2nd Lt. Herman Schwetze, of the 1st New Orleans Volunteers.

"In early February, I was on patrol duty in the city and visited a house at 200 Saint Louis Street on my usual patrol. There I found Dr. Murray. It was about 10:00 o'clock in the morning. In the house there was one old nigger woman and two young colored women. Dr. Murray was in bed wearing his pants and a black citizen's hat. I don't know what else he was wearing, as I went into the parlor to wait while he dressed. I don't know if he was drunk but he appeared to be a little shaky. I told him to consider himself under arrest and took him to the Provost Marshal's Office." There, Murray was officially placed under arrest and ordered to report to the commander of his regiment.

Acting that day as assistant provost marshal was 1st Lt. Benjamin P. Powell, First New Orleans Volunteers. He recalled: "Colonel [William] Dickey, commanding the 84th U.S. Colored Troops, had come to my office and said that his assistant surgeon was in a house of ill fame on Saint Louis Street and that he wanted the man arrested. After the arrest, I think that Dr. Murray did not report to his regiment, but was re-arrested the same day, and by Lieutenant Schwetze, the same officer who had arrested him earlier. To the best of my opinion, Dr. Murray was very much intoxicated on both occasions."

Lieutenant Schwetze returned to the witness chair and recalled that the place of the second arrest was "Bianca Robinson's house," on Union Street, between Baronne and Phillipe Streets. Special Detective A. B. Ward (whose employer is not given) had been employed in that capacity for the previous three years. He told the court: "The place on Saint Louis Street is a house of ill fame run by a colored woman. Bianca Robinson's place is also a house of ill fame and has been for years."

Then 1st Lt. William F. Adams of the 84th USCT added a prior offense to the Court's knowledge. The day before Dr. Murray's visits to the houses on Saint Louis and Union Street, Lieutenant Adams had been sent by his commanding officer to find the missing doctor. "I went to the house of ill fame on Custom House Street, run by the colored woman Eliza Skinner. All the inmates of that house are colored. Mrs. Skinner told me that the doctor had left and gone to the house at 200 Saint Louis Street. There I found him, in a room with a colored woman. He was too drunk to walk, so I returned him to the regiment in a wagon."

There was a delay in the proceedings while the court awaited a witness. When the court reconvened, Dr. Murray himself was missing. Detective Ward found him passed out, drunk, "on the banquette on Custom House Street." The court noted that "for the past two days, Dr. Murray has been so much under the influence of liquor as to render it almost impossible to continue his trial." The Judge Advocate arranged confinement until Murray became "properly sober."

When this condition of relative sobriety was achieved, the court reassembled to hear the final witness, Murray's commanding officer, Col. William Dickey, who described the doctor's character as excellent, up until February 4th, 1866. "Since then, he has failed to attend sick call and failed to prescribe for the sick."

This closed the testimony. Murray was found guilty and sentenced to be dismissed, a decision approved by Maj. Gen. Edward Canby. There, the record ends. There is no pension application.

>—⊶⊳•─O─⊲•⊷—<

COMMENT: It appears that Dr. Murray had a successful career until February 4, 1866. What prompted him to throw it all away in six weeks of drinking and whoring? One possible explanation might be that his problems became manifest near the time of Mardi Gras—then, as now, a carnival of excess before the onset of Lent. But this is only speculation.

New Orleans has long had a reputation as an open city, with vices and excesses of all sorts tolerated by the authorities and by the laissez-faire culture. The Mediterranean antecedents of Crescent City society brought with them the relatively tolerant Catholicism of France and Spain, unlike Boston with its Irish interpretation of the same religion and the other Yankee enclaves with their dour north European Protestantism. Murray's stupefied tour of the flesh-pots gives us something of the details of New Orleans life not so long ago.

Chapter Thirty-One

William H. Lakeman

"I thought it strange that there was a dead leech in the bottle of medicine," exclaimed a witness (and former patient) at one of Dr. Lakeman's three court-martials.

Lakeman claimed to be a graduate of St. Thomas Medical and Surgical College in London, England. "I have served as a dresser to the surgeons and clinical clerk to the physicians connected to the hospital." He began his American career as a private in the 13th New York Infantry, but by late 1861 he had been promoted to hospital steward in that same regiment. In February 1862, he had two encounters with justice. In his first trial, he was charged with neglecting his patients during a four-week drunk. He was acquitted. In his second trial he was again charged with drunkenness, neglect of duty, and with giving the wrong medicine. It was at this trial that a former patient told of seeing the dead leech floating in a bottle of medicine from which Lakeman was dispensing the prescribed medicines for patients on his ward. Lakeman wrote a lengthy defense, claiming that all the charges were a mistake, and signing himself "William H. R. Lakeman, M.D." His explanations did not satisfy the court; he was convicted and dismissed from the army.[1]

Only eight months later he reappears in the records, on the muster roll of the 76th New York, as assistant surgeon, charged with being drunk at South Mountain, Maryland—specifically at Crampton's Gap on October 27, 1862, about a month after the battle of Antietam. He pled not guilty to all charges.[2]

The first witness was the major of Lakeman's regiment, Charles G. Livingston. He told the court, "Dr. Lakeman was on duty at his proper position behind the regiment and was the only medical officer on duty about that time. In the forenoon, he was sober, but in the later afternoon, he was under the influence of liquor. He was not decidedly drunk, but he was decidedly under the influence. I think it would have been sufficient to have been observed by any person who should look at him. We were on the march most of that day." In cross-examination, Dr. Lakeman asked, "Would you not have reprimanded me had you seen me in an unfit condition to perform my duties?" Livingston's answer was certainly reasonable: "I did not see you performing any particular medical duties or I should have done so. You were certainly not in a condition to perform an operation."

The next man to speak was Lt. Jacob Chur, Acting Assistant Adjutant General for the 2nd Brigade. "I was at headquarters for the 2nd Brigade when a young man reported to Colonel Hoffman, commanding the brigade, that Lakeman was intoxicated. I was directed by the colonel to see if such was the case. I went over and from my own observation saw that he was intoxicated. I reported this fact to headquarters and was directed to make out these charges. This was about 4:30 in the afternoon, and his condition was obvious at a distance of twenty yards, from his manner and from his gait."

Chur's place on the witness stand was taken by Pvt. Newton Baldwin, of the 76th New York:

> On October 27th, I was driving an ambulance, transporting hospital stores for our regiment. I saw Dr. Lakeman most of the day, as he was riding directly in front of my ambulance. He was sober in the morning, and intoxicated during the day. He called to one of the nurses who was in my ambulance for a flask of brandy, which was kept in the medicine knapsack. The nurse got it out and gave it to him. Dr. Lakeman took a drink from the flask and then put it in his pocket. At noon, when we halted for dinner, he was intoxicated to some extent and took a drink again when we started. He was so much intoxicated that he could not sit still on his horse and at night, when we camped, he got off his horse and was so intoxicated that he staggered about.

Cross-examining again, Lakeman asked the witness, "Was it not through malice that you reported me to Colonel Hoffman?" The answer, as might have been predicted, was, "No!" In response to a question by the President of the court ("After the doctor had taken the flask and drank, did he waver to and fro like a drunken man?"), the witness responded, "Yes, he did!" Here ended the prosecution's case.

Appearing for Dr. Lakeman was Lt. James S. Godard. He stated that he had seen Lakeman about once every hour during that day. "I went to you around noon for medicine, which you gave me, and I saw nothing out of the way. Then I saw you at night, after we halted. I got out of the ambulance, went to my company, and did not see you again until about 9:00 o'clock in the evening, when you sent for me to come and sleep in the ambulance with you." (The meaning of this action is not explained in the trial record.) Lieutenant Godard was of the opinion that Dr. Lakeman did not look intoxicated that day or evening. "If I had seen you look intoxicated, I would not have consulted you.

It is true that I saw Dr. Lakeman drink from a flask of brandy, and I had some of it myself. My brandy had laudanum in it."

Pvt. Edward Bolston, of the 76th New York, told the court that on October 27th, he had seen Dr. Lakeman several times and saw him as "somewhat intoxicated" in the afternoon. The President of the court then asked, "You said you saw him intoxicated in the afternoon. Had the effects worn off by the time you saw him in the evening?" Private Bolston said that the doctor was still intoxicated when seen late in the evening. Lakeman tried to establish his sobriety by asking about Bolston's care of the doctor's horse. The private replied, "You told me to take good care of your horse, and see to his feet. The horse was tied up to the ambulance, unsaddled, with the bridle off and blanketed." (Lakeman seemed to be trying to establish that he was able to unsaddle his own horse and therefore sober.) The final witness was Pvt. David Snooks, also of Lakeman's regiment. He recalled that there was "nothing in the doctor's behavior to prevent him from going about his business, as far as I could see. When we halted for the night, the doctor came in and said the sutler had come and asked what we wanted. I told the doctor that I wanted bread, cheese and cookies and he said if we wanted anything else to get it. He then came by again and told me to get a can of butter for him. There was nothing about his manner which attracted my attention. He had supper that evening with the chaplain, the major and Lieutenant Godard. I noticed nothing unusual about his behavior during the day, but at night there was 'some pitching around.'"

Before the court closed for their final deliberations, they reviewed the following written statement submitted by Lakeman:

> To state I had not had a drink would be false. I had been suffering from acute dysentery previously, and the heavy, wet march the night previous aggravated it. I got wet through. I asked Dr. Duffid [sic] what I should do to ease me. He recommended me to take opium in full doses, which I did. I was not absent from my regiment at any time during the march, before or since. I attended to those who fell out and were sick on the road, and got them in ambulances. When I arrived in camp, my servant not being there, I attended to my own horse, as the groom found him.
>
> During supper, the order for my arrest arrived, which alike astonished Major Livingston and myself, so much so that the major went to see Colonel Hoffman at my urgent request to inquire into it and ask for an interview, which was not granted. I solemnly swear I was not drunk, and feel punished enough on account of the charge, after having served nearly 20 months with an unblemished character in the volunteer service and through 16 engagements, having fought my way to my present position from a private. I hope that your honorable Court will take these things into consideration and I am thankful for the courtesy extended to me.

The court did not extend him much courtesy. They found him guilty on all charges and ordered him cashiered, a verdict approved by Maj. Gen. William B. Franklin, who "confirms the proceedings of the court martial and the doctor ceases to be an officer in the service of the United States as of this date, November 26, 1862."

In a puzzling later development, although there is no record of Lakeman serving further in the military, on December 2, 1864, he was charged with drunkenness, and sent to Old Capitol Prison in Washington, D.C., as a "prisoner of war, being in the city of Washington without proper authority." He was reported dead in 1886, but a letter from William H. Lakeman, Jr., in 1893 stated that "Dr. Lakeman is alive and resides at 101 Ravine Avenue, Rochester, New York."

He did not apply for a pension and does not appear in the American Medical Association directory of deceased physicians.

>─┤─◆>─O─<◆─┤─◄

COMMENT: If Dr. Lakeman was, indeed, a medical graduate of St. Thomas College in London, his education was of better quality than most. The record of four different trials involving drunkenness strongly suggests that it was alcohol that unraveled his career. (One cannot but wonder how many of these doctors might have been salvaged if Alcoholics Anonymous had existed in 1861.) As for his professional competence, there was no direct criticism of his actual medical activities, only some understandable concern that he might be impaired for doing serious surgery when he was so drunk that he swayed back and forth on his horse.

Chapter Thirty-Two

William B. Hezlep

Must a surgeon be sober to perform an amputation? When is a drinker drunk? And can one tell intoxication from "excitement?" These were the fundamental questions in the court-martial of William B. Hezlep (also spelled Hezless and Hezlop).[1]

Hezlep had graduated from Philadelphia's Jefferson Medical College in 1854, when he was twenty-two, and two years later had married Sarah Bushness of Swissvale, Pennsylvania. He spent the first two years of the Civil War with the 3rd Pennsylvania Cavalry and, in February 1864, was court-martialed for being drunk on duty the previous November, at the battle of New Hope Church, Virginia, just west of Spotsylvania. Five medical officers and several line officers were called upon to testify.

Surgeon Gordon B. Hotchkin of the 1st Pennsylvania Cavalry and acting surgeon in chief of the First Brigade, 2nd Cavalry Division, told the Court:

> I was with the command at New Hope Church on November 17, 1863, as we were marching on the plank road, when the first shells were fired by our advance. Almost immediately afterwards, I fell in with Dr. Hezlep, who was the surgeon in chief of the brigade at the time and as soon as wounded were brought in under the direction of Dr. Phillips, Surgeon-in-Chief of the Division, we took possession of the New Hope Church for a hospital. From the time we took possession until the last man was carried away was from noon until about 11:00 P.M. Dr. Hezlep was there with us all the time except for a short time when he was out on the field of action. I saw him in the latter part of the afternoon, and also after he returned from the field. He was drinking liquor and was somewhat excited by it; after dark, he showed the effect of it much more, so much as to interfere with our duties at the time. His movements were rapid and unnatural in his manner

of speaking to the surgeons about him; he spoke in a harsh and authoritarian way with frequent repetitions of the same words. During the action itself, he assisted and did not seem unfit for this job. I can say I positively saw him drinking.

Surgeon William R. Rezner of the 6th Ohio Cavalry recalled that day well:

> I was present the day of the battle. It was customary for the surgeon in chief, which was Dr. Phillips, to select a certain number of the medical officers to remain at some site chosen as a hospital. Dr. Hezlep was one of those and the site chosen was New Hope Church. [This is one of the few descriptions of surgeon assignments in combat.] I was present during the whole engagement, until we fell back the next forenoon and I think Dr. Hezlep was present during the entire day, taking charge of the hospital and assisting in dressing the wounded during the day as they came in. There was a great many wounded on that occasion and the entire time there was a great deal of confusion. I did not notice anything unnatural with Hezlep except his loud conversation in the afternoon, which may have been due to drink, but it was common for the doctor to talk loud with the excitement of battle. Our custom is to do simple dressings of the wounded brought into the hospital during the time of the engagement, and after the engagement ceases, we then perform any operations that may be necessary on that day. Because of our falling back in the evening, only two amputations were performed, one of which Dr. Hezlep performed. In that operation, there was a mis-cut, but that could be produced by any excitement of the moment. I cannot say that it was due to the excitement of liquor. The operation was well completed and terminated well. The second operation, I did not consider to be under his charge, only so far as his general superintendency would extend, as surgeon in chief of the brigade. Dr. Hezlep's superintendency was merely to direct that some operation should be performed and assign some surgeon to perform it. I did see the doctor drink once during the afternoon. I cannot say that loud conversation or the mis-cut were due to drink or not. I saw Dr. Hezlep perform an amputation of an arm. He first made a deep incision which is liable for any operator under excitement. I would not consider it as evidence of intoxication. I did think that he was slightly under the influence of liquor early in the afternoon, but not by the time later on when surgery was done. His duties were general supervision of the hospital and dressing of the wounded. The deep cut during the arm amputation had no effect on the outcome.

John M. Junkins, a surgeon with the 4th Pennsylvania Cavalry, was also present at the battle of New Hope Church. "At 9:00 in the morning, when I first saw him that day, there were no signs of intoxication. Between 2:00 and 3:00 P.M., at the church where we were together until after dark, dressing the wounded, I noticed that Dr. Hezlep took several drinks of whisky during the afternoon. I noticed that it had a considerable effect on him, but not when he did the operation, around 5:00 P.M. He performed the operation well, and dressed it well. I was annoyed when he gave *me* directions on how to do surgery. From my observations, Dr. Hezlep discharged all of his duties and I cannot say that he was unfit."

The next witness was Assistant Surgeon Isaiah F. Everhart of the 8th Pennsylvania Cavalry. "At New Hope Church, I assisted Dr. Hezlep doing an amputation of the left arm. At the commencement of the operation, I did not notice anything unusual about him, but during the operation, before it was completely closed, I judged him to be slightly under the influence of alcohol, but not sufficient to unfit him from performing his duties. When the operation was done, I noticed that he was talking louder and seemed to be more excited than usual. I did see him take one drink, but I never thought he was unfit for duty that day." Dr. Everhart's testimony ended the prosecution.

The first witness for the defense was Lt. Col. Edward S. Jones of the 3rd Pennsylvania Cavalry:

> I saw Dr. Hezlep on the skirmish line two or three times and I saw him carry one of the wounded men off the field on his back; I also saw him direct men to prepare litters to carry men off the field. When the battle was over, I rode up to New Hope Church and saw Sergeant Crous of my regiment lying on a door or a table. A number of surgeons were there and they asked Dr. Hezlep if [Crous's] arm should be amputated. He came forward and probed the wound with his instruments and finger; the probing effected me so much I had to go away. During the time I was there, Dr. Hezlep did not appear intoxicated. This engagement was the biggest skirmish we had participated in. This may have influenced Dr. Hezlep, who I consider to be an excitable man, but not a drinking man.

Maj. James M. Walsh of the same regiment as Colonel Jones saw the arm amputation and thought that Dr. Hezlep was not intoxicated, he was simply his usual, excitable self. Major Walsh also saw Dr. Hezlep out on the skirmish line and thought that he was not intoxicated.

Lt. John West of the 16th Pennsylvania Cavalry was the ambulance officer for the 2nd Division. "I saw the doctor off and on all day from the skirmish line, to loading ambulances and to his work back at the hospital. He did not seem any more excited than usual and I did not see him drink that day."

Surgeon Henry L. Durans of the 3rd Pennsylvania Cavalry had been with Dr. Hezlep all that day and found no reason to think that he was intoxicated. Lt. William F. Potter of Duran's regiment told the same story.

Dr. Rezner, who was called upon to testify again, added some chilling details. "When Dr. Junkins did the leg amputation, Dr. Rezner gave him some instructions, since Junkins' knife was going in the wrong direction. While Rezner was giving operating instructions, Dr. Hezlep made suggestions about the tourniquet, since the patient was losing so much blood." The court asked if there were any "embarrassing things" that happened during the amputation of the leg. Rezner responded, "Dr. Hotchkin was to do the surgery. He got his instruments all ready and then refused to do the amputation. This meant that Dr. Junkins had to do this procedure under short notice and the chloroform proved defective and did not operate kindly. It did not relax the muscles as much as usual, consequently rendered the operation tedious and more difficult to perform." (The man whose leg was sawed off might well have used a word other than "tedious.")

In brief, most of the witnesses thought that Dr. Hezlep had been drinking, but it was not enough to effect his surgical skill, in spite of the fact that they saw him make both a "mis-cut" and an [incorrectly] "deep" incision during the arm amputation. The court reflected the witness' opinions and found Hezlep not guilty of being drunk on duty.

A few weeks after his trial, Hezlep made two requests for leave: He wanted ten days to visit home and an additional twenty days to recover from severe diarrhea. After these two absences, he served until his regiment was mustered out at the end of their enlistment, in August 1864, and was then immediately transferred to the 6th Pennsylvania Heavy Artillery, where he stayed until the end of the war.

He apparently liked army life—within limits. In 1864 he wrote to the Surgeon General, saying that his wife's health was poor, and he would like to remain in the army but not to serve "in the field." The reply was not what he wanted to hear: "No such promise can be made. Contract surgeons are having their contracts terminated daily, there being an excess now on duty."

As the 6th Pennsylvania Heavy Artillery was being mustered out in June 1865, Hezlep wrote again, asking for employment elsewhere in the medical corps. He was granted a post with the 7th Pennsylvania Cavalry until they, too, became civilians.

The record is then silent until 1874, where he appears conducting a medical practice in Allegheny, Pennsylvania; fathering a daughter in 1875; receiving a state license as an allopath in 1881; and dying in August 1884 at Swissvale.

His widow filed for a pension, stating that she was penniless, and in 1890 she began receiving $8 a month. She passed away in 1911. Their daughter, then thirty-six, submitted two bills to the Pension Bureau. The itemizations illuminate the sad truths of terminal illness. The $75 for a casket, $10 for embalming, and $3 for a half-dozen death notices are poignant enough, but the bill for "scouring" twenty-four yards of carpet and the "renovation" of a hair mattress and fourteen pounds of feathers are grim reminders of the process of human dissolution.

><del>+</del>+><del>+</del>><del>+</del>O<del>+</del><><del>+</del>+-<

COMMENT: Four doctors saw Hezlep as influenced by alcohol but not unfit to do amputations. This certainly seems to be one area where standards have changed. While discipline of doctors today is not perfect, it is almost certain that Hezlep's medical work in the current world would be subject to some serious limitations.

Another observation relates to his widow being left without funds. When Hezlep died, he was fifty-two. Doctors today are usually able to accumulate some estate by that age, whereas a century ago most physicians' income was more modest. But to die leaving nothing at all raises the question of a drinking problem continuing into postwar life, interfering with community acceptance and professional work. A further possibility was that his service-connected diarrhea went on after the war (certainly a common event) and limited his productivity through weakness and illness.

Yet another issue arises. Colonel Jones saw Dr. Hezlep probing the arm wound. The colonel became so disturbed that he had to leave the hospital area. When the war began, most of these men may have thought of glory and of gold braid, not of shattered bones, extruded intestines, and dying screams. The doctors, who could not walk away from the wounded, may have used whiskey to deaden their own horror at the scenes of mutilation.

A final note relates to Hezlep being issued a license as an "allopath." Before the advent of physiology-based medicine, there were many competing schools of thought: naturopaths healed with herbs, hydropaths used water cures, osteopaths adjusted bones and joints, and homeopaths used extremely dilute medicines. Allopaths, who used medications that counteracted the symptoms of the disease, were doing, in brief, what doctors do today.

Chapter Thirty-Three

James L. Van Ingen

The 5th New York Infantry, better known as Duryee's Zouaves, was an extraordinary group. In Gaines Mill, Virginia, having lost a third of their men, they paused while still under fire to count off anew, to rearrange their ranks in the absence of fallen comrades. At the second battle of Manassas, they lost 297 men in ten minutes. Dr. Van Ingen, their first surgeon, was extraordinary in his own way and was court-martialed twice, both times for events that occurred in Baltimore, Maryland.[1]

After sustaining twenty casualties in Big Bethel, Virginia, the regiment spent the winter of 1861–1862 in Baltimore, assisting in the construction of a large fort on top of Federal Hill and practicing bayonet exercises. It was at this time, February 1862, that the doctor had his collision with military justice. In his first trial, Van Ingen was charged with assaulting and cursing Pvt. Edward Read, with beating up a drunk in a Baltimore saloon, and with stalking and harassing a woman on the city streets. There was also a little problem with being drunk while making a house call to see a sick captain.

The issue of Read, the assaulted private, was first addressed by witness Robert L. Wells, the twenty-one-year-old hospital steward:

> Dr. Van Ingen was making his morning visit to the hospital, in company with two ladies. The doctor looked out of the second-story window, saw Read in conversation with a woman, and shouted for him to come in. When the doctor returned to the ground floor, he demanded that Read explain why he was on the sidewalk, talking with a woman; Read replied, "I had just stepped outside when she spoke to me." The doctor said, "Do you call me a liar?" Read referred the doctor to the sentry, who had been close by on the sidewalk. When the sentry was called in, Read spoke to him and the doctor said, again, "So, you call me a liar!" Dr. Van Ingen then struck Read with his fist, hit him so hard that he turned around twice and fell on

the floor. Read's only words as he went down were, "Oh, Doctor! I was never treated so before." The doctor then ordered Read taken to the guard house in handcuffs and leg shackles.

Read had come to the hospital as a patient, suffering from phimosis. [a condition preventing the foreskin of the penis from retracting, often resulting in infection and adhesions between the glans and the prepuce]. When he recovered, he was detailed [assigned] as a nurse. Dr. Van Ingen had ordered that no lewd women be allowed near the hospital. When I saw her later, I thought she was of lewd character.

The next witness was nineteen-year-old Read himself, recipient of Van Ingen's mighty blow:

> I had just been detailed as an assistant cook at the hospital of the 5th New York, and I did not know that we were forbidden to be on the sidewalk. I stepped outside, when a young lady approached and told me that a man in Company H had taken her watch. That was all of our conversation. Then the doctor called out, in a coarse voice, from the window, "Sentry, clear that walk!" and I returned to the kitchen. When the doctor called me, he asked what I was doing with her, and he insisted that I knew her. The sentry said that he could not hear our conversation, then [the doctor] struck me on the left side of my face with his fist and I fell down.
>
> When he came to see me in the guard house, he called me a rascal and a scoundrel, and asked me, "What do you mean, bringing whores around here, when I have respectable women?" It is true that the woman on the sidewalk made a remark which made me think she was of bad character.

Here, the doctor accused Read of knowing who had stolen the watch, of having entered the hospital with a loathsome disease, and with refusing to salute him, all of which Read denied.

On Cemetery Ridge in Gettysburg stands a bronze statue of Maj. Gen. Gouverneur K. Warren, the man who blocked Confederate Maj. Gen. John Bell Hood's threat to the Union left. In 1862 Warrren commanded the 5th New York, and was the next witness in the trial of Dr. Van Ingen. He was to clarify the matter of the doctor taking, without authority, Pvt. Rulif Van Brunt of the 5th New York as his orderly, to carry his sword, belt, and sash, to a court-martial in Baltimore. Colonel Warren told the court that the hospital was under his command, that Van Ingen had no authority to take anyone as his orderly, and he had issued no orders authorizing Van Ingen to have an orderly.

The next witness was Private Van Brunt himself. "I was a patient at the hospital. Dr. Van Ingen ordered me to go with him to a court-martial in the city. About noon, we went into Geekie's Saloon on [123 West] Baltimore Street. Some men came in, one of them drunk, and asked me if I had come to fight for the niggers. I did not answer him. The doctor took off his hat and gloves, set aside his cane, picked up a chair, and tried it to see if it was sound. He then raised the chair and struck at the man who had spoke to me. Another man warded off the blow, and after a few words, the event passed." The next day proved even more memorable than the visit to Geekie's.

The next day, I went to the city again with Dr. Van Ingen. We were going into Pollock's Photographic Saloon, also on Baltimore Street. As we were going into the entrance, we passed four ladies. The doctor gave them part of the room, and did not take up any too much room himself. As we passed, one of the ladies ran aside, pulling her dress away from the doctor. [During the Civil War, secessionist women signaled their distaste for Union men by ostentatiously avoiding the possibility that even the hem of their dresses should touch the hated Yankees. Since a hoop skirt might occupy the entire sidewalk, this ritual of contempt involved some rather dramatic maneuvering.]

The doctor took offense, went to her, and tendered his card; she declined receiving it. [Here, too, we see a long-forgotten bit of etiquette, involving the rules of the calling card. Tendering an unwelcome card and refusing to receive a card were both ritual insults.] The party of ladies then went on and turned down a by-street. The doctor and myself passed along behind them. The ladies went into Barnum's Hotel, at Fayette Street, and went into the Ladies Room. [A "ladies room" where ladies gathered while men congregated in another room, to chew, smoke, drink, and discuss manly topics.] The doctor stood in the hall and sent me into the room where the ladies were, to present the lady again with his card. She declined again. Then the doctor sent his card to the proprietor of the hotel, but before the proprietor came, the ladies passed out of the hotel and went up Fayette Street.

The doctor and myself passed along at a distance behind them. The ladies, in crossing the street, spoke to two or three young gentlemen, and then passed on. One young man came to the doctor and asked him what reason he had for following the ladies. The doctor told him what happened and offered the young man his card. The young man took the card and crushed it in his hand; the doctor then said that this act had freed him of all obligations.

Van Brunt went on to describe a hostile crowd gathering around the doctor and his rescue from peril when an onlooker took him into a private office until the crowd dispersed. Now the court asked for further details about Van Brunt and the doctor following the women.

"We walked no closer than [15 feet] behind the ladies. After the gentleman crushed the doctor's card, we did not see the ladies again. At the photographic saloon, the lady ran for some distance, pulling her dress aside, as if the touch would be contaminating, as if she was afraid to be touched by the uniform." The only cross-examination question was about Van Brunt's pre-War occupation: "I was a student at New York City Academy." (Two months after his testimony Van Brunt was discharged for a preexisting condition of pulmonary tuberculosis.)

The next witness, Capt. Churchill Chambreleng, also of the 5th New York, had been under Dr. Van Ingen's care for two weeks. "He treated me very well; on only one occasion did he appear to be under the influence of stimulants, and was not then in a condition to attend to his professional duties." Sgt. Gardner Pattison was working at the guardhouse of the 5th New York when the doctor ordered Private Read confined. "Dr. Van Ingen came in and asked, 'Where is that scoundrel?' and insisted that Read had deliberately insulted him. He demanded that I put a ball and chain on Read. Read claimed that some people thought him to be of good character, and the doctor said, 'Are you being impertinent to me, you who came to the hospital with that filthy disease?'" On cross-examination, the sergeant recalled that Van Ingen was a competent doctor, having never lost a patient.

There were four defense witnesses. Surgeon William G. Salley of the Adams House Hospital had known the defendant for sixteen years. "His reputation as a surgeon is very high. I have never seen him unfit for duty from intoxication. I examined him once on surgery and anatomy. He passed a first rule examination, and knows almost as much as I do." Private Van Brunt appeared again, to add, "Dr. Van Ingen cured me of remittent fever. I know he is very successful in curing patients in the hospital. I have never seen him intoxicated."

Pvt. Jacob Hulsart, also of the 5th New York, had been a nurse in the hospital through nearly all of Van Ingen's tenure. "He took good care of the patients. Some cases were thought not to live from one moment to another, and he treated them until they got to be well again. I had charge of the doctor's private liquors. I never saw him intoxicated. He was never absent from his duty a single day until he was taken sick." (In two years a bullet would kill Hulsart, at Weldon Railroad, Virginia.) Brig. Gen. Abram Duryee said that he had never heard of Van Ingen's ability being questioned. "I have a letter sent to me by the Surgeon General of New York, highly endorsing Dr. Van Ingen." (Duryee survived five wounds and lived a quarter century past the end of the war.)

The final defense action was a long, written statement by Van Ingen himself, in which he told the court that he had arisen from a sick bed ("chills and fever," probably malaria) to attend the trial and that his illness was due to overwork. "In addition to the 5th New York, I took care of 45 convalescents of the 4th Wisconsin; I took 15 men to the General Hospital at my own expense, as their quarters were not suitable. I treated the sick of the gunboats in the harbor, as they had no medical officers."

As to Private Read: "This regiment has been plagued by venereal disease. Read disobeyed a long-standing order about talking with prostitutes and then denied to my face that he had done so." His version of the Geekie's Saloon incident was that he had been treating patients since before dawn, that he had had no breakfast, and that he was at the saloon for lunch, not for drinks.

He was even more adamant about the propriety of his actions regarding the secessionist woman at the photographic saloon. "She acted as though the touch of the uniform would contaminate her. With her nostrils dilated, and eyes shooting fire, her dress drawn aside to the extreme of decency, she was the personification of hate."

He went on to hint at a plot to remove him: "Colonel Warren suggested that I resign, but he could not give me a reason. They thought I would resign because I had a good practice at home." He described his prewar naval service in the West Indies, on the ships *Ohio* and *Falcon,* where, he said, he had been very successful in treating cholera, Chagas fever, Mexican diarrhea, and yellow fever, although he personally was exhausted by the experience, losing almost a hundred pounds. He also claimed great success in reducing sickness in the New York recruit camp near Albany. The court deliberated and found him innocent of all charges except those of cursing Private Read and of putting Read in irons without proper authority. He was sentenced to be privately admonished by Maj. Gen. John A. Dix.

However, this did not end the doctor's troubles. He was immediately court-martialed on a second set of charges, of conduct unbecoming an officer and a gentleman. The first specification states that at 3:00 in the morning, on January 21, 1862, he called Pvt. Charles Frye, of Company I, a "God damned son-of-a-bitch" and threatened to "blow his damned brains out." This so terrified Mrs. Frye, who "had been lying seriously ill in a contiguous room, that she sprang from bed to interfere which caused her to faint and go into convulsions." Frye testified that his wife, who had been seriously ill for weeks, was boarding at 16 Warren Street, near Camp Federal Hill. He had permission to visit his wife and look after her, since there was no system of health care for dependents. He was alarmed by her "violent fit of coughing" and went downstairs to get some medicine; this disturbed Dr. and Mrs. Van Ingen, who were staying on the first floor. The doctor demanded that Frye be quiet, and harsh words passed between them. Two witnesses at the same boardinghouse remembered no harsh words spoken by the doctor, and he was acquitted.

Colonel Warren ordered that Van Ingen return to the fort from his rooms at 16 Warren Street. The doctor sent word that he was too sick to walk. He was then ordered to appear before a medical examining board to determine his "professional qualifications, physical ability, and moral standing." He did not appear for the examination; the board then went to him, at 16 Warren Street, where he refused to be interviewed. (A refusal to be examined meant automatic dismissal from the army.) The board concluded that he was not too sick to be examined and ought to be discharged because of "insufficient professional knowledge and bad habits, involving intemperance and violence."

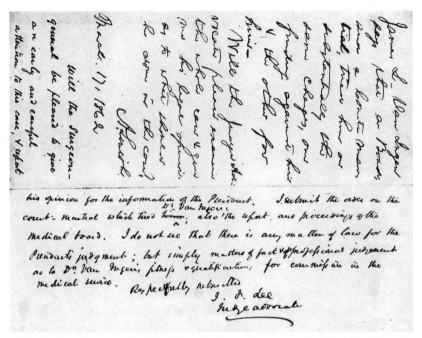

After Dr. Van Ingen was dismissed from the Army, he wrote to President Lincoln, who made this note: "James L. Van Ingen says a Board and a Court-martial tried him on substantially the same charges, one finding against him and the other for him—Will the Judge Advocate General please examine the whole case and give me his legal opinion as to what [should] be done in the case?" This unusually long note does not appear in Basler's index of Lincoln's writings.

This recommendation for discharge was approved by General Dix, Secretary of War Edwin Stanton, and by the Surgeon General. Van Ingen appealed to the President, who asked the Judge Advocate General to prepare a report, as shown by this note in Lincoln's own hand:

> James L. Van Ingen says that a Board and a Court Martial, tried him on substantially the same charges, one finding against him & and the other for him. Will the Judge Advocate please examine the whole case & give me his legal opinion as to what [should] be done in the case? A. Lincoln March 17, 1862.

Holt noted McClellan's favorable view of Van Ingen but concluded that the Act of Congress, governing such examining boards, mandated that their recommendations be followed. On February 14, 1862, James L. Van Ingen was out of the army. He died on July 26, 1881, in Schenectady, New York.

>–+–+›–•–O–‹+–+–‹

COMMENT: It is of interest that Van Ingen was dismissed in part because of "insufficient professional knowledge," when all testimony described him as skillful and successful in his medical work Regarding drunkenness, as many men testified to his sobriety as did those who said he was intoxicated. The heart of the matter seemed to be his hotheaded response to provocation, his irritability, and his quickness to take offense.

Without doubt, many officers suffered from the wearing effects of disease, responsibility, and the frustrations of military life. Van Ingen bore these burdens less gracefully than he might have.

His review by Lincoln indicates the remarkable degree of "hands-on" attention during that administration. Lincoln's willingness to interest himself in the miseries and quarrels of individuals, in the military and out, has not been seen in generations, and is difficult to imagine now. Father Abraham seemed willing to exhaust and deplete himself in the service of America and all of its inhabitants.

The doctor's clash with the law, disappointing as it must have been to Van Ingen himself, has left us with yet another insight into the social beliefs and behaviors of America in the 1860s. Crumpled calling cards, lifted hems, and sword-carrying orderlies are as far from life today as the rules of chivalry followed by King Arthur, yet as the last two Civil War widows (alive when these words were written) could tell us, the great conflict is still part of living memory.

Chapter Thirty-Four

Andrew McLetchie

The Highlander Regiment, with its strong Scottish flavor, seemed an ideal place for Andrew McLetchie and, indeed, his comrades spoke of his bravery and gallantry at the First Battle of Bull Run. McLetchie, praised by his regiment (also known as the 79th New York) and by the mayor of Annapolis—even by the postmaster of that city—had a dark side to his personality, one that led him into a courtroom in January 1864, charged with being drunk on duty. The trial record is a monument to the obfuscatory talents of legal counsel—a lawyer's ability to introduce doubt and confusion where before all was clarity and sunlight. In the end, even Abraham Lincoln had a hand in the saga of Andrew McLetchie.[1]

On July 21, 1861, the Union army marched forth to smite the Rebels and end the war in a single blow. The next day, while the demoralized Yankees streamed north from Bull Run to rethink the consequences of modern warfare, McLetchie was on a Confederate train, headed for prison in Richmond, Virginia. There he languished for two months until paroled. His new assignment was as assistant surgeon at Camp Parole, on the outskirts of Annapolis, Maryland, where thousands of men waited in utter boredom for the wheels of exchange to function. He was still working there, twenty-seven months later when his trial got under way.

The first charge was that of being drunk while in charge of the hospital at Camp Parole, being drunk January 6th through March 6th, 1863, and drunk March 21st through April 4th, 1863; on June 10th, 1863, he was so drunk that he needed to be helped to bed. He was also charged with being drunk in August 1863 and in January 1864.

Under the heading of "conduct unbecoming an officer and a gentleman" was the offense of trying to force his way through a sentry post—a very serious crime in military law. The specifics listed were as follows: On the night of January 22, 1864, he had been in Annapolis, without permission. He returned to the camp around midnight, drunk, and was challenged by the sentry, who asked

156

for the countersign (password). McLetchie did not know it (which is surprising, considering its common use in camp security) and tried to ride his horse past two different sentry posts. About 1:00 in the morning an officer admitted him on the condition that he report himself to headquarters at 8:00 in the morning, which he failed to do.

The first witness was Col. Adrian Root, the camp commander. He headed the 94th New York Veteran Volunteers; nearly all the witnesses were from that regiment. Root had not been present at the midnight encounters and could only cite what his staff members told him. Lt. Henry Swan knew much more. "I was Officer of the Guard that night. I had several encounters with Dr. McLetchie that night. He was drunk, wanted to enter the camp, and did not have the countersign. He demanded that he wake the camp commander, Colonel Root, which I would not do. His speech was thick; when he dismounted, he staggered, and when mounted, ran his horse up and down the boundary of the camp in a reckless and furious manner. When I let him in, I ordered him to report to headquarters in the morning, which he did not."

Lt. Henry Fish, who had been Officer of the Day, saw McLetchie at midnight. "His face was flushed and his speech was thick." Sgt. Fayette Wise confirmed these observations and added that McLetchie was "reeling in the saddle." Here the case was adjourned for seven days because the defendant had a severe attack of malarial chills and fever and was spitting up blood.

When the trial resumed, McLetchie's attorney increased his efforts to destroy the evidence of the witnesses. Henry Spurr, who had been Corporal of the Guard that night, described the defendant as "weaving about on his horse." Counsel asked the same question in several different ways, seizing upon small and irrelevant discrepancies and accusing the witness of being confused to the point of unreliability. The corporal complained, "I have never been a witness before. I am confused by so many different questions." This admission told the attorney that he was being successful in his approach. After trying to destroy Spurr's credibility with further questions about how to be sure someone was drunk, he switched ground—to the horse. "Did the doctor *ride* his horse over the [boundary] line, or did the horse *step* over the line?" In spite of this effort to shift the blame onto a supposedly unruly horse, the corporal stuck to his story, as did several other guards, who in their own turns were subject to relentless questioning—enough to fill nearly a hundred pages of transcript.

The next witness was a doctor, Joshua Sweet, Acting Assistant Surgeon at the "Naval School" in Annapolis and McLetchie's tent-mate for nine months. "Dr. McLetchie went into town every evening but Sunday, and returned at 12:00 at night or at 2:00 in the morning, very much under the influence of liquor." Counsel asked, "In what manner did he show he was under the influence of liquor?" Sweet had a ready answer: "Thick tongue, inability to express himself clearly, and the distinct odor of liquor." "Well," came the question, "*how far* was he under the influence of liquor?" The answer: "Enough to be

unfit to transact [medical] business properly." When pressed to justify this opinion, Sweet added, "I could tell he was unfit by his manner at morning sick call;
he could not concentrate his mind on the case before him." The attorney then
asked, "Dr. Sweet, how did you judge this?" Came the reply, "Dr. McLetchie
would ask the same patient the same question several times. He could not
remember either his own question or the patients' answers." Now the witness
was asked to specify exactly which patients with which diagnoses were the ones
that the defendant could not concentrate on. "I cannot answer that question. In
the last nine months, we have seen hundreds, maybe thousands, of men at
morning sick call. I cannot tell you particular cases."

Here the attorney tried a new tack. "Just exactly do you mean by a diagnosis?" Every attempt by Dr. Sweet to explain the concept of a diagnosis and
the classification of symptom patterns was met by a set of new questions, each
going further afield from the offense with which his client was charged.

Having exhausted the possibilities of discrediting medical concepts of disease (not an unworthy quest but irrelevant and amateurish in this venue), counsel returned to the central issues.

Q. Were there nights when Dr. McLetchie did not return at mid-
    night?
A. Yes, some nights he did not return at all!
Q. What occurred on other occasions to make you think he was
    under the influence of liquor?
A. I witnessed his constant drinking. I saw it with my own eyes. Many
    nights, the orderlies had to undress him and put him to bed.

Through days of such cross-examination, all the prosecution witnesses
remained consistent in their stories.

The two principal defense witnesses were both medical men. Civilian surgeon James Norval described McLetchie as "one of the most efficient and reliable
surgeons in the army, with excellent behavior at the Battle of Bull Run. Dr.
McLetchie's speech is naturally not distinctly articulated." (Here counsel suggested
to the court that his client's "thick speech" was merely the result of his Scottish
brogue.) Norval continued: "Dr. McLetchie was never drunk, but a single glass of
cider will flush his face." The final witness, James W. Pettinos, Surgeon of U.S.
Volunteers, waxed eloquent regarding the reliability, sobriety and all-around special qualities of the defendant. (Pettinos was not the best character witness, being
under arrest himself for drunkenness, scandal-mongering, and sadism.)

The court deliberated, found McLetchie guilty, and recommended dismissal from the army, a decision approved by Brig. Gen. Henry Lockwood, a
man who knew the Annapolis scene quite well, having taught for many years at
the U.S. Naval Academy. (He is the only army officer buried there.)

However, the McLetchie story was far from over. J. R. Magruder, Mayor of
Annapolis, wrote to Lincoln, urging reinstatement of this "worthy gentleman,"

an opinion seconded by the town's postmaster (an important political post in those days). Twenty-three officers of the self-described "Gallant 79th New York Highlanders" wrote the President, describing the convicted man as a fine fellow, worthy of every consideration.

All of these missives converged on the desk of Judge Advocate General Holt, whose summary concludes, "It is submitted to the President whether the cool bravery manifested by this officer in the performance of his professional duties on the bloody field of Bull Run, until captured, and a good opinion which appears to be universally entertained, both by his peers and superiors in the service, of his personal and professional character ought not to relieve him from the disability inflicted on him by sentence of the court-martial that tried him."

The next entry in the file is in the hand of John Hay, one of Lincoln's two secretaries: "Executive Mansion May 5, 1864 Let the disability now resting upon Surgeon McLetchie be removed so that he be rendered eligible for reappointment." This note is followed by the distinctive signature, "A. Lincoln."

McLetchie celebrated his victory by signing a contract to work as a private physician for the Federal government in Baltimore at $100.00 a month. Four weeks later, the *Baltimore American & Commercial Advertiser* carried the notice that the Rev. Cyrus Dickson had joined the doctor and Miss Mary C. Brashear in marriage.

His records show brief periods of service in 1865, at Annapolis, Baltimore, and with the 8th Infantry. A pension application filed by his twenty-six-year-old daughter in 1891 states that her father died in 1867 of "disease contracted in the service," and that her mother followed him in death in 1873. After nine years of correspondence between the daughter and the Pension Bureau, this application was rejected, because "there is no record of disability or treatment found" in the service files. (To give credit to Dr. McLetchie, the Pension Bureau seems to have overlooked the attack of malaria described in the court-martial transcript.)

>-+-<>-+-O-+-<>-+-<

COMMENT: A doctor who is out drinking past midnight every evening is unlikely to be very efficient the next morning, and Dr. Sweet's testimony confirmed this. A doctor who cannot keep patients' stories in mind for more than a few minutes is simply too incoherent and befuddled to be trusted with medical care. His colleagues in the Highland Regiment, who were out fighting a war while McLetchie—for reasons unclear—stayed in Annapolis, may have recalled the more efficient McLetchie of 1861, rather than the besotted midnight rider of 1864.

Holt's relatively benign acquiescence to political pressures for clemency, an attitude endorsed by Lincoln, shows that even with Honest Abe, political considerations might loom larger than the implications of a drunken doctor. McLetchie's ability to mobilize political support suggests that for some, a life of public service may require less cerebral functioning than the calling of Hippocrates.

Chapter Thirty-Five

William Robinson

The career of Dr. Robinson was like a meteor: a sudden bright streak across the dark firmament of the Civil War, then vanishing as if he had never existed. If he had not made an inappropriate demand upon the often-flexible boundaries of Southern hospitality, he might have lasted longer and made more of a mark in our nation's records.[1]

He was born in 1836—where is not recorded. In January 1862 he was mustered into the newly formed 16th Kentucky Infantry at Camp Kenton, Kentucky, and served with them as a hospital steward, as they marched through their native state, to Piketon, Prestonburg, Louisa, Bowling Green and on to Shepherdsville. In November 1862 he was sent to Louisville on medical leave, on the recommendation of Dr. John Pirtle of the 8th Kentucky, who noted "severe diarrhea, hemorrhoids, and extreme debility, in association with five weeks of gastroenteritis."

While Robinson was recuperating, Pirtle was discharged from the army, and in February 1863 Robinson was mustered in as surgeon, to fill the vacancy in the 8th Kentucky. His new regiment was still recovering from the battle of Stone's River, and they stayed in Murfreesboro, Tennessee, until June, breaking the months of relative calm with the Tullahoma campaign of late June and early July 1863. While the regiment paused for a few weeks in McMinnville, Tennessee (sixty miles southeast of Nashville and noted for its Cumberland Caverns), Robinson took the action that ended his army career. The story was told by three witnesses, one military and two civilian.

The first witness, 2nd Lt. George Wood of the 51st Ohio, told the Court, "I was Lieutenant of the Guard and was ordered by Colonel McClean to go to Mr. White's house and arrest Captain Robinson. I found the accused sleeping under a tree in the front yard. He was so intoxicated he did not know what he was about."

William T. White told the Court:

> I live at McMinnville on the north side of the town on the Smithville Road, near the Female Seminary. I have a wife, two children, and three Negroes. I was at home around 12:00 o'clock; a boy came to me and said there was a gentleman at the door. I went to the door. The accused was on horseback. He said that he wanted his dinner. I told him that we had company, that my family was at dinner, but he should have some as soon as they were through. I got him to dismount and I gave him a seat on the front porch and I then stepped back into the house.
>
> When I came out again, he was lying down on the floor of the porch. I asked him to get up and said to him that his dinner would soon be ready. He got up and went into the yard about twenty steps, to the fence, and made water. Then he lay down under a tree. Where he made water was not in view of my family and guests. He would have been in view of anyone who might have been on the porch. I don't think he intended any disrespect, he had his back to the house when he made water. I don't suppose he knew where he was.

The third witness, Mr. William B. Hill, was one of the dinner guests at the White house. "The accused was in the yard on his horse when I first saw him. He wanted dinner. He also asked if we knew where the army was moving to. I told him I had no idea where the army was or where it was going. He then got down and hitched his horse and lay down on the porch. He slept there a few minutes on the porch. When Mr. White woke him up, he began to unbutton his pantaloons, for the purpose of making water. Then he walked across the yard to the fence."

(While the witnesses used the term "making water," it should be noted that the actual charges filed described Dr. Robinson as having "committed a nuisance." This term, common in the Civil War court-martial records, was used for both inappropriate urination and defecation; the context distinguished one from the other.)

Dr. Robinson offered no testimony in his own defense. The trial was over. The verdict was "guilty." He was sentenced to be dismissed and he was. The official records show him leaving the army on August 4, 1863. He never applied for a pension.

>─┼─◄►─○─◄►─┼─◄

COMMENT: That he was drunk is evident. That he was so drunk, so early in the day, suggests that his alcohol intake was beyond the norm.

The act of arriving at a stranger's door and demanding supper is seen by us today as somewhat peculiar, but long experience in reading Civil War records has yielded many occasions where a soldier testifies, "I went to a house on the road to get my supper." And it would seem that some sort of supper would be forthcoming. Whether the householders feared violence if they refused such a request or whether they simply accepted it as normal behavior for that time and place is unknown, but feeding strangers was hardly rare in the 1860s. The army supply systems frequently collapsed, and the roads of the whole southern half of the country were filled with men, singly or in groups, roaming from place to place: deserters, stragglers, paroled prisoners, robbers, wounded soldiers, refugees, bushwhackers, and those simply lost. When they had had homes, they probably fed strangers; now they were the strangers, and they were hungry.

(One of the authors recalls the late 1930s, when "hoboes" and "tramps" would come to his grandmother's door in a rural area, requesting a handout or offering to work for food. This one aspect of the Great Depression suggests that the custom may have persisted well past the nineteenth century.)

However, Robinson certainly exceeded the bounds of social propriety. His potential host, Mr. White (whose political leanings are not recorded), seemed willing to feed a total stranger, a very drunk stranger, even a stranger so rude as to not dismount before greeting his host. But "making water" in the front yard at high noon, even with his back to the house, tipped the balance and exceeded the limits of fabled Southern hospitality.

Robinson's records are of interest in yet another dimension: the description of his medical training and qualifications. There is none. Today a person applying for a medical position, military or civilian, would be expected to produce copies of a dozen different diplomas and certificates. By contrast, documentation of schooling of any sort is extremely rare in the Civil War medical officer files. More to the point, the records of our Civil War doctors rarely mention anything of their technical training. We know something of what they were supposed to know from the written examinations preserved in a few medical officer files. How and where they learned such information is almost never given. This is regrettable because it makes it hard for us today to evaluate the background and competence of a Civil War doctor by the standards of his own time.

Chapter Thirty-Six

William A. Gardiner

As late as 1960, alcohol was classified as a "stimulant"—at least in the California laws allowing involuntary commitment for addiction. As Dr. William Gardiner ended his career in 1863, his problems were also described as "recourse to stimulants." A key issue in his case: Was such "recourse" caused by his military service?[1]

Gardiner was better qualified than many surgeons, with an 1842 M.D. from the medical department of Pennsylvania College. He entered the federal records at the age of thirty-seven, when he was mustered in on September 19, 1861. After a few weeks with the 36th Pennsylvania Volunteer Infantry, he spent the remainder of his service as Surgeon of the 81st Pennsylvania. He was first court-martialed only three months after he joined the army, charged with being drunk on November 19, 1861, in the office of Dr. Charles Tripler, the Medical Director of the Army of the Potomac.

As was said of Queen Victoria, Tripler was "not amused." He had become McClellan's chief doctor just three months earlier and was struggling to raise his department from the chaos, confusion, and abysmal inefficiency that had become manifest at the first battle of Bull Run, and continued, as waves of measles, scurvy, and diarrhea swept through the camps. Tripler had been an army doctor for thirty-two years before this; he knew what he needed at this critical period, and the last thing he needed was a drunken surgeon. He preferred charges against Gardiner, and the issue came to trial in January 1862.

The principal prosecution witness was Dr. A. K. Smith, who was working on that day in Tripler's office. He told the court that Gardiner looked "very stupid" and "smelled of whisky." However, Smith was even more impressed with Gardiner's odd behavior: "Dr. Gardiner came into the office late in the morning with some requisitions for Dr. Tripler to sign. They were approved and he went away with them. He came back in a while and asked me if the requisitions had been approved. I looked at them and assured him that they were, indeed, approved, and handed the papers back to him. He left again but was back again in five minutes. Dr. Gardiner asked me then why he could not have the requisitions. I told him that he already had them and that they were in his own hands, if he would only look. Then he went away again."

Dr. Gardiner defended himself by pointing out that he had successfully filled out the forms and therefore could not have been drunk. He then called his star defense witness, Pvt. Michael Garny of the same regiment. This young man had accompanied the surgeon on the errand and his replies are the very model of evasion and discretion:

Q. Was I drunk that day?
A. Not in my presence.
Q. Was I drunk in Dr. Tripler's office?
A. Not in my presence.
Q. Were you with me when I got into the ambulance to drive the horses?
A. I was standing on the street when you got into the ambulance.

This testimony—which, of course, said nothing—seemed to deeply influence the court. They found Dr. Gardiner not guilty and sent the case for review to Brig. Gen. Samuel P. Heintzelman, commanding.

Like Tripler, he was not amused: "The decision of the Court in this case is most extraordinary. There is not the shadow of evidence to contradict the clear and direct testimony of Dr. Smith. The findings in the case of Surgeon William A. Gardiner of the 36th, now 81st Regiment Penn. Vol. are disapproved. Trusting that Surgeon Gardiner will profit by his experiences, the Court will not be reconvened in this case. Surgeon Gardiner will resume his sword and return to duty."

Heintzelman clearly felt that a reconsideration of the case by this board of officers would have been a waste of time and effort. He also trusted that Dr. Gardiner would have learned something from being court-martialed. The general was to be disappointed. Dr. Gardiner's medical-officer file contains the following, produced verbatim.

Charge One. Drunkenness on duty. Specification. Dr. Gardiner was drunk about January 4, 1862, while on duty in charge of the regimental hospital and has continued, more or less, in a state of intoxication from that date to January 10, 1862. Charge Two. Conduct to the prejudice of good order and military discipline. Specification 1. Dr. Gardiner did encourage and did allow the drinking of ardent spirits to intoxication in his hospital department about January 6, 1862, and the same conduct has been continuous from that date to January 10, 1982. Specification 2. Dr. Gardiner used profane and abusive language directed toward the assistant surgeon and others of his regiment about

January 7, 1862 and continued to use similar language between the 6th and the 9th of January 1862. Specification 3. Dr. Gardiner did lie in the apothecary tent under the influence of liquor from day to day, not properly attending to Surgeon's Call, not properly attending to the sick in hospital, and not allowing the assistant surgeon to do so without personal abuse. This at Camp California [near Fairfax Courthouse, Virginia], about January 4, 1862.

For reasons unclear, this case never came to trial and does not seem to be in the 1880 index to Civil War court-martials. Perhaps Gardiner was too sick to be tried. In February 1862 the 81st Pennsylvania was stationed in the Defenses of Washington, D.C. There was not a Confederate in sight, but an invisible enemy was at work. The brigade surgeon wrote to Dr. Tripler that Gardiner was confined to his bed by dysentery; at that moment there was no assistant surgeon, and the regiment wanted entirely for medical care.

The next month Gardiner's regiment joined the Peninsular Campaign, south of the Confederate capital, and was engaged at Yorktown, Malvern Hill (both in Virginia), and all the battles in between. During the Union retreat from Richmond, the regiment lay at Harrison's Landing on the James River, awaiting their August 1862 evacuation. As they waited, Gardiner resigned his commission and went home.

Seven months later he was admitted to the Pennsylvania Hospital for the Insane. His physician wrote, "Dr. Gardiner had returned from the army with chronic diarrhea, which he knew could not be cured, could entertain no hope of getting better, and as such was the case and the severity of his complaint so great that to alleviate his sufferings recourse was made to stimulants, which he partook of as a relief, which only effected temporary relief, so that finally in the last part of April 1863, his suffering became unbearable and he took an unusual quantity of stimulants, which brought on Mania a Potu." This latter condition was the cause of death. What is "mania a potu"? It is literally an excited psychosis caused by drinking, most likely a form of delirium tremens. Dr. Gardiner breathed his last on April 29, 1863.

His widow, Mary, now left with three children under the age of twelve, applied for a pension. Supporting her claim was a letter from Lt. Col. William Wilson of the 81st Pennsylvania, which noted that Dr. Gardiner "was very sick in the bowels on the Peninsula," and a report from a Dr. Rush Vant Dyke, stating that Gardiner's illness arose in, and was caused by, military service. She was awarded a pension that continued until her death in 1912.

Her estate made a final claim upon the Federal Treasury: $116 for the funeral, $10 for embalming and $8 for the hearse. Her personal physician, J. L. Van Tine, wrote, "I made no charge, as she was the widow of a physician." Such a decision seems poignant, even quaint, in today's era of Medicare, HMOs and computerized billing.

>—+—+>—+·O·+—<+—+—<

COMMENT: The issues here are administrative: Dr. Gardiner impaired his usefulness by being drunk. In the pension application are three opinions that his condition arose out his military service. His first drunken offense occurred in November 1861, while his regiment served in the relative safety of the District of Columbia, so it could hardly attributed to the horrors of combat. As to his bowel problems, these were most likely real enough. During the war, over 44,000 Union men died of diarrhea/dysentery, and tens of thousands suffered from these conditions for years, even lifetimes, after the war. The conclusion that Gardiner drank to alleviate his despair over intractable diarrhea is one open to endless debate. That he might have used whiskey to treat his diarrhea is possible, since whiskey was prescribed for a wide variety of ailments.

Chapter Thirty-Seven

James G. Buchanan

In the days before blood-alcohol levels, the definition of drunk was all art and no science. An objective measure might have put a quicker end to the eleven-month career of Dr. James G. Buchanan of the 32nd Ohio.[1]

The records reflect nothing of his medical training, but the very first notation in the file, February 7, 1862, suggests that he would be delayed in joining his new regiment in Virginia because he was drunk back in Ohio. When he was court-martialed in 1862, the first charge was "habitual drunkenness," and it was alleged that he "has been in the habit of habitual drunkenness since April 1, 1862, that he was in a state of intoxication at the Battle of McDowell [Virginia] May 8, 1862, and also on the march with his regiment on the 27th of May and when acting surgeon of the Academy and York Hospitals at Winchester, Virginia, from the 13th of July 1862 to the 20th of August 1862."

The second charge raises again the subject of hospital rations and the doctor's mess. According to the specifications, at Winchester, he traded "large portions of the rations of the inmates of the hospital—sugar, coffee, salt and rice—for milk, butter, cherries, cucumbers, and green beans, which he and his family ate themselves." The court turned first to the subject of Buchanan's sobriety or lack thereof.

Capt. Joseph Gladden said, "I thought him intoxicated at McDowell." Pvt. A. M. Yolan of Company A recalled, "I know he was intoxicated at McDowell, and on the march from Franklin [Virginia] to Petersburg [Virginia]. I saw him drunk at Academy Hospital when he was in charge. I was a cook at the hospital and he was cutting up in a playful manner. At the hospital, we traded coffee, sugar and rice for vegetables and butter, which were used at the doctor's table. Occasionally, if one of the patients was very sick, the doctor might furnish him toast with some butter on it. Mrs. Buchanan was made matron at the hospital. When the Buchanan family finished eating, the cooks and nurses could eat what was left over, but there was seldom any left."

Private Yolan was then asked about the doctor's drinking habits. "At the hospital, he lived upstairs. He was able to go up the stairs without help. At

McDowell, the doctor was intoxicated. He lay down and slept for an hour and a half during the engagement."

In cross-examination, Dr. Buchanan asked the witness, "Did I not frequently give you money to purchase provisions for the use of the hospital?" Yolan replied, "Well, sir, you gave me a two-dollar counterfeit bill which I gave back to you. Then you gave me a dollar and a few days later a second dollar. That was all the money."

The next witness was Capt. Jefferson Hibbetts of Company K. "I saw him intoxicated at the Mountain House [Virginia] at McDowell, then near Moorefield [Virginia] and again, while encamped at Franklin [Virginia]. At McDowell, he was drunk around 5:00 P.M., while we were crossing the first mountain. Going up the second mountain, he was very boisterous and using strange and unusual gestures. After the battle, I saw him standing on the patio in front of the hospital. I talked with him and could judge from the conversation that he was intoxicated."

Alfred H. Brundage, Assistant Surgeon, was asked for his recollections. "I saw him intoxicated a lot of times." Chaplain Russell Bennett was asked, "Did you consider him unfit to perform his duties by reason of intoxication?" The man of the cloth replied, "I would not have trusted for him to have prescribed for me or my family at these times."

Company F of the 32nd Ohio was also known as "Potts' Battery." Captain Jefferson Potts himself testified that, "In respect to the doctor's habits, they are not good. At McDowell, I do not think he was in condition to do his job. I saw him intoxicated a lot of times." Pvt. Jacob Griffith of Potts' Battery, who had been a patient in Buchanan's hospital said, "The doctor was often very lively, with variations, probably through the influence of intoxication. The doctor and his family ate at the same table as we did. I know that he purchased some food."

Capt. W. L. Malory, Assistant Commissary General, detached brigade, had a glass of whiskey with Buchanan. "He was affected by the whisky to an undue degree, much more so than it was proper for a man holding his trust to be." Pvt. William Kay, another member of Potts' Battery, was asked what made him think Buchanan was intoxicated at Franklin. "He played cards with one of the boys. When it was the doctor's deal, the cards fell on the floor. He could not count his game well."

A man of Company A, whose name is illegible, said that Buchanan was drunk at McDowell and at Franklin:

> When we drew two kegs of whisky, Buchanan was so drunk he had to go to bed; he was more or less drunk for two weeks. After the battle of Cross Keys [Virginia], he filled a bottle with whisky and put it in his breast pocket. After his noon meal, he fell back when he tried to get on his horse and saved himself by holding onto the reins. He succeeded on the second try but broke his pipe in the attempt. Then he fell forward

twice and saved himself only by holding on to the horse's mane. In July at Academy Hospital he drew a barrel of whisky and was drunk, more or less every day. At the hospital, the doctor and his family ate first. If there was anything left, the nurses and cooks could eat that.

This witness, too, had noted Dr. Buchanan asleep at the battle of McDowell. At this point the witness was cross-examined by Buchanan. "Did I or did I not give you money for the purpose of purchasing articles of food for the hospital?" The answer was brief: "Never!"

Lt. John P. Pearce, the regimental adjutant, said of Buchanan, "I've seen him drunk, but not what I would call real drunk." Lt. J. B. Yost of Potts' Battery added, "I've known him to be intoxicated a number of times. At McDowell, he gave confusing orders."

At this point in the court-martial, the issues seem fairly clear: Buchanan was drunk nearly all the time—in fact, so drunk that he fell asleep in the midst of a major battle. As hospital director, he robbed the patient's food supplies to buy delicacies for his own family and offered a counterfeit bill to pay for his provisions. But, it is said, a difference of opinion is what makes a horse race. So, too, with a court-martial.

Lt. Col. Ebenezer Swinney testified that Buchanan was "a moderate drinker; I never saw him intoxicated. He was certainly not a habitual drunkard. At the battle of McDowell, there was no liquor. I saw the doctor that day and the next and he was perfectly sober. Before the battle, as well as on the march to Cross Keys, we shared a tent and marched together. I never saw him intoxicated." The colonel did admit, "I seen him take a drink occasionally from day to day. When he did so, it had a tendency to make him more talkative, more animated and humorous. At Cross Keys, he was cool and sober. Crossing the river at Moorefield, he carried two persons on his horse and went back for more." The court then asked the colonel: "Define intoxication as you understand the term." He answered, "A man is unfitted to discharge the duties of his calling by reason of the use of liquor."

Col. Thomas H. Ford, Commanding, appeared for the defense. "I have been with the regiment since April, except for several weeks in July when I was sick. All the time I have been in command, Dr. Buchanan was sober and ready for duty." Two more men chimed in for the defense. Chaplain James P. Hyndshaw said that he had seen Buchanan daily at York Hospital and never saw him intoxicated. Hospital Steward Charles Ludlow said that he had been with the doctor nearly all the time at Winchester and McDowell and never saw him drunk. As to the food at the hospital, "The cooks and nurses as well as the patients all had the benefits of what was traded for."

Pvt. Ludwell Buzzard, who had been a nurse at the hospital, disagreed with the falling-off-his-horse story. "I saw him after he had lunch at Cross Keys. He was not drunk." William Kay, who had commented on Buchanan's tendency to drop playing cards, was recalled by the defense. He had been wounded at McDowell and recalled, "I went to Dr. Buchanan and he gave me attention. I saw him again that evening. I thought he had been drinking, but not so as to make him incapable of attending to his business."

Maj. S. M. Hewitt, who had been a physician in civilian life, denied that he had ever seen Buchanan intoxicated and told the court that the hospital at Winchester, under Buchanan's direction, was well run.

The court found Buchanan guilty of selling hospital rations and fined him $36. He was acquitted of the charges and specifications of being intoxicated. The next month, the entire regiment was captured at Harper's Ferry [Virginia] and paroled. Buchanan resigned from the 32nd Ohio in January 1863. An unexplained note in the record says, "Dismissed by order of the President of the United States, March 13, 1863." That June, the Governor of Ohio commissioned him assistant surgeon of the 125th Ohio, and he served with them until the end of January 1865.

After the war, he worked for many years for the Pennsylvania Company at Allegheny, Pennsylvania. He began receiving a pension in 1907 and died two years later. One record says that he was age seventy-five; another says eighty-four. One of them is wrong.

>─┼─◆─○─◆─┼─◄

COMMENT: The records show again the uneasy relationship between state authority and federal authority. Buchanan was dismissed by order of the President of the United States, yet reinstated by the governor of Ohio.

Deciding whether Buchanan was a drunk or not presents the same difficulties as deciding how old he was. All we have is the written record. Were his colonel, lieutenant colonel, major, and hospital steward drinkers themselves, oblivious to the value and importance of having a truly sober surgeon? Or perhaps the dozen witnesses who saw him tipsy and unsteady were personal enemies? And would not paying a debt with a counterfeit $2 bill be considered "conduct unbecoming and officer and a gentleman"? The reader today, in a different place and time, can only puzzle over these issues.

PART FIVE

Rules and Authority

Chapter Thirty-Eight

Clement A. Finley

Honolulu, Hawaii has two Pink Palaces: one is the old Royal Hawaiian Hotel on Waikiki; the other is halfway up the green tropical mountainside—Tripler Army Hospital. It is Tripler, not Finley, and for good reason.[1]

Dr. Clement A. Finley was a toddler when George Washington died. The seniority system in the old Army assured that the oldest men had the most power; energy and competence counted for naught. Finley had been on active service since 1818. (He received his bachelor's degree at Dickinson College in 1815; his M.D., from the University of Pennsylvania, was not until 1834.) During the year that Finley served as Surgeon General, he embodied all the characteristics of the pre–Civil War army medical department: penny-pinching, narrow-mindedness, pettifogging and an almost-bottomless well of painful jealousies regarding privilege, rank, and caste. (The contempt that line officers had for doctors certainly played a part in developing these characteristics.) His nemesis in the December 1861 court-martial was Dr. Charles S. Tripler, Medical Director of the Army of the Potomac, who accused Finley of "conduct unbecoming an officer and a gentleman," in having "insultingly ordered Dr. Tripler from his office when on urgent duty on behalf of the sick and wounded." Tripler himself was no youthful, wild-eyed radical (he was born in 1806 and had served in the Mexican War), but in his official actions he embodied much of the army of the future, not the army of the past.[2]

Finley's prior court-martials invoke a veritable Who's Who of American military and medical history. In the early 1830s, a shotgun blast had left a permanent hole in the side of a young French trapper, a hole that oozed gastric acid. Army surgeon William Beaumont studied digestion by inserting little silver cages of food into this unnatural orifice and, after a time, hauling them out by means of a string. With this, he established the modern science of physiology. At Jefferson Barracks, Missouri, in 1834, Finley was court-martialed for disobedience in failing to report for duty as ordered by Surgeon Beaumont.

In 1847 Army medical officers were given military rank. Two years later, Finley was court-martialed again for disobedience. A Captain Macrae had ordered

Surgeon General Clement A. Finley, in his pre-war career, had clashed with many of the famous officers of that era. The Civil War brought further conflict with his colleagues. MASSACHUSETTS COM-MANDERY, MILITARY ORDER OF THE LOYAL LEGION, USAMHI

Major Finley to attend a muster and inspection. Finley replied that he did not respond because: (1) he outranked Macrae, and (2) he had to answer "a call of nature," due to a chronic intestinal problem. Winfield Scott played a prominent part in the proceedings. One outcome was that in the future, medical officers were never assigned to posts where the doctor outranked the post commander.

In 1851, in yet another court-martial involving a famous name, Finley was tried on charges filed by Bvt. Lt. Col. Braxton Bragg while at the same time, Finley filed countercharges against Bragg. A Private Siler of the 3rd Artillery was under treatment at Finley's hospital in Jefferson Barracks. Bragg ordered Siler to duty without consulting Finley, "in violation of the 88th Paragraph of the Medical Regulations of the Army." This feud had been simmering all that spring. In mid-May, Finley had written to Bragg, his commander, "Your conduct in relation to my application for an attendant for the three recruits taken sick yesterday is so incompatible with any respect or regard for me officially or personally, that I decline any intercourse with you that is not strictly official." Finley went even further. A few days later Bragg sent his orderly to Finley with an official communication, which Finley returned, with a note saying that he did not take orders from Bragg since although Bragg was a *brevet* lieutenant colonel, he was a *regular* captain and therefore outranked by Finley. The next month, at parade, Bragg ordered to be read out loud Order No. 69, which contained "false and malicious charges" against Finley. The outcome of the Finley-Bragg litigation was that Finley was convicted and sentenced to be dismissed. President Millard Fillmore remitted the sentence of dismissal, although he upheld the conviction. The relationship of line and medical officers continued to be a source of friction and ill will for many years to come.

Ten years later fate brought Finley the once-in-a-lifetime chance to show his ability to rise above petty quarrels and demonstrate a benign and productive concern for literally millions of sick and wounded Union soldiers under his jurisdiction.

At the opening of the Civil War, the army medical department was still under the command of Col. Thomas Lawson, who was not only over eighty years old but also literally dying. Seniority, and lack of rules on retirement, had kept him in charge well into a penurious senility. Even when he lay at home in his final hours, he was replaced only by an *acting* director. At last in June 1861, when Lawson stopped breathing, Finley assumed command and soon showed that he regarded young reformers and the Sanitary Commission as greater enemies than either the Confederates or disease.

The Union's largest force was the Army of the Potomac, with the popular (and politically powerful) George B. McClellan at its helm. McClellan appointed Dr. Charles S. Tripler as his medical director. The first problem to be solved was bed space for the thousands of sick and wounded in the vicinity of Washington, D.C. The Sanitary Commission fully supported Tripler's efforts to build a vast network of new hospitals in the District of Columbia and in northern Virginia, but it soon became apparent that there was not the political or financial support for such a scheme. Tripler's alternative plan was to stabilize patients in the Washington area and then move them to Annapolis, Baltimore, and Philadelphia for long-term recuperation, thus constantly opening new bed space near McClellan's troops.

There was nothing wrong with his plans from a rational point of view, but it overlooked the established chain of command. The Secretary of War, Simon Cameron, had told Finley that he had jurisdiction over the general hospitals of the Army of the Potomac, an arrangement that McClellan ignored.

The growing power struggle between McClellan and Cameron, with Tripler and Finley as surrogates, reached a climax on October 19, 1861. Tripler had been in Philadelphia, arranging for hospital space, and came by appointment to Finley's office in the War Department to discuss this matter. Tripler was accompanied by Dr. John Neill, a "prominent member of the medical profession." The interview was unpleasantly brief. At the court-martial, Dr. Neill, as directed by Maj. John F. Lee, Judge Advocate of the Army, submitted a "Memorandum of Remembrance," regarding the meeting.

T. I have here, in my memorandum book, data concerning buildings in Philadelphia suitable for hospitals.

F. In making such a visit to Philadelphia, you have undertaken to do what I have already done. Are you not aware of such arrangements being made under my direction in this city, Alexandria and Baltimore?

T. I acted under orders from General McClellan.

F. This order was of your own suggestion and you went to Philadelphia without conferring with the head of your own department.

T. I went by orders of the general and had not a moment to spare
after its reception.

F. Do you pretend to say that you had not time between the order
and your departure to communicate with me upon the subject?

[It was three blocks from McClellan's office to Finley's.]

T. I acted under orders.

F. You can leave my office, Sir.

It would be only fair to note that Tripler here may having been playing the
role of a provocateur since informing his medical superior, Finley, could have
taken only a few minutes from the trip to Philadelphia. Whatever the motivation, Finley responded as might be expected. Neither man was an innocent
when it came to bureaucratic infighting.

At the court-martial, Dr. Finley also sent a note to Maj. John F. Lee, who
was acting here not just as Judge Advocate for the entire army but also as Judge
Advocate for this court-martial. Finley wrote:

> I have read Dr. Neill's statement . . . and consent that it shall be
> read in evidence . . . if his private business shall compel him to return
> to Philadelphia. My own impression of the matter is that I thought Dr.
> Tripler had failed in official respect to me. I did not consider that he
> offered me any respectful explanations.
>
> But I willingly accept his own statement . . . and I am glad to dis-
> avow and retract anything I said to him which he or Dr. Neill may
> consider as rude or insulting. I have no wish to treat him with official
> injustice or to wound his personal feelings.

Tripler wrote on the back of this letter that he forgave Finley. With that,
McClellan ordered the court-martial dissolved.

However, Finley's troubles were not over. Three months before this court-
martial, the Sanitary Commission had begun to publicly agitate against Finley
for his "devotion to routine" in the face of growing crises, and his "undisguised
hostility" to improving the medical department. A few weeks after the court-
martial, Finley was denounced by the powerful *New York Tribune* for opposing
construction of a Union hospital in South Carolina because the mild climate
made such a facility "unnecessary." (One does think of malaria, among other
fevers.) The editor concluded that the army medical department "is not accused
of misfeasance or of malfeasance but of nonfeasance." In April 1862 Finley was
removed from office and retired for "disability." He died in 1879.

Tripler was not so long-lived, passing away a year after Appomattox. In 1865 both men, along with dozens of others, were breveted as brigadier generals, Finley for "long and faithful service" and Tripler for "faithful and meritorious service." These subtle differences speak volumes, and history—that great winnower of reputations—is perhaps the force that stirs the Hawaiian breezes, rustling the palm fronds in the gardens of *Tripler* Army Hospital.

COMMENT: Finley's problems reflected several intertwined issues of command and control. McClellan commanded the Army of the Potomac, yet his medical, supply, and transportation units were under the direct control of the Secretary of War, Simon Cameron, a man politically powerful, administratively corrupt, and remarkably ineffective in military manners. McClellan's enormous ego met its match in Cameron. Tripler seems to have been McClellan's willing cat's-paw in an end run around both Finley and Cameron. From the patients' point of view, it made more sense for an army's military, administrative, and medical functions to be under one unified command. Whether McClellan's first priority was the patients' welfare or extending his own area of jurisdiction must be speculation, but this court-martial outcome was a useful step in giving commanders control over their own medical workers.

Could Tripler have accomplished his goal of finding hospital space by working directly with Finley in the first place rather than going around him? Or would Finley's intransigence, as manifested by his own numerous court-martials, have stood in the way of such cooperation? Further, Finley had suffered much at the hands of line officers over the decades. What pleasure it must have been to tweak the nose of McClellan, the very epitome of the arrogant military man.

Chapter Thirty-Nine

Warren Webster

Throg's Neck in New York Harbor marks the division between the East River and the western reaches of Long Island Sound. Today, traffic flies far above the water on Interstate 295. In 1864, the point of land marking Throg's Neck held Fort Schuyler, and nearby lay McDougal General Hospital. There, Dr. Warren Webster, an assistant surgeon in the regular army, was court-martialed.[1]

Although new to the field of medicine (he received his M.D. from Harvard in 1861), the twenty-six-year-old Webster had already spent time on the frontier, at Fort Larned, Kansas. There he reported on the dreadful effects of untreated syphilis upon the Kiowa and Arapaho Indians. "[They are] victims of the most desperate forms of constitutional syphilis, evidencing itself in lost noses, vacant palates and the vilest cutaneous affections." Webster opposed the use of mercurials in syphilis, believing that destroying the initial chancre with a caustic would effect a cure. Later in the war he would submit additional medical reports on such subjects as trephination of the skull, treatment of wounds of the face, ligation of the common carotid and axillary arteries, and the diagnosis of typhus, but the charges in his court-martial related not to specific diseases, but to a crucial issue of control: Who has authority over a sick patient—the line officer or the medical officer?

The other principal actors in this January 1864 drama were two war heroes and a wounded Irish immigrant. Brig. Gen. Edward R. Canby's Fabian tactics in the Rio Grande valley of New Mexico Territory (combined with a Union victory at Apache Canyon) had expelled the Texan invaders and ended the Confederate dream of extending Rebel territory to the Pacific Ocean; in May 1862, the forty-seven-year-old Canby assumed staff and administrative duties in the New York City area. Harvey Brown graduated from West Point in 1818 and was sixty-six years old when he arrived at beleaguered Fort Pickens at the mouth of Pensacola Harbor, Florida. All the surrounding territory was held by the Confederates, who launched a series of attacks culminating in a November 1861 artillery duel. For his gallantry in the successful Union defense, Brown was breveted brigadier general. At the time of Dr. Webster's trial, Brown commanded the Defenses of New York Harbor.

That accounts for the two war heroes. As for the third player, he was the focus of the trial, Pvt. Philip Fitzsimmons of Company G, 38th New York Infantry. He had been in the army exactly four months when his regiment fought at Fredericksburg, Virginia. On December 13, 1862, a Confederate bullet shattered his sternum and left clavicle and lodged behind the scapula, leaving him with a painful and useless left arm. Five months after his wound, he deserted from Judiciary Square Hospital in Washington, D.C., but in November 1863 he was back as a patient, this time in Fort Schuyler's McDougal Hospital.

Dr. Webster was court-martialed on two charges. The first was disobedience:

> Warren Webster, Assistant Surgeon, U.S. Army, in charge of the McDougal General Hospital, having received an order from Brigadier General Canby, commanding the City and Harbor of New York, through Brigadier General Brown, commanding Fort Schuyler, based upon an order from the War Department, which said order accompanied the order of Brigadier General Canby and was read by Surgeon Webster, to arrest and send to Fort Columbus, Pvt. Philip Fitzsimmons of Company F, 40th Regiment of New York Volunteers [upon his return, he had been transferred to a different regiment], a deserter and inmate of his hospital, did refuse to obey the said order. This at or near Fort Schuyler, New York, between the 10th and 15th November, 1863.

The second charge arose when a captain, carrying an order for the arrest of Private Fitzsimmons, was refused entrance to McDougal Hospital by Webster's orders.

The first witness was General Brown.

> About the 12th of November, I received an order to arrest Fitzsimmons and sent the paperwork to Dr. Webster. About the 14th, I received a reply from Dr. Webster that, since the hospital is under the sole control of the Surgeon General of the Army, he cannot respond to [this] patient transfer but only to one coming from the Surgeon General. Dr. Webster had recently been thrown from his horse and was confined to bed at this time. Not wanting too much trouble, I went to Webster's quarters and tried to get him to obey. He refused and further stated that Fitzsimmons was unfit to travel. I sent back to Department Headquarters for further instructions, but also told Dr. Webster that I would take the man from the hospital by force, if necessary. Dr. Webster asked me to wait for an hour. I then wrote an order for Captain Hannan to take six guards and some men to carry Fitzsimmons, if necessary, and go and arrest him. Since I did not know

Fitzsimmons' condition, I also sent the post surgeon, Dr. Peas, along. The man was brought to the post hospital by Captain Hannan and sent by my orders the next morning to Fort Columbus.

During cross-examination, Dr. Webster asked General Brown to clarify the difference between the post hospital and McDougal General Hospital. "Dr. Webster is in control of the interior of the general hospital, but General Brown is in charge of the exterior and the guards. I consider that Dr. Webster should obey my orders, like any other officers on the post. It is true that Dr. Webster's name is not on the Post Returns. I asked Dr. Webster to arrest Fitzsimmons, instead of asking his adjutant or another of the hospital's officers, because Webster was in command of Fitzsimmons, and I needed to go through the proper chain of command. In my opinion, all hospitals in the command area, which includes Fort Schuyler and New York City and Harbor are under my command." Here there was reference to an October 1863 agreement between General Brown and Dr. Webster that General Brown would not interfere with the internal workings of McDougal General Hospital.

Provost Marshal at Fort Columbus was 1st Lt. J. P. Thacey of the 10th U.S. Infantry. "Private Fitzsimmons had been turned over to me as a deserter by order of General Brown, along with his descriptive roll. Fitzsimmons had been declared to be a deserter by the commanding officer of his regiment. My recall is that the order for arrest said that Fitzsimmons could be removed to Fort Columbus, but not to his regiment, until his health was better." Here, the prosecution closed.

Webster's first witness was Surgeon William J. Sloan, who had been in the army twenty-seven years and was presently in the Medical Director's office in charge of correspondence and executive duties. He was formerly in charge of the construction of all of the general hospitals in the New York Harbor area, and in 1866 he was breveted brigadier general for his control of a cholera epidemic. "Dr. Webster stands very high in the corps, professionally. From hospital records and from our inspections, we find that the staff at McDougal General Hospital shows great ability. One of the best tests of a hospital's functioning is the number of complaints made to our office, and there have been very few complaints about McDougal Hospital." Webster asked the following question: "Please state whether or not there is a well-understood distinction in the military orders and correspondence of this department, between Fort Schuyler and the McDougal General Hospital?" Sloan replied, "There is and always has been. In the original instructions to me to erect a hospital in the vicinity of Fort Schuyler, I was directed to go beyond the fort boundaries and erect the hospital on ground belonging to the United States. At the time the hospital was built, it was my understanding that the grounds were beyond the precinct of Fort Schuyler and entirely separate from Fort Schuyler. The grounds and facilities of McDougal General Hospital are entirely distinct and under different regulations."

Now Dr. Webster submitted several papers in evidence. The first was an October 6, 1863, letter by Henry W. Halleck, General in Chief of the United States Army, which said in part, "The regulations and orders of the War Department place all general hospitals under the control of the medical department. Subordinate military commanders have no authority to interfere in their management." A second document, issued by the Surgeon General of the Army on August 13, 1863, noted, "The duties of military commanders in connection with inmates of general hospitals are specifically defined in General Order No. 36, of 1862, which same order declares general hospitals under the direction of the Surgeon General. In a recent case of interference with general hospitals by Brigadier General [Benjamin] Roberts, Commanding District of Iowa, which was submitted to the Secretary of War, the Secretary decided in conformity with General Order No. 36."

Based upon these documents, Webster further cross-examined Surgeon Sloan, asking if he was familiar with the letter of General Halleck of October 6, 1863. Sloan replied:

> Yes, I am. Any orders should go through the medical director to the surgeon in charge of the general hospital. Even orders from the War Department, transferring patients from the hospital, should bear the words, "If able to travel"; for general hospitals this is an invariable rule. Post hospitals are covered by other regulations. The military commander has no control over the patients in a general hospital; he can discharge a man from the service, but only with a surgeon's certificate. I have reviewed the papers regarding Private Fitzsimmons and note that he was ordered transferred from the general hospital on Governor's Island [in New York Harbor] to McDougal General Hospital and that transfer was made October the 16th. The direct interference in general hospital management by subordinate military commanders has been the source of great trouble and controversy, and sometimes contradicted the regulations adopted by the medical department. Interference with those regulations without the knowledge of the medical director has caused a great deal of trouble and annoyance.

At this point in Dr. Sloan's testimony, the Judge Advocate of the court (who did not seem to have listened to the testimony) asked him, "Is it not true that McDougal Hospital was built as part of the Fort Schuyler reservation?" "No," said Sloan, "at the time the hospital was built, there was no commanding officer or troops at Fort Schuyler." There were further questions regarding this ongoing jurisdictional battle in which considerations of turf and territoriality seemed to loom as large as any concern regarding common sense or patient welfare.

The next witness was Dr. Eugene H. Abadie, a Frenchman with twenty-seven years of U.S. Army service. "Dr. Webster served under me for a while, and I have the highest regards for him." The defendant asked Abadie whether a wound that shattered the clavicle was dangerous. Dr. Abadie understood the question quite well and replied:

> The apex of the chest containing the [collar] bone is closed imme-
> diately behind the seat of operation by a dense membrane from the
> neck and neighboring parts, strengthened by two loops, one on each
> side of the deep cervical fascia, through which loop passes a tendon of
> a muscle which goes from the neck to the shoulder. These loops are
> attached immediately behind the articulation of the breastbone and
> clavicle. This closing of the chest, at this point, sustains the whole
> weight of the atmosphere [apparently referring to air pressure outside
> of and within the chest] and in case of destruction by inflammation or
> ulceration, would promptly destroy the patient's life [probably by
> pneumothorax]. In addition to this, there is the danger of injuring the
> blood vessels that pass out of the chest to the neck and upper extrem-
> ities. The [subclavian artery] after passing out of the chest, ascends to
> pass over the first rib, just below the collarbone, near the seat of the
> operation. The most important point to guard against in such an oper-
> ation is to avoid accumulation and burrowing of matter that might
> endanger, by pressure or inflammation, the important parts described.
> A patient undergoing such an operation would not be fit in fourteen
> days to be removed from the hospital. Granting that the operation has
> succeeded and that the case is progressing favorably, exposure to the
> weather or accidental injury or too much exercise might increase to a
> dangerous extent the inflammation already present.

In brief, the witness did not think that Private Fitzsimmons should have been moved.

Another regular army doctor, Acting Assistant Surgeon J. J. Caldwell, on duty at the McDougal Hospital, recalled the following:

> I had Fitzsimmons under my care from October 15 to November
> 15, 1863. When he was admitted to the hospital, he had a gunshot
> wound of the left breast and clavicle, with evidence of dead bone in
> the clavicle. A surgical operation was performed on November the
> first, to remove the dead bone, by making an incision, two and a half
> inches long, parallel with the clavicle, and deep enough to remove the
> dead portion of the bone from the external surface and under the bor-
> der of the clavicle. On November the 15th [when the patient was
> moved], the wound was still open, discharging pus, and the patient
> had made very little progress toward healing, and there was still evi-
> dence of the disease [infection] in the clavicle. In my report of
> November 15th, I stated that Private Fitzsimmons was unfit for travel,
> and still had a wound requiring dressing twice a day.

The silver-haired General Brown was called back again, this time for the defense. Brown was asked: "You stated in your cross-examination that while in command of the City and Harbor of New York, you understood that you had authority from Washington D.C. to command all the general hospitals in your command. Would you please give the date and source of your authority." Brown replied:

> I have left that command and do not have all my records. At the time, I considered that I had control of all the hospitals. I had been recognized as such by the department at Washington by the Surgeon General's Department, by the Medical Director and by the Medical Inspector, as I understood it. I habitually visited the hospitals [and was responsible] for the discharge of all men leaving the hospital. I never considered it any part of my duty to interfere with what is called the interior management of the hospital, except in cases where my action was necessary. On a regular basis, I inspected McDougal Hospital, in conjunction with the Medical Director. I considered that all the soldiers, all the sick, were under my command. All the sick that came under the jurisdiction of the City and Harbor of New York, I considered to be under my command, and under my control. I was the issuing authority for all such matters, including furloughs. [In this Brown seemed to have ignored all the orders and memoranda issued by the Secretary of War and the General in Chief.]

The final witness was Dr. Peas, the Post Surgeon at Fort Schuyler. He had been designated to accompany the officer and soldiers sent to arrest and take away Private Fitzsimmons, and his apparent function was to examine Fitzsimmons and assure that there was no medical contraindication to removing him. Under cross-examination, he admitted that neither he nor the arresting officer made an examination at the time that Fitzsimmons was picked up and carried out of McDougal Hospital. Under further cross-examination, he further admitted that this removal was made during a heavy rainstorm, which recalls the testimony of Surgeon Abadie, who noted that exposure to inclement weather might be harmful to Fitzsimmons's recovery.

This concluded the testimony. Dr. Webster then submitted a written defense, which recapitulated the major parts of the testimony, and this was followed by a twenty-page rebuttal to Dr. Webster's defense, a rebuttal prepared by the Judge Advocate of the court. After reflecting upon the testimony and the written statements, the Court found Dr. Webster guilty of both charges and specifications, then sentenced the defendant to be confined to the limits of his post for six months and to be reprimanded in general orders by the general commanding the department. The major general commanding the department reviewed the court-martial and approved both the proceedings and the sentence, but added:

In consideration of his high standing, and his reputation for subordination anterior to the events which led to his trial, I note that the Court recommends the remission of the sentence. While acknowledging, as the major general cheerfully does, the professional merits of Assistant Surgeon Webster, he cannot permit so marked a breach of discipline as that which was clearly proved before the Court, to go unpunished. Believing, with the Court, that the offense was founded in some degree on a misconception of duty, which, however, would have been more pardonable in an officer of less intelligence, the sentence of confinement to the limits of the post at which Assistant Surgeon Webster is employed, is reduced from six months to 60 days.

It is of note that in the *Official Records,* January 1864, Dr. Webster was listed as in command of David's Island and the detachments of the Invalid Corps there (David's Island lies in Long Island Sound, five miles north of Throg's Neck). Webster's medical officer file has disappeared, so it is difficult to tell whether the move to David's Island was a promotion or a demotion. Whatever its meaning for Dr. Webster, it certainly did not kill him. He lived another twenty-two years, dying on January 13, 1886, in Baltimore, Maryland. He made no application for pension.

>—+·+>—·O—·<+—+—<

COMMENT: It would appear from the record that Webster was correct in refusing to give up his patient, both on legal and medical grounds. Certainly, many orders and letters were presented in evidence, showing that general hospitals (but not post hospitals) were under the jurisdiction of the surgeon general rather than the line officer commanding. To sentence a physician to six months of virtual house arrest for apparently carrying out the instructions of the War Department seems an injustice. (To put a finer point on the matter, the authors suggest that it was Webster's line officer superiors who should have been punished; they clearly disregarded the policies enunciated by both the Secretary of War and the General in Chief. A charge of insubordination seemed in order.)

The medical corps of the Confederate army faced similar problems and attempted similar solutions. On July 21, 1863, the surgeon in charge of the general hospitals at Atlanta issued this order: "Soldiers in hospital are under the charge of the surgeon and not of any military commander and no interference whatever with authority should be permitted. They should not be examined while in hospital with reference to any other disposition than that provided for in the regulations."[2]

The medical record in the case of Webster and Fitzsimmons tells us several things. The surgeons seemed clearly aware of the relevant anatomy and the many dangers created by accidental piercing of the various organs in the upper chest. Private Fitzsimmons's own pension records confirm the seriousness of his wound. Although he was returned to duty on paper, his discharge, on a disability certificate issued in July 1865 at Sickle General Hospital in Alexandria, Virginia, described "impaired use of the left arm from gunshot wound of the left sternum and clavicle." In 1886 it was reported that the musket ball was still in his wound, and that he had little use of his arm. His death in 1900 was attributed to "asthenia, uremia, acute nephritis, and gunshot wound of the left shoulder, which resulted in blood poisoning, from which he died." His widow received a pension for another nine years, and—in one of those pathetic little footnotes to history—in 1949 Fitzsimmons's daughter wrote to President Harry Truman to request pension payments. The official reply informed her that she would be eligible if she was under age sixteen. She was seventy-one.

Chapter Forty

Floyer G. Kittredge

Dr. Floyer Kittredge, surgeon of the 31st Massachusetts, had the distinction of being court-martialed twice in one year. His first offense was being absent without leave. On March 13, 1863, he left his regiment as it marched from Baton Rouge, Louisiana, to Port Hudson, Louisiana, and was gone for twenty-four hours. Three days later his regiment was on picket duty in Cypress Bayou, Louisiana, and this time he was gone nearly a week. He was found guilty and sentenced to be cashiered.[1]

Maj. Gen. Nathaniel Banks disapproved the sentence, writing, "The evidence does not show to the satisfaction of the major general commanding that this officer was guilty of an intentional neglect of duty. The execution of the sentence is suspended until the pleasure of the President can be known." Lincoln's decision is not in the file, but it must have been favorable, since Kittredge did not leave the army. Nine months later, he was tried again, this time for extorting money from free black men at Baton Rouge.[2]

The charge was conduct unbecoming an officer and a gentleman. The first specification stated that Kittredge, "professing to be, and acting as examining surgeon for the Corps d'Afrique in Baton Rouge, . . . did join and connive with other officers engaged in the conscription of Negroes, and with Samuel Harbor, a citizen, in extortions of money from Negro conscripts, for exempting them from service in the Corps d'Afrique." He was charged with issuing a medical certificate of exemption to "Jacob Church (colored)" and also to "Louis Francois (colored)," without having examined either man.

The trial began by Kittredge challenging a court member, Lt. Col. William Hopkins, his own commander, on grounds of enmity. Hopkins replied, "I court-martialed Dr. Kittredge last March by order of my Brigade Commander. I have no personal enmity against Dr. Kittredge, other than what arises from his repeated disobedience of my orders. I would like to be relieved of sitting on this case." The court voted to retain Colonel Hopkins, and the trial commenced with the testimony of Jacob Church, "F.M.C." (free man of color).

I do not know the accused. I never saw him till I saw him at the office of the provost judge, where we had the preliminary trial of this case. I never was conscripted by any officer for service in the Corps d'Afrique. I received a certificate from Mr. Samuel Harbor that said I had been examined for a soldier and was unfit for duty, for which I paid him $25.00. Mr. Harbor first met me on the Sunday morning when they were going to burn candles in the graveyard, and told me that they had conscripted one Charles Crow and that they would conscript all us free niggers, but he told me he thought he could get a paper for me so that they would not trouble me.

I told him all right, and he left me. The next day, he told me that he could not see the colonel that day, but he expected to see him at the theatre that evening and would try to get the paper from him for me. On Tuesday morning, Mr. Harbor told me that the colonel said his paper would not do but he must get one from the doctor and brought me the paper from the doctor at noon of the same day and told me the pay was $25.00. I told him I thought it was very hard for me to pay that much after he had stated that he would give me the paper for nothing. He said, "I do not charge you anything. It is the doctor who charges you this and he wants the money." I then paid him the $25.00 and said to him, "Mr. Harbor, if this is not the law, I want my money back." He said that if it was not the law that I should have my money back.

This paper was then introduced in evidence. It read, "Headquarters, Recruiting Station, Corps d'Afrique, Baton Rouge, November 2, 1863. This is to certify that Jacob Church has been examined for a soldier and is unfit. F.G. Kittredge. Assistant Surgeon, 31st Massachusetts Volunteers in Charge. Examining Surgeon." The paper was shown to the witness, who was unable to recognize it, as he could neither read nor write. At this point, Kittredge cross-examined the witness. "At the time Mr. Harbor gave you this piece of paper, did he not tell you that there was another [person named] Church examined?" The witness said that he had heard no such thing.

Church then stepped down, and the next witness was Samuel Harbor, "citizen."

I know Dr. Kittredge by sight. I have known him for about three months. I do not know that he ever acted as Examining Surgeon for Colored Troops at this post. I know that one Jacob Church (colored) received a certificate stating that he had been examined for a soldier and found unfit. I gave [the paper] to him myself. I received it from some officer at the Penitentiary [then used as Union headquarters], but do not know who it was. He was a thick-set man and I think was a lieutenant.

Jacob Church came to me and told me that he wanted me to see if a paper could not be obtained for him that would free him from being conscripted, as he did not consider himself on a level with other Negroes, was over age, and had plenty of money. I told him I would try and went to the Penitentiary and asked Captain [Martin] Durham if such a thing could be done. He told me, "Certainly," and it was through him that I got the paper. Dr. Kittredge had nothing to do about the paper that I know of. I never had any conversation with him about it.

I received $25.00 from Church for the paper and expended it for champagne and oysters, together with officers of the regiment of the 18th Corps d'Afrique, according to agreement. Captain Cunningham [perhaps Lieutenant Thomas Cunningham of the 18th Corps d'Afrique] told me that Dr. Kittredge was invited to attend the supper, but he did not come. Captain Durham, Captain Cunningham, Lieutenant [John] Meade, Lieutenant [Albert] Dinsmore and others agreed to the proposition that I was to charge enough for the exemption papers to pay for the supper, and they were there at the supper. We had two suppers at Victor's and one at another time. The reason assigned that Dr. Kittredge was not present was that he had enough to drink and did not want to come up.

I received a paper of the same kind for Louis Francois (colored), which I received from Captain Durham, for which Francois gave me $40.00 [about three months pay for a soldier]. I never spoke to Dr. Kittredge about the affair till today, when he told me he had been arrested and wanted me to give in my evidence. The $40.00 I received from Francois was spent for champagne and oysters. Dr. Kittredge was not present [at the dinner]. Captain Cunningham told me he was expected to be present, but he, Captain Cunningham, thought probably the doctor was heavy enough without coming to the supper. Dr. Kittredge was reckoned as one of the party who was to partake of the supper paid for with the money obtained for the exemption papers. I wish to change one part of my evidence. Captain Durham refused to take any of the money and was not present at any of the suppers. Dr. Kittredge was not present at any of the meetings. The arrangements were made at the Penitentiary one day while I was sitting on my horse and the officers standing about the door. I kept the money in my own possession until it was time to pay for the supper. The cost of the dinners used up almost every dollar obtained for the exemption papers.

When further questioned by the court, he indicated that he had told Mr. Church that the money collected was for himself, rather than anyone else. He also recalled an erasure on the paper, turning the first name of "James" into "Jacob," but he did not recall who made the erasure.

The next witness was Louis Francois, who recalled that he had seen Kittredge before but did not know him personally. "I first saw Dr. Kittredge in the office of the Provost Marshal. I have never been conscripted and was never examined. I did receive an exemption paper from Mr. Harbor, who told me that the expense was on account of some officers. I do not understand a medical paper exempting me, because I have no physical defects." The next witness was a handwriting expert, Sgt. Maj. Henry D. Barber, of the 31st Massachusetts. "I have been in the habit of seeing the handwriting of various people and comparing and examining signatures for some years before coming into the army. The signatures on the two letters are in Dr. Kittredge's handwriting, but the rest of the exemption papers were written by a different person." This opinion was seconded by the next witness, Hospital Steward George W. Bears. "I have seen Dr. Kittredge's signature frequently, and that is his writing."

The final witness was 1st Lt. John F. Meade, who gave an illuminating insight into recruitment for the Corps d'Afrique, at least in the area of Baton Rouge.

> The surgeon and some officers would go into the building where the conscripts were confined. The conscripts were then drawn up in lines, and examined by the surgeon. The surgeon took their names on a sheet of foolscap paper and those who passed, he wrote, "Fit for a soldier," against their names and those who did not pass he wrote, "Unfit." For boys, he wrote, "Fit for drummers or cooks." This paper was copied in the office and certificates made out accordingly. The business was conducted very loosely and the papers were left lying on the table and any person could go in at any time. A great many of these conscripts made their escape. As many as eleven men have got away in one night. The records made by Dr. Kittredge were all thrown into a box, which was taken to Port Hudson, when the 18th Regiment of Corps d'Afrique left for there. I was engaged in conscripting colored soldiers in Baton Rouge for about two months. I remember that we took two wine suppers with Mr. Harbor, but I don't remember who paid. One supper was at Victor's and the other was at Free Market Hall. Lieutenant [Charles] Pine was the officer who filled up all the enlistment papers, and also wrote the certificates for exemption. All of the certificates were signed by Captain Durham and by the surgeon.

The court acquitted Dr. Kittredge but left an ominous record signed by six members of the court. "The Court, while thus acquitting the accused, *upon the evidence* [original emphasis], consider it proper and feel it their duty, to call the attention of the Commanding General, to the exceedingly loose and reprehensible manner in which the duties of the accused, as Examining Surgeon for the Corps d'Afrique, were discharged; and also to censure in the severest terms the conduct of such of the officers of the 18th Regiment of Corps d'Afrique as are proved by the evidence to have been associated in the conspiracy to fraudulently extort money from certain Negroes who either had been or were liable to be conscripted, and recommend them [these officers] as eminently fit subjects for a general court-martial." General Banks merely noted that without the signature of the President of the Court or of the Judge Advocate that such a recommendation was "very irregular and cannot have the force of an act of the Court."

Dr. Kittredge stayed with the 31st Massachusetts until receiving his discharge on February 15, 1864. The only postwar notation in his military files is a brief statement that he died on June 1, 1878, in Peabody, Massachusetts.

>─┼─◆>─●─<◆─┼─<

COMMENT: Kittredge's two trials do not raise any medical issues since we have no clear description of his actual technique of physical examination. The relevant themes are ethical, administrative, and legal. The testimony sheds considerable light on the process of recruiting colored troops in Louisiana, and it is not a pretty picture. The officers involved apparently saw the prosperous black bourgeoisie of the Baton Rouge area not as a nidus for a renaissance of black culture and prosperity but rather as targets for extortion. For them, the Day of Jubilee had not arrived; the Day of the Locust had. The money extorted from the two victims, equivalent to five months' wages for a skilled artisan, were expended on champagne and oysters. It would appear that "free men of color" in Louisiana had merely exchanged one set of oppressors for another.

Kittredge's part of this swindle is not what one would hope for in a Harvard man.

Chapter Forty-One

Joseph A. Kerrigan

The home front in the Civil War has been called a Carnival of Fraud. The case of Dr. Joseph Kerrigan brings to mind a melange of the Marx Brothers, W. C. Fields, and the Threepenny Opera, and gives us a chance to meet little-known Brig. Gen. Francis Baretto Spinola, even more of a "political" general than Dan Sickles or Ben Butler. Spinola will appear later in this drama, which begins with the court-martial of Kerrigan, charged with "violation of recruiting regulations."[1]

As a beginning point, consider Section 1261 of the Revised Regulations for the Army, 1861. "In passing a recruit, the medical officer is to examine him stripped to see that he has free use of all his limbs, that his chest is ample, that his hearing, vision and speech are perfect, that he has no tumors, or ulcerated or extensively ciciatrized legs, no rupture, or chronic cutaneous affections, that he has not received any contusions or wound of the head that may impair his faculties, that he is not a drunkard, is not subject to convulsions and has no infectious disorder, nor any other that may unfit him for military service." With those admonitions in mind, consider the following.

Kerrigan was charged with these shortcomings, all occurring in New York City, between November 28 and December 7, 1862.

> Surgeon Kerrigan did examine and pass into the service of the United States, [three men] L'Hote, Anger, and Roue, sailors of the French Merchant *L'Armide,* to sign rolls mustering them into the service of the United States, knowing at the same time that they were entirely ignorant of the nature of the transaction and that they were under the influence of liquor at the time.

> Surgeon Kerrigan did examine and pass into the service of the United States, Vincent Ruelland, a sailor of the steam corvette *Tisiphone* of the French Navy, who at the time of his examination was under the influence of liquor, and did not know the nature of the

service for which he was examined, and it was not explained to him by said Kerrigan.

Surgeon Kerrigan did examine and pass into the service of the United States, Anthony Riker, a Negro, who at the time of the examination was entirely ignorant of the nature of the service for which he was examined, and that he was unfit for it on account of his age and other disqualifications and that the said Kerrigan did fail to explain the nature of the service to him.

Surgeon Kerrigan did examine and pass into the service of the United States, Joseph White, alias William White, a Negro, who was unfit for the service both on account of his age and other disqualifications, that he was entirely ignorant of the nature of the service for which he was being examined, and it was not explained to him by said Kerrigan.

The first witness called was Count Henri de Marivault of the French Navy, commanding His Imperial Majesty's Ship *La Tisiphone* (Tisiphone was one of the three furies in Greek mythology), a steam corvette. He, like the other Frenchmen, spoke through a sworn interpreter. Captain de Marivault reported that Vincent Ruelland, a sailor of the third class of the ship *La Tisiphone,* was a member of his crew. (In other adventures, De Marivault evacuated French citizens from the Confederacy, corresponded with Gen. Benjamin Butler about exporting tobacco, and was assaulted by a Yankee soldier at New Orleans.)

Ruelland, also speaking through an interpreter, made the following statement to the court. "I was just going to the ship for clean clothes about 3:00 in the afternoon and I met a man who made signs to me and made me drink. The next morning, I did not know where I was or what I did. After this, they led me into a place like a grand house where there were many persons. I was so drunk I did not remember I had been examined by a surgeon. I could not remember in the room with many people. I went to a camp and put on a uniform." He was shown his enlistment papers and asked if the writing on the paper was his. "My writing is much better than that. I don't think I signed anything while I was drunk. My ship came to New York in September, and I had been ashore maybe 30 times. I have never been drunk on shore before. When I woke up in the morning after this encounter with the army, I found in my pocket handkerchief a paper dollar that was not mine."

The next witness was Ferdinand de la Hay, a French-speaking recruiting officer. "I saw Dr. Kerrigan acting as a surgeon at General Spinola's headquarters at Lafayette Hall. I remember that Ruelland came to Lafayette Hall to enlist as a soldier in the United States service. A man came to me and said that there were some Frenchmen who wanted to enlist, and that I should be kind enough to make out their papers, they not speaking English. I done so, and brought this Frenchman to Dr. Kerrigan to be examined. I saw Dr. Kerrigan examine the

Frenchman according to the regulations. Then I brought the Frenchman to the mustering officer, who mustered him after the interpretation of the oath. I saw the Frenchman get his bounty and counting out some money. He was perfectly sober when I did the interpretation. He was wearing his sailor clothes." In cross-examination, Kerrigan asked De la Hay, "What is your rank in the service?" De la Hay replied, "I am an authorized recruiting officer, but with no particular rank. My papers are from the Adjutant General of the State of New York." When asked by the court to describe the scene at Lafayette Hall, De la Hay gave the following description. "The man, the recruit, is first brought in by a broker into a large hall on the second story, a big room of the 5th New York Militia. General Spinola, mustering officers, paymasters and other functionaries are employed in that office. Here the recruits are mustered and sworn in. In the other corner, there is a large table where the enlistment papers are made out by citizens employed by the recruit broker. The surgeon's room is off from this hall. I helped with the examinations, since some men do not speak English. I think Dr. Kerrigan's examinations are very thorough; that doctor has a name among the recruit brokers of being a hard case."

Who is this General Spinola who plays such a large part at Lafayette Hall? Francis Baretto Spinola was born in 1821 on Long Island, New York. As a Democratic politician, he served five years as a Brooklyn alderman, six years as a member of the New York State Assembly, and four years as a state senator. In 1862 he was appointed a Brigadier General "for meritorious conduct in recruiting and organizing a brigade of four regiments and accompanying them to the field." Officers who accompanied Spinola on his failed expedition to Washington, North Carolina, considered him to be a coward and an utter fool. Later, he was wounded near Manassas Gap, Virginia, after the battle of Gettysburg; following the consolidation of several corps he was declared supernumerary. His next assignment was recruiting duty in New York City in the winter of 1863-1864, where he was court-martialed for "conniving with bounty brokers to defraud and swindle recruits." He was sentenced to be dismissed, but in June 1865 he was allowed to resign. He spent the postwar years in the insurance business and as a member of Congress. His wartime experiences were, no doubt, helpful during his service as a member of the Committee on Military Affairs.

The next witness, described as "Anthony Riker (colored)," remembered seeing Dr. Kerrigan at Lafayette Hall:

> He examined me. He asked me to look at a pencil and say which end was up. I said the sharp end. He then examined my eyes and said I should pass. I asked him if I could take care of the colonel's horse now. I did not enlist to be a soldier. I had no idea of being a soldier, no sir, none at all. I thought I was hired to take care of the colonel's horse. I told them my age, which was 63 at the time. I have difficulties which would make me not fit for a soldier. I got a lame ankle, a bone

shooting out on my right leg. I hurt my back 12 years ago, lifting a barrel. Then I hit my back again and was laid up once more. The doctor never noticed my shooting bone or asked me if I had any ailments. The doctor gave me a glass of something to drink and after that he asked me to drink again. Then I took a cigar. Then they took me to a large room, one end of the room full of muskets and about four or five people there. After the examination, the doctor took me to where they swore me in.

When shown some papers by the court, Riker said, "It looks like the paper the gentleman was writing and I thought he was signing an agreement about taking care of the horse. I can't sign my name, but I touched the pen and he did the writing. They gave me $50.00 to buy clothes, but when I counted it, there were only $14.00. After I got the money, I took up my hat to go and they stopped me and told me to sit down. When it got dark, they marched us all downstairs and locked us up. I am not in the army any more. I got my discharge after someone helped me write to Mrs. Schultz, my last employer, and she helped me."

Joseph White, a colored waiter at the Metropolitan Hotel, testified as follows:

I left the hotel at 11:00 in the morning the last day of November to go home. I got dinner at 2:00 o'clock and met a man at the corner of Prince and Broadway. He said that he wanted a hostler to tend a couple of horses for an old man on 16th Street. He told me to go and see the old gentleman and I could come back afterwards. When I got opposite Lafayette Hall, he said I should go in to see a man there. Inside there was a cavalry man, and he said, "Here is the man who wants to be a hostler." They told me to go upstairs and see the doctor. I told them I could not go out of the city, that I had to work nearby, and they told me I wouldn't have to travel and they would pay me two months in advance. When I came into the doctor's room, he told me to pull off my clothes. He told me to walk up to him, stoop down and then go back. He held up a card and I told him it was the ten of diamonds, then he told me to put on my clothes. I held up my broken finger, but he told me it was nothing. The doctor did not ask me if I had anything which would disqualify me as a soldier. I didn't have a chance to tell him that a tree fell on my side, broke my finger, hurt my back and it gives me giddy feelings, and I cannot tolerate the sun. When I was at Port Royal [South Carolina], I volunteered for General Hunter to go into a colored regiment, but I was discharged because I was not sound. I am 48 years old. I did not know that I was being mustered as a soldier, no sir! I didn't want to be a soldier because I was not well enough. When I came out of the doctor's office, there was a man at a desk who asked me if I could read, and I said I could not. He told me to touch the pen and then he signed four or five papers for me. The man I met on the street was given some money, and he gave $40.00 of it to me and he kept $10.00. Then I was placed under guard and sent to a training camp on Riker's Island [New York Harbor], where I have been drilling and learning to be a soldier ever since. When they asked me to do the stooping, I thought it had to do with horses, because I always have to stoop down to clean the horses.

In an unlikely turn of events, it seems that White had important friends in high places. He was acquainted with Gen. William Tecumseh Sherman and Gen. David Hunter. The Judge Advocate of the court-martial wanted to introduce a letter from General Sherman to Senator Hays, concerning Mr. White. The counsel for Dr. Kerrigan objected to the introduction of the letter on the grounds that it was not under oath. The members of the Court overruled this objection on the grounds that "official papers do not require to be sworn to." The letter, describing White as of "good character," was admitted. This closed the prosecution, whose witnesses had mainly been those persons recruited under very dubious circumstances. The next witnesses, all for the defense, were Kerrigan's work associates.

Col. Isaac V. Reeve, a veteran of twenty-eight years in the army, stated that he had served with the 13th Infantry, and from August 1862 he had been mustering and disbursing officer of volunteers in New York City. "During my service in this position, Dr. Kerrigan was one of our examining doctors. He was always available for duty, I have never had complaints about him, and to the best of my knowledge, he has never passed anyone who was under the influence of liquor. He has examined thousands of men and I believe his methods of examination are proper." In cross-examination, Kerrigan asked, "Could a man be examined by a surgeon and apparently sober, and be drunk a few minutes later?" Reeve answered, "He could, without drinking in the meantime." Kerrigan then asked the colonel, "Do you think it is the duty of the surgeon to explain to the recruit the reason for the examination?" Reeve replied, "Definitely not. The responsibility of the surgeon is to ask about disabilities of any type, not to explain the reason for the examination."

Lt. Robert B. Smith of the 11th U.S. Infantry described his duties at the mustering office and stated that Kerrigan was excellent in every way. Lt. Michael Dolan of the 2nd U.S. Infantry was a mustering officer in the same office, working every day with Kerrigan, whom he described as reliable and honest. Dr. A. B. Mott, surgeon of U.S. Volunteers, had known Kerrigan for six years and echoed his colleagues in praising Kerrigan's virtues. Kerrigan's long written statement in his own defense can be easily paraphrased as: "I have done my duty and am without blame. The witnesses are unreliable liars."

Kerrigan was found guilty of improperly passing into service Anthony Riker and Vincent Ruelland but acquitted of the other charges. He was sentenced to be "forever disqualified from holding the office of surgeon under the United States government."

Two years later, an attorney, Nelson Taylor, wrote to Secretary of War Edwin M. Stanton on behalf of Kerrigan, asking that his administrative disability be removed. The letter was referred to the office of the Judge Advocate General, who recommended that Kerrigan's request be honored. The reason for this reversal was that the only evidence had been presented by the recruits. Stanton approved this recommendation, and Kerrigan was free of any burden imposed by the court that tried him.

COMMENT: Was Stanton's largesse a reflection of a general post-War amnesty (after all, Robert E. Lee had not been punished), or did it reflect a genuine feeling that a witness who had been harmed is a less reliable judge of the truth than a witness who is defending his own behavior?

Kerrigan's commander, General Spinola, who ran this busy recruit mill in Lafayette Hall, was also court-martialed, convicted, and dismissed. The sordid stories of the recruit brokers, who brought drunks and innocents off the street to be processed, mustered, imprisoned and shipped to camp, lend credence to the prosecution witnesses.

Late in the war, the reservoir of patriotic volunteers was nearly dry. Perhaps the shabby near-kidnappings described in this trial were necessary to feed the war machine as Grant's meat-grinder offensive wore down the Confederate defenders. Perhaps the dubious routine at Lafayette Hall only reflects the corruption inherent in a bounty system. Whatever the explanation, Kerrigan was pleased to be part of this operation and felt that his actions were beyond reproach. He was universally supported in the testimony of his colleagues at work. It is difficult not to suspect collusion—on top of corruption and graft. The ends of justice were most likely served by Kerrigan's conviction.

The medical examinations performed by Kerrigan seem superficial, but then the descriptions of these examinations were given by men variously illiterate, drunk, or fluent only in French, which makes an objective appraisal quite difficult. (The quality of Kerrigan's medical work should have reflected his education: A.B., St. John's University, 1852; master's degree, 1855; M.D., New York College of Physicians and Surgeons, 1858.)

The court-martial members, who lived by their standards, not by today's, concluded that Kerrigan's approach fell well short of the mark. We would be unwise to argue with them.

Chapter Forty-Two

William J. Fleming

At the battle of Malvern Hill, south and east of Richmond, Virginia, there were 8,000 casualties. Dr. William J. Fleming of the 102nd Pennsylvania was a casualty, too, though not a single bullet touched him.[1] He was court-martialed for leaving his post.

His trial raised as many questions as it answered. Was he a coward, shirking his duty? Was he sick himself, unable to obtain the medical care that could have restored his efficiency? Was he unwittingly a victim of a system of medical organization, pitifully obsolete, in which a wounded patriot might receive less care than a dog run over on the road?

Fleming's difficulties did not occur in a vacuum but reflected the unsolved problems of a medical corps that, after fifteen months of war, had not come to grips with reality or necessity.

George B. McClellan's grand plan, of landing at the tip of the York Peninsula and marching north to Richmond, came to grief in the Seven Days battle, a few miles from the Confederate capital itself. The medical director of McClellan's Army of the Potomac, Charles S. Tripler, had requested a minimum of 250 ambulances for this campaign; only 177 were provided. By the time of Malvern Hill, one Union army corps had only enough ambulance transportation for 100 men—when the wounded were in the thousands.

Even though a vast armada of steamboats serviced McClellan's forces, and could have evacuated those unfit for duty, Tripler kept the sick men with the army. He feared that if they were removed north and recovered from their malaria or typhoid or dysentery or wounds, they would not return. The result was that when battle casualties poured in, the hospitals were already overwhelmed. The Federal hospital at White House Landing, on the Pamunkey River, when it began to receive 4,500 casualties from the battle of Fair Oaks, Virginia, had on duty five surgeons, one hospital steward, and no nurses.

A further flaw was the regimental surgeon system, another remnant of the old army. In small-scale wars, a regiment might constitute the entire force, and the regimental surgeon's place of duty could be nowhere else. In the vast aggregations of the new warfare, it became unworkable for regimental surgeons to treat only "their" wounded. The unlucky man who limped into the "wrong" field hospital was resented because food was issued to regiments, not to men.

On the Fourth of July 1862, Dr. Tripler was replaced by Jonathan Letterman, whose ideas of medical organization were further advanced than Tripler's and eventually set the pattern for the entire Union army. It was in this shifting context that Dr. Fleming was charged with not being with his regiment on July 1, 1862—more specifically, that on the march from Haxall's Landing (on the James River), June 30, he left his regiment, missed the battle of Malvern Hill, and returned on July 2nd to Harrison's Landing, five miles downstream from Haxall's. Six witnesses spoke.

Col. Thomas A. Rowley (a former captain in the Mexican War and a future brigadier general) went first. "On June 30th, we left Haxall's Landing and spent the morning in a woods this side of the clover field [no grid coordinates in this war!]; that night we halted beyond Malvern Hills [sic]. At 3:00 in the morning of July 1st, we moved back to Malvern Hills, where we were engaged from 9:00 A.M. until after dark. I did not see Dr. Fleming in the field. Assistant Surgeon Matthew Morrison was present with the regiment during the engagement and after the battle."

Dr. Morrison himself was the next witness. "Dr. Fleming joined the regiment when the regiment moved into the woods near Haxall's Landing, but I didn't see him again until July the second." In cross-examination by Fleming, Morrison said, "We left the woods about 4:00 in the afternoon on June 30. I discovered you were absent when Dr. Warren, the brigade surgeon, asked where you were. By then, we had marched about half a mile from the woods. I was in my position at the rear of the regiment and you were not there." Hospital Steward Jervis Brown confirmed Morrison's story.

Lt. James Bishop of Fleming's regiment said that he first saw the doctor back at Haxall's on July 2nd. "I was with the regiment the entire time. After the battle of Malvern Hill, our regiment passed Haxall's Landing and went on to Harrison's Landing. I had just delivered some wounded to the sawmill and I saw Surgeon Fleming in the open field near Haxall's. He told me he had been sick for two or three days and was still very unwell. He told me he had been at Malvern Hill."

Brigade Surgeon S. R. Haven had been on duty at Malvern Hill and had not seen Fleming at all that day. "I did see Dr. Fleming the evening after the battle [probably July 1st] at a barn which was the rearmost depot established for wounded of Couch's Brigade, about a mile from the battlefield." In response to Fleming's cross-examination, Dr. Haven had not heard of Fleming being sick.

The next testimony, by Surgeon Robert M. Tindle of the 61st Pennsylvania, sheds light on the organization of medical care in 1862. "I saw Dr. Fleming between 5:00 and 7:00 o'clock in the evening of July 1st. It was at General

Depot for the wounded of Couch's Division; we had established the depot in a barn. From experience, it is my opinion that surgeons close to troops engaged are of very little service. When I saw Dr. Fleming at the barn, he was acting professionally; he was not there as a patient." The Court asked Tindle, "Was the depot a proper position for a medical officer of the 102nd Pennsylvania to attend to his duties as a surgeon of his regiment?" The answer: "If it was fully understood he was there, and if there was proper transportation [probably meaning ambulances]. A doctor at such a depot could discharge his duties with the severely injured; slight wounds could be taken care of on the field. I do not know of any wounded from Dr. Fleming's regiment being brought to the barn depot."

The final witness was Dr. Richard Simmington of the 93rd Pennsylvania. He had seen Fleming June 30th on the road leading to Malvern Hill, during the daytime of July 1st "near the brick house in the rear of our position," and during the evening of July 1st, "at the general depot in charge of Dr. Price of Couch's Division. It was dark enough then so that we needed candles." Simmington remembered the defendant as not feeling well and giving Fleming all of his quinine. "On the way to Malvern Hill, Dr. Fleming's regiment was not riding in the rear of the brigade, but Dr. Fleming himself was riding in the rear of the brigade."

Fleming submitted the customary written defense statement, which contained these high points: On June 30th, he was exhausted and sick with fever, intense headache and pain in the back and limbs. That night he slept in the woods. On July 1st, "My suffering returned, giving me the first idea that intermittent fever [malaria] was the disease." He could not find his regiment, so he dismounted and lay down for a while. Then he found a surgeon and obtained some quinine. Feeling a little better, he went to the battlefield but still could not find his regiment, so he returned to the depot in the barn, received some more quinine, and took care of the wounded. "I left the next morning when it was clear that the enemy was going to take the hospital. I had lost my coat. It was raining heavily and since then I have suffered from inflammation of the leg veins and irritation of the lungs."

On the subject of medical organization, Dr. Fleming's defense contains some illumination: "The position of the surgeon during battle was very indefinite previous to the last general order to the subject, which was made subsequent to the last battle of Malvern Hill. In this general order, it is specified that the surgeons will be close by their respective regiments, which was different from the general impression of surgeons on the subject previously, or there had been no necessity for the order." (That general order is not included with the trial records.)

The court was not sympathetic. Dr. Fleming was dismissed from the army. He worked again as a contract surgeon from July 1863 to November of the same year. In May 1864 a new contract was annulled when he failed to report for duty.

He was an unusually qualified doctor for his era, with three degrees from the University of Pennsylvania: A.B., 1848; A.M., 1851; and M.D., also 1851. In the decade after the war, his office was at 2207 Callowhill Street, Philadelphia, while in 1886 he was listed at 2048 Vine Street in the same city.

In 1827 London physician Richard Bright described a kidney disease characterized by albumin in the urine, often progressing to total kidney failure and death. When Fleming died in 1889, the cause of death was given as "Bright's disease."

>—+—◆>—O—<◆—+—≺

COMMENT: While the court saw Fleming as a laggard, failing in his duty to his regiment, he could just as well be seen as a sick man, racked by the chills and fever of malaria, who, bolstered by some quinine, continued to minister to the wounded. On the other hand, Fleming failed to notify assistant surgeon Morrison, or the brigade surgeon of his whereabouts, thus confusing the situation. The testimony also speaks to the conflicting opinions about the best use and position of doctors, hospitals, and medical supplies.

Considering that McClellan's Peninsular Campaign was probably the largest amphibious operation since Xerxes' invasion of Greece in 480 B.C. and used an almost-overwhelming flotilla of steam-powered supply ships, remarkably little attention was given to the medical needs of the Union soldiers.

Chapter Forty-Three

Edward Flynn

It was rare for a commissioned officer to be sent to prison. It was even more unusual for a doctor to be imprisoned. Yet in August 1863, Dr. Edward Flynn was locked in the unpleasant confines of the Myrtle Street Military Prison in St. Louis, Missouri.[1] The story is a complex one, with issues not only of diagnosis and medical causation, but more sinister ones of corruption and entrapment. Was Flynn a venal doctor, abusing his position to sell discharges from the army, or was he an innocent victim of an overzealous detective? And, finally, can a doctor diagnose heart valve disease by pressing his ear to the patient's chest— when that chest is covered with a towel?

Flynn began his military career in April 1862 as an Acting Assistant Surgeon at Stone Farm Hospital, where he served—apparently successfully—for nine months before being transferred to Mount Pleasant Hospital (probably in Washington, D.C.). In March 1863 he received a new contract for service at Benton Barracks, near St. Louis. Four weeks later his duties as a ward physician were enlarged to include service on a medical examining board for sick and wounded soldiers being considered for discharge from the army. Assigned to the same board were Drs. James E. Hall and Tracy E. Waller. (Waller was dismissed a few months later for drunkenness.) It was this new duty that proved Flynn's undoing.

In late August 1863 he was charged with accepting a $50 bribe from Pvt. Benjamin S. Wilkins, Company F, 41st Illinois; in return for this money, Flynn recommended a discharge, based upon valvular disease of the heart and inflammation of the liver. Flynn pleaded not guilty.

The trial's first witness was Pvt. A. G. Johnson, 8th Kansas Infantry, who worked in the discharge office of the general hospital at Benton Barracks. He told the court that when a medical examiner arrived at a conclusion, these findings would be written on a slip of paper that Johnson would then copy onto a "blotter." These same findings and conclusions would then be copied onto a blank discharge certificate. The certificate became final only when signed by the director of the hospital.

Johnson recalled that Private Wilkins had been employed as an "acting druggist" at the hospital and was examined on June 13, 1863, for possible discharge:

> When I walked through the room, Wilkins had his upper garments off. Dr. Flynn may have had a towel over his breast, as he usually uses one in his examinations; he uses it for the purpose of avoiding the contact of the man's flesh with his ear. When he examines the heart or the lungs, he places his ear to the man's body and uses the towel to prevent the connection. After the examination, Dr. Flynn wrote on a piece of paper which the clerk handed to me, to be copied onto the blotter. There are three doctors on the medical examining board, but there are never more than two ever present at one time.

The next witness was Wilkins himself, the man who allegedly bribed the doctor. This twenty-five-year-old private, who had already served two years, told this story: "I had a position in the hospital but Dr. [Ira] Russell was down on me. I thought I'd be sent back to my regiment and I preferred not to go. I was very anxious to get my discharge and I told Dr. Flynn that I would give him $25.00 now and $25.00 after he got me the discharge. I had been captured in the fight at Holly Springs [Mississippi] and had been paroled. I couldn't work in the hospital as a paroled prisoner, but I could as a patient. That's why I was admitted as a patient."

When the court asked him if in his own opinion he was fit for duty and able to stand the hardships of camp life, Wilkins answered "Yes" to both questions. He further stated that he knew the meaning of valvular heart disease and that he had no symptoms of that condition.

"Dr. Flynn examined me, followed by Dr. [David] LeRoy. The first examination was about five minutes, but Dr. LeRoy's examination was very short. When I had first spoken to Dr. Flynn, he said that he would not examine me for money, but if he found a reason, he would discharge me. After the examination, I asked him to go into the next room with me and I gave him the $25.00. The doctor made some slight objection, but then took the money and asked me not to mention it to anyone. Both Dr. Flynn and Dr. LeRoy said they thought I was a fit subject for discharge."

In response to direct questions, Wilkins added several additional bits to the puzzle: His principal symptom was "dyspepsia" and decreased appetite; he had received no medical treatment during his stay in the hospital; he was suffering with "inflammation of the eyes," which had been present for about four months; in the past, he had suffered two attacks of "bilious fever"; and, finally, he had never received any discharge papers, even after the examination by Flynn and LeRoy.

Wilkins further recalled that Dr. Flynn had told him, "I don't blame any soldier for getting his discharge when he can. This infernal war is about played out. The whole thing is in the hands of a clique of officers, and the privates and non-commissioned officers have a poor show."

Wilkins's testimony took a whole new direction in response to the cross-examination by Dr. Flynn. Wilkins had an unusual background: He had read medicine for one year and law for two years but enlisted as a private because he thought the country "needed his services." He had not really wanted a discharge but applied for one under orders from the surgeon in chief at Benton Barracks, Dr. Ira Russell.

> It was disagreeable to me to offer money for a discharge, but I was ordered to do so. I must go back and state some of my own circumstances. When I worked at the hospital, two soldiers had been discharged without their final statements. This meant that they could go home, but without receiving their back pay. They asked me to draw their back pay and send it to them. Each of them gave me power of attorney to do so. I had no idea that this was wrong.
>
> Dr. Russell found out about it from Private Johnson, who wanted to get me in trouble. That is why I gave Private Johnson $5.00 to speed up the copying of my blotter onto a discharge certificate: I wanted to get Johnson in trouble, to pay him back. But that has nothing to do with my giving $25.00 to Dr. Flynn. That was done as requested by Dr. Russell and the Surgeon General. I understood that they were investigating skullduggery.

Wilkins's testimony closed by describing a scene in Dr. Russell's office. Ordered to report there, Wilkins found both Dr. Flynn and Dr. Russell. "I saluted Major Russell, who then turned to Dr. Flynn and said for him to return the $25.00 to me. Dr. Flynn counted out the bills to me. I had copied down the numbers on the bills, so I know it was the same ones."

The next witness, Dr. Russell, shed some light on these mysterious transactions.

> Assistant Surgeon General [Robert C.] Wood had received an anonymous letter saying that discharges were being sold. It was thought that a legal gentleman was behind the business, so we sent a corporal to the legal gentleman who said that for some compensation he could find a surgeon to do the papers. However, the legal gentleman smelled a mice and concluded to do no more for the corporal. Then Assistant Surgeon General Wood said to try some of the doctors directly. I had nothing previously against Dr. Flynn, in fact, was on friendly terms with him. I sent Hospital Steward W. D. Wiley to Private Wilkins to instruct him to offer money to the doctor. Dr. Flynn was not the only one being tried with this method.

When I examined Wilkins myself, I could find no evidence of heart disease. I examined him by percussion, auscultation, and by having him exercise rapidly. I did not use a stethoscope; I used my ear. I repeat that I had a favorable opinion of Dr. Flynn as a man and as a surgeon. I had Wilkins examined by two other doctors in addition to me, Dr. Flynn and Dr. LeRoy.

The first of these two doctors was William Grier, who made a diagnosis of "slight hypertrophy" but no heart valve disease. (This began a long discussion on the difficulty of diagnosing such conditions, the different ability of doctors to hear sounds, and the causation of some kinds of heart disease by rheumatism.) The second examiner was Dr. Charles Alexander of Lawson General Hospital in St. Louis. He had no idea why he had been ordered to examine Wilkins but did so and found no disease. Here the prosecution closed.

Benjamin F. Gilman, a contract surgeon at Benton Barracks, was the first defense witness. He told the court that he had been in practice for twenty years and was familiar with Wilkins's medical history. "Wilkins told me that he had been out of health for two or three years before he enlisted. He had been treated for liver disease and dyspepsia. Where there is dyspepsia, there is almost always heart palpitation. Disease of the liver also follows dyspepsia. Wilkins is not a healthy man in general terms; he has irregularity of the pulse. He appears in the convalescent stage of liver disease, with sallow skin and a slight pain in the right upper quadrant. As to Dr. Russell, I believe he did not like Dr. Flynn and did not treat either him or me right."

Dr. James E. Hall, who served on the same medical board with Drs. Flynn and Waller, said that he had been called to see Wilkins two weeks before the alleged bribery. "Wilkins had an ordinary bilious turn and I gave him the ordinary medicine for this condition. He had torpidity of the liver, which can cause dyspepsia or cardiac disease. These liver conditions are incident to the climate here and would not need to lead to a discharge."

The court weighed all these opinions and observations and made a finding of guilty. Flynn was sentenced to be dismissed from the service of the United States government, to forfeit all pay due to him, to have his contract canceled, and to be imprisoned in a military prison for sixty days.

About four weeks later, John L. LeConte, Surgeon of Volunteers, Acting Medical Inspector of the Department of Missouri, wrote in protest. The salient points of his letter were that Flynn was not the examining surgeon but was only a junior member of the board and therefore did not have the power to discharge. In regards to the $25, Flynn did not seem to know that he was accepting money. "Wilkins simply thrust an unmarked package into the doctor's hands and then left." LeConte requested Flynn's release. Joseph B. Braun, Acting Assistant Surgeon General of the U.S. Army requested that the rest of Flynn's sentence be canceled. On September 15, 1863, Brig. Gen. William K. Strong revoked both the remainder of the prison sentence and the forfeiture of pay. Flynn's dismissal remained. Eighteen years later, he wrote regarding a pension, but did not receive one.

⊱—⊷⊶•❀•⊷⊶—⊰

COMMENT: This trial raises both administrative and medical questions. As to the former, it would appear that Flynn may well have been the victim of entrapment because his superiors conducted a rather heavy-handed investigation into charges raised in an anonymous letter (which is not in the court-martial file).

The medical issues illustrate the gulf between today's concepts of disease and physiology and those of 1863. In some aspects, Victorian medicine was modern: the sounds of diseased heart valves and their correlation with autopsy findings was quite accurate by today's standards. The causation of mitral valve disease by rheumatic fever was clearly recognized. Cardiac hypertrophy (excessive development of the heart muscle) was understood to be related to obstructed circulation, though such hypertrophy was more easily diagnosed at postmortem than in the living patient. As for the use of the stethoscope, many Civil War surgeons owned one, and each regiment was supposed to receive one as standard equipment.

Gastrointestinal functioning was much murkier to the Victorian medical man without today's barium studies and endoscopies. The concept of "dyspepsia" was a vague one, implying many types of indigestion. In 1892 William Osler defined chronic dyspepsia as a type of gastritis, with changed stomach acid, weakened musculature of the stomach wall, and excessive gastric mucus. Whatever the exact meaning of dyspepsia, textbooks of the time clearly listed it as one of the causes of heart palpitations. Even stranger to modern readers are notions of liver function. "Torpidity" of the liver meant underfunctioning, although there was no way to measure such a thing. "Bilious fever" cases had increased temperature and vomiting of bile but were without jaundice. "An ordinary bilious turn" escapes modern classification.

What was called "hepatitis" rarely exhibited jaundice, so it must have been something different from today's version. Victorian "hepatitis" had chills and fever, impaired appetite, white tongue, and diarrhea.

Of course a physician in the 1860s, as now, could not be expected to have medical knowledge in advance of his time—but bribery, or even the suspicion of it, was just as abhorrent then as now.

Chapter Forty-Four

Ferdinand Brother

A muster roll is not just a list of men. It also includes horses. In the Civil War many men furnished their own horses and were paid by the government for the use of the horse as well as receiving rations of hay, oats, and other forage. If one were to imagine the confusion that would arise if in today's army each man brought his own vehicle, with all the potential claims regarding prior condition, wear and tear, mileage, gas and oil, loss in combat, responsibility for maintenance, and fraudulent claims as to the value of vehicles destroyed, it would serve as an analogy for the difficulties of Surgeon Ferdinand ("Ferd") Brother of the 8th Regiment of Cavalry, Missouri State Militia.[1]

In Lebanon, Missouri, on January 7, 1864, Dr. Brother was charged with "causing a false muster to be made, whereby the government of the United States was defrauded."

The text of the first specification reads:

> Surgeon Brother, on or about the 25th day of April 1863, did make to Lieutenant Hunter, adjutant, 8th Regiment of Cav, M.S.M., a statement that William Crisswell, hospital steward, 8th Cav., M.S.M., had a horse in the service of the U.S. from the date of his enlistment to that date, he, Surgeon Brother, well knowing at the same time that Crisswell's horse had died at the post several months previously.
>
> On Surgeon Brother's presentation, the said adjutant made out the muster and payrolls to the 30th day of April, 1863, in accordance with Surgeon Brother's statement and the said Crisswell received payment for the use and risk of a horse in the service when he had not a horse at all, his horse having died during the month of December 1862, thereby defrauding the government.

A second specification charged that Dr. Brother had made the same false claim to Col. J. J. Gravely, the commander and mustering officer. The first witness was the colonel himself.

Q. Did Surgeon Brother make a statement to you that Hospital Steward Crisswell had a horse in the service from his enlistment until April 30, 1863?

A. Surgeon Brother made no statement concerning Crisswell's having a horse in the service.

Q. Did Steward Crisswell have a horse when mustered?

A. Crisswell appeared on the field on the day of the muster, mounted, and was mustered by me with horse and equipment. It appears that there are hard feelings between Adjutant Hunter and Surgeon Brother. The original muster rolls were made out by Hunter. I have been here only a month and had to depend upon the papers provided to me.

Q. Adjutant Hunter make any vindictive statement regarding Surgeon Brother?

A. About two weeks after the muster, I heard Hunter threatening to file charges against Brother. Hunter said, "I will make you sorry for this. I know enough about this, God damn you, to ruin you!"

Hospital Steward William Crisswell's testimony went further to discredit the prosecution, as well as to suggest a certain thickness in Crisswell's own mentation.

Q. Did you own a horse on the day of muster, April 30?

A. I think I did.

Q. Had your horse died previously to that muster?

A. He had. I think he died in January or February 1863.

Q. Did you report the death of your horse to Adjutant Hunter?

A. Yes.

Q. Did you report the death of your horse to the adjutant prior to the muster?

A. Yes.

Q. Did you report the death of your horse to Dr. Brother prior to the muster?

A. No.

This closed the testimony. The court acquitted Brother. He continued to serve with the 8th Missouri State Militia Cavalry until the end of the war, except for a month in New Jersey on sick leave. After 1865 he moved to Bunkerhill, Illinois, where he practiced for several years before finally settling in Beatrice, Nebraska; he was active in the Grand Army of the Republic.

In 1893 he was still living in Beatrice, in the southeast corner of Nebraska, and receiving a pension for "injury to the left shoulder and side, right knee, vertebrae and also heart." In spite of these limitations, he served as county physician (the county refused to reimburse him for the expenses of his horse) and maintained a medical office until 1904. In 1919 he spent six months at the State of Kansas National Military Home, where he was treated for painful stiffening of his joints, especially the right knee. He had "total loss of sight in the right eye and a cataract over the left eye, which obscures vision of at least four-fifths of normal sight; by reason of said disabilities, he requires the regular personal aid and attendance of another person." In May 1920 he re-entered the Military Home for a three month stay. He died at his own home on December 7, 1920. The next day, the *Beatrice Daily Sun* headline read: Oldest Nebraska Mason Passes Away. In June 1930 his widow, Martha, joined him in Evergreen Home Cemetery.

In the eighty-seven years from his birth in Philadelphia, he had seen a whole nation change. His uniform and sword are preserved at General Sweeney's Museum in Republic, Missouri. The coat still bears the black band of mourning, placed there in 1865 after an assassin's bullet plunged a hopeful nation into grief and despair.

>─┼─◆>─○─◆┼─◄

COMMENT: This court-martial appears to have been totally unnecessary because there was no evidence of wrongdoing. Its basis seems to be personal enmity on the part of the regiment adjutant, Lieutenant Hunter. The civilian equivalent process, in which the district attorney's office evaluates whether a case is worth prosecuting, was apparently absent in these military trials.

Dr. Brother may have felt that his services were undervalued; after all, he was better trained than most, educated at Missouri Medical College, McDowell Medical College, and the Medical College of Thomas Jefferson University in Philadelphia. Whatever Lieutenant Hunter's reasons for harassing the doctor, it certainly did not benefit the Union cause.

PART SIX

Where's that Doctor? AWOL!

Chapter Forty-Five

Louis H. Junghanns

The German revolution of 1848 was an uprising for freedom and democracy. Its failure sent thousands of "Forty-Eighters" fleeing to the United States, many settling in Missouri. When the rebellion by the slave states shattered their new home, most Germans rallied to the Stars and Stripes. Such was the case with the 12th Missouri, a St. Louis regiment and its first colonel, Peter J. Osterhaus, an 1848 refugee trained in German military schools and destined for success in the Union army. (His performances at Elk Horn Tavern, Arkansas, and Missionary Ridge, Tennessee, earned him brigadier's stars and postwar consulships in France and Germany.)

In the first two years of the regiment's service, three doctors guarded the health of the 12th Missouri: Frederick Hohly, who was promoted; William Fritz, who resigned; and Charles Cook, who was discharged. Our protagonist, Surgeon Junghanns, arrived in December 1862. He, too, was destined to serve only briefly; his court-martial was convened in September 1863.[1]

In April of that year, his regiment had camped at Milliken's Bend, Louisiana, sixteen miles northwest of Vicksburg, Mississippi, part of Grant's often-frustrated campaign to capture the City on the Bluffs. Soon the St. Louis Germans joined the great march south to Hard Times Landing, Louisiana, traveled across the Father of Waters on a steam armada, and in the state of Mississippi described a great counterclockwise arc around Vicksburg via Grand Gulf and Big Black River Bridge, ending at Walnut Hills, on the northeast edges of the besieged city.

Three charges were leveled against Junghanns. In the first, "conduct prejudicial to good order and military discipline," it was alleged that he had sent an insolent letter to his commander, Col. Hugo Wangelin. Further, he had also written to Samuel C. Plummer, Medical Director of the Division, excusing himself from duty on the basis of sickness and accusing his colonel of positioning noisome animals around the hospital tent—in Junghanns's words, "arranging all the animals of the regiment round his hospital, making it, after a few days, a perfect pest house."

Under the second charge, "neglect of duty," he had reported himself as too sick for duty, leaving the regiment with no doctor, but was still well enough to visit the camps of the 3rd and 17th Missouri and have a few glasses of beer with old friends.

The third charge, "conduct unbecoming an officer and a gentleman," was based on the letter he wrote to Plummer about Wangelin and his animals. Plummer passed the letter on to Gen. Frederick Steele (who doubtless had more urgent business), whose inquiries with the colonel raised the irritation level in the 12th Missouri. The formal charge adds that Junghanns "knew the charge to be false at the time, as no other animals except those over which he exercised exclusive control, these belonging to the hospital wagons and ambulances," were at issue. All these pesky events occurred at Milliken's Bend on April 18, 1863.

Later, several more charges were filed. On May 2, 1863, when the regiment began its march south from Milliken's Bend to Hard Times Landing, Junghanns did not go with them, leaving the regiment without a doctor. On May 22, 1863, Maj. Gen. U. S. Grant launched his third and final frontal assault on Vicksburg. In this bloody and fruitless affair, there were 3,000 Union casualties. Once more in the great war, direct attack was proved useless, and the Union settled in for a prolonged and traditional siege. On May 25, just three days after the Federal disaster, Junghanns returned to his regiment, which had suffered 116 men killed and wounded during his absence, but he "failed to report himself for duty and utterly neglected to discharge his duties as a surgeon, although the hospital was full of sick and wounded soldiers of the regiment, but, contrary to his duty, when application was made to him by some of the sick soldiers, he refused to listen to their demands for treatment, but told them to wait for the assistant surgeon as he [Junghanns] was not doing any duty."

Almost as an anticlimax, he was also charged with being absent without leave from May 2 to June 4, 1863. It was apparent that testimony would be needed to decide whether Junghanns would be best seen as a loafer, moving about Vicksburg at his leisure and having a beer with friends while his comrades fought and died, or whether he was a man too sick to march with his regiment or care for the wounded who lay all about him. The first prosecution witness was Joseph Speigelhalter, Assistant Surgeon of the 12th Missouri.

Speigelhalter first identified copies of the letters to Dr. Plummer and to Colonel Wangelin as being in Junghanns's handwriting. He also confirmed that he himself was absent sick from the regiment from middle April until May 4, 1863.

> At the time I rejoined the regiment, they were on the march, between Grand Gulf, Mississippi, and Fourteen Mile Creek, Mississippi. Surgeon Junghanns was not with the regiment. The sanitary condition of the regiment was tolerably good, since we had left most of the sick behind. We had skirmishing almost every day, which

continued after we got near Vicksburg on May the 18th. From May 20th to June 4th, we were camped on the extreme right of the army surrounding Vicksburg, in Walnut Hills. Our regiment was exposed to fire all the time and also participated in the assault of the 22nd of May. In the four days around that time, we lost 31 killed and 85 wounded. I was the only surgeon on duty. I attended our wounded in one of the hospitals, as well as a dozen sick and wounded men in the regimental hospital and the men sick in camp able to come to sick call. I think they were properly cared for. What I did not have time to do, surgeons from the other regiments did. When Dr. Junghanns appeared, I invited him to come over to the hospital and see the cases. He said he had no interest in the regiment at all and had forwarded his resignation.

When asked about Junghanns's physical condition, Dr. Speigelhalter replied, "He was sickly, as he always was, but was not sufficiently so to incapacitate him for the performance of duty. He had diarrhea and, I believe, intermittent fever [probably malaria]. He was sick but not too sick to do duty."

The next witness was Lt. Frederick Kessler, the acting adjutant of the regiment. (Kessler would soon be killed at Chattanooga.) He confirmed that the regimental books showed that Junghanns had been absent as appeared in the charges. He recalled having no surgeon for a long time until Dr. Speigelhalter joined on May the 11th.

Samuel C. Plummer, Surgeon of the 13th Illinois Infantry and Acting Medical Director of the 1st Division, clarified the responsibilities of a surgeon who feels that he should be excused from duty on a plea of physical disability.

He reports through the Medical Director of the Division to the Medical Director of the Corps, having presented himself for examination to the Medical Director of the Division. The corps medical director then assigns another surgeon to take his place. I examined Dr. Junghanns on April the 18th, when he was complaining of neuralgia and diarrhea. I did not excuse him from duty because his appearance did not indicate a lack of strength sufficient to be a disqualification for the performance of duty. I told him that I thought exercise in the open field would benefit him. He did not accompany his regiment from Milliken's Bend to Grand Gulf, and the regiment had no surgeon on this march.

When asked why the regiment would need a surgeon in such a situation, Plummer replied, "I never knew of a regiment marching a day when the presence of a surgeon was not required." Plummer was also of the opinion that from May 12th to June 4th there were enough killed, wounded and sick in the 12th Missouri so that it was more than one surgeon could handle.

Dr. Junghanns cross-examined the witness, asking, "After I notified you by my letter of April 25th of my physical disability, did you not relieve me by sending Assistant Surgeon Wetherell?" Dr. Plummer agreed with this and stated that he had forgotten that event. When asked by the defendant if he had examined his pulse or his tongue, Dr. Plummer replied, "No, I did not examine either one; I did it on general appearance." Junghanns pursued this line of thought. "Has chronic diarrhea or severe neuralgia ever been improved by exercise as severe as that connected with a military campaign?" Plummer was not about to be trapped by this line of logic and answered, "I want it understood that I did not consider that there was any disability when you applied to me to be relieved from duty. I was aware that you had remained behind during the expedition to Greenville, and I believe that your indisposition was caused by enervation for lack of exercise in the open air, rather than any consequential sickness."

Sgt. Gustavus Benthe testified that he had been sick on May 22nd and unable to see Dr. Speigelhalter because he was taking care of the wounded from the charge against the Confederate fortifications. "The regimental hospital was two miles away from the regiment and the doctor was away the whole day, going away in the morning and coming back in the evening. There was no one to take care of me." Lt. Hermann F. Mons, the quartermaster of the 12th Missouri, was questioned on the subject of animals around the hospital. "By the time the teams were ready to move the regimental property over to the camp from the boat, it had become perfectly dark. The teamsters took whatever ground they wanted. Some of them may have been near the hospital, but I can't say for sure; it was too dark. The ambulance teams were all mixed up with the regular transportation teams and remained there all night."

Charles Doering, Acting Hospital Steward, appeared as the first defense witness. He stated that there were horses all over the encampment making it difficult to put up a hospital tent. He did recall that about fifty yards separated the hospital tent from the draft animals. On further examination, he changed this estimate to twenty yards but stated, "The patients did not suffer anything from the proximity of the mules." Doering also recalled that on the 28th of April, although Junghanns was sick and vomited several times, he continued to prescribe for the patients and that he, Doering, had filled the prescriptions. Pvt. John Biddlingmier confirmed the story of Dr. Junghanns's vomiting. Here the testimony ended, and Junghanns wished to introduce into evidence a medical certificate given to him by "Surgeon Wetherell, of the 31st Iowa." (The only Iowa surgeon listed by that name is George F. Wetherell of the 26th Iowa.) There was much discussion of a subpoena being served on Brig. Gen. John Rawlins, Adjutant General of the Department of Tennessee, whose office was supposed to have had this medical certificate. The court took a several-day recess while the Judge Advocate traveled to locate the original certificate. It could not be found; however, he did locate an abstract in a "letters received book," which confirmed that such a document had existed.

The court found Junghanns guilty of all the charges except the one related to visiting other camps and drinking beer. He was sentenced to forfeit all his pay from May 2nd, 1863, onward and be dismissed from the service. The sentence of the court was approved by Maj. Gen. U. S. Grant, and the verdict became final. There is no pension application, and at that point Dr. Junghanns disappeared from the military records.

>-+•>-O-<+-+-<

COMMENT: Was Dr. Junghanns really sick? He says he was. Dr. Speigelhalter suggested diarrhea and malaria, and one lieutenant and one private saw the doctor vomiting. On the other hand, Dr. Plummer thought there was nothing wrong with Junghanns that could not be improved by "exercise in the open field." (It is hard to know whether Plummer's suggestion was facetious or reflected contemporary notions about humors, asthenia, and health. In those days doctors prescribed sea voyages, and even today French national health insurance will pay for thalassotherapy, in which patients exercise in sea water.) Junghanns's appearance at the regimental camp outside of Vicksburg, when so many of his own regiment lay wounded from the recent assault, and his refusal to treat soldiers who begged him for help certainly did not set well with his peers or with the court. It was mid-summer in Mississippi at a time in history where over half the country was subject to malaria. If anything, such epidemics would be worse in the Deep South. While Dr. Junghanns himself may have been sick, it is very probable that half the soldiers around him were just as sick or worse. In an era when many generals went into battle missing an arm or a leg or both, just "being sick" did not get much sympathy. That was certainly the position of the court-martial board.

Chapter Forty-Six

George H. Mitchell

Abraham Lincoln, legendary for his compassion, apparently drew the line at this doctor. Perhaps if Mitchell had not been court-martialed three times, he might have been a better candidate for forgiveness. In July 1862, while the 88th Pennsylvania was on campaign near Warrenton, Pennsylvania, Mitchell left for three days without permission. A week after his return, he was in a fistfight with the regimental quartermaster, Lt. Frederick R. Fritz, after an exchange of profanity. At his court-martial, Mitchell illustrated the use of the leading question—but with only limited success.[1]

The first witness was Brigade Surgeon Abram L. Cox, who began with the statement, "I have a voluntary admission made to me by Dr. Mitchell that he was gone without authority and had gone to Alexandria [Virginia] on his own hook. He agreed that he should have had permission to go beforehand; he never mentioned to me that he was going to leave camp." Mitchell then asked the witness, "Did I not receive the written permission of General [Zealous B.] Tower to go to Alexandria to purvey medicines, predicated upon the verbal permission of Colonel [George P.] McLean?" Dr. Cox said, "I know nothing of such permission. What you said to me was, 'I have gone up and come back and escaped with nothing but a scolding from the general.'" Dr. Mitchell posed another leading question: "Did I not mention that medical supplies of the regiment were exhausted and that the departmental medical director suggested that I go in person and have the articles purveyed?" Cox replied, "No, you did not."

Andrew Smith, surgeon of the 94th New York, told the court that on the 6th of July, Dr. Mitchell had come to him and asked him to look after Mitchell's regiment while he was gone. "He was gone for three days, while I took care of his patients. After he returned, he told me that Dr. Cox did not even know that he had gone and I heard directly from General Tower that Mitchell had no permission to leave." (It is of interest that in these discussions, no mention is made of any specific regulation governing the comings and goings of doctors. Most of the witnesses make statements such as, "It is my understanding that . . ." Exactly how doctors were to conduct themselves appears to be a mystery, even in the formal proceedings of a court-martial. Perhaps the answer is a simple one: None of the parties to the trial had read the regulations.)

The next testimony focused on Dr. Mitchell's fisticuffs. The regimental commander, Colonel McLean, told the court, "Dr. Mitchell and Quartermaster Fritz were quarreling. Blows had been struck. I told them both to go to their quarters, and supposed they had obeyed. I then turned to superintend the putting up of my own tent, soon heard a noise behind me, and saw them still quarreling. As I turned, Lieutenant Fritz again struck the doctor. I ordered them to their quarters again and they obeyed." Dr. Mitchell, cross-examining, asked, "Was it not possible that the doctor did not hear the first order to go to his quarters?" Colonel McLean admitted that it was possible but unlikely. Capt. David Griffith of the 88th Pennsylvania said, "I was present during the difficulty between Lieutenant Fritz and Dr. Mitchell. They were ordered to their quarters, but they did not obey. After they were given that order, there were further blows and further bad language. I repeated that order and put them both under arrest."

Dr. Cox was called back to the witness stand, this time as a defense witness. Mitchell opened with a question that not only inferred the answer but was a compound question. "Did I not show you a permission from General Tower to go to Alexandria for a specific purpose and upon my return to report my success with General [James B.] Ricketts and you replied, 'I thought so'?" Cox replied, "I have no recollection of anything of the kind!" Cox's testimony was of little help to Mitchell, and he now turned to Lt. William Fairlamb, also of the 88th Pennsylvania, who recalled that the altercation between Fritz and Mitchell lasted about five minutes and that he had not seen Mitchell strike a blow or say anything further to Fritz after the first order was issued. But then he added that he was not in a good position to see what was going on. Two more witnesses were called, neither of whom knew anything about the issues. On a new subject, the hospital steward, Frank Murphy, was asked about the condition of the regimental hospital supplies. Before he could answer, there was a sustained objection, and he was excused from further questioning.

Dr. Mitchell submitted a long defense statement that, greatly summarized, covers the following points: He went to see Colonel McLean for permission to go to Alexandria to obtain medicine. McLean had no objection, but he did not have the power to give written permission. Mitchell then went to General Tower, who wrote a note stating, "Assistant Surgeon Mitchell had my permission to go to Alexandria for the purpose of purveying medicines and to return as soon as possible." Mitchell explained, "General Tower told me I should show it to General [James B.] Ricketts, which I did, but he did not approve it. I then returned the permission to General Tower. I then consulted with the colonel and redacted my permission to leave on the previous permission received from General Tower. The important medicines and stimulants were entirely exhausted. As everyone gave me permission to leave, I did not think I was committing a breach of discipline." (He omits the refusal of Ricketts, the commanding general.)

Mitchell did admit that he had used harsh words with Lieutenant Fritz, "[b]ut the quarrel was precipitated upon me. Ten minutes afterwards, I wrote a note to Colonel McLean asking for pardon for the offense, and permission to withdraw the words used. The permission was not granted. Subsequently, I asked the same permission of General Tower, but that was not granted, either." (One wonders whether these requests were standard features of Victorian etiquette or Mitchell's own peculiar code.) Regarding the charge that he had struck Lieutenant Fritz, Dr. Mitchell proposed a highly original defense: "I was so enveloped in an India Rubber Coat that it was impossible for me to use my arms for the purpose of striking a blow. I was utterly unable to obey the order of the colonel until he took me by the shoulder and gave me a movement." (In trying to visualize this implausible scenario, one thinks of a child in a too-thick snowsuit.)

Mitchell was found guilty on all three charges and ordered dismissed from the service. A river of correspondence began with a variety of petitions and testimonials. Three months after his conviction, this great clot of paper reached the Executive Mansion. John Nicolay, Lincoln's private secretary, referred the matter to the Judge Advocate General on November 22, 1862. Two days later, Holt made his reply.

> The object of this petition of Assistant Surgeon Mitchell is to induce the President to revoke the sentence of a general court-martial by which in August last, he was dismissed from the service. It is not competent for the President to exercise such a power, though if satisfied that injustice had been done by this sentence, he might aid in giving relief against it by consenting that the Governor of Pennsylvania should make a reappointment. Although examination, however, of the record, leaves no doubt but that this officer, while in charge of the sick of his regiment, his superior officer being ill, left without leave and was absent for three days. On his return, he spoke of his absence, not in a spirit of regret, but rather of exultation. For this offense, I think he was very properly dismissed.
>
> But this discussion need not be pursued, since by general order dated 22 of November, he has been again dismissed by direction of the President with loss of all pay and allowances that are now or may become due for having absented himself without authority while awaiting sentence of court-martial. This action [by Mitchell] was doubtless taken under the mistaken impression that the records of the court-martial had been lost. It seems that in the face of such decisions, no further application for the restoration of this officer should be entertained.

After an unexplained gap of six months, the final notation is: "Petition refused. A. Lincoln June 23, 1863."

While his first set of offenses were wending its way through one year of administrative procedures, Mitchell had been court-martialed a second time, in October 1862, charged with being absent without leave from August 15th to September 22nd, 1862, with neglect of duty by not taking care of his patients during that time period, and with conduct unbecoming an officer and a gentleman, in which he appropriated to his own use "twenty pounds of beef, two cans of condensed milk, three cans of preserved fruit, and one package of Oswego starch, all supplies meant for the sick and wounded." The final specification in "conduct unbecoming" was that his current absence without leave occurred while he was awaiting sentence for his first court-martial.

Familiar names appear in the second court-martial. Brigade Surgeon Cox noted that Dr. Mitchell had been absent during the battles of Cedar Mountain, South Mountain, and Antietam. "Previous to the battle of Cedar Mountain, the accused had made several applications for leave of absence on account of alleged sickness, and three medical gentlemen were ordered to examine him. They reported that he was not sick, and his leave of absence was consequently not granted. It is the custom in our brigade that all leaves of absence for surgeons come through my office. The doctor got no leave of absence from me. When he returned to the regiment, he stated that he had been at Alexandria, Keedysville [Virginia] and several other places which I do not remember." Dr. Mitchell asked in cross-examination, "Did you not sign a requisition for rations in the provost marshal's office, thus acknowledging my being on duty?" Cox had no difficulty with this question: "I have no recollection of signing any such thing at all. I had thirteen hospitals under my charge then, and if my name ever got on any paper acknowledging this doctor as being on duty, it was done so fictitiously and not with my knowledge." Mitchell tried another tack: "Did I not report myself in your tent at camp on the morning of 14th of September, the day preceding our entrance into the city of Frederick?" Cox had no recollection of such an event. Mitchell tried again: "Have you not from time to time publicly asserted your intentions of driving me out of the regiment and the service?" Cox had no recall of having done such a thing. The court now summoned General Ricketts, whose testimony was brief. "I have never given Dr. Mitchell permission to be absent."

Daniel Biedler, ambulance driver with the 88th Pennsylvania, addressed the subject of stolen food:

> I was at Keedysville. I had stopped the ambulance by Dr. Mitchell's order while the battle was going on. The doctor brought out to the ambulance two cans of condensed milk, one can of beef tea and some liquor in a bucket. He used the condensed milk, and gave me some of it. The beef tea was made into soup and taken to the hospital, but I do

not know what was done with the liquor. The next day, I met Dr. Mitchell on the road, coming from the battlefield toward Keedysville. He told me to go back with him and said he had got some beef. When we came to camp, it was cooked and we all ate of it, the doctor, myself, two or three men from Company C, stragglers from our regiment and the doctor's colored servant. The day we left Keedysville, the doctor drew several cans of preserved things and put it in his trunk.

Biedler also recalled that the doctor drew an additional twenty-five pounds of beef, twenty of which were delivered to a "civilian house" while the other five was "cooked and eaten by us. Maybe four or five sick men ate some of the meat."

As part of Mitchell's defense, three different surgeons testified, creating a very confused story about the assignment of doctors during the fighting in that part of Virginia. The only two aspects that came across clearly were that Dr. Mitchell had been examined and found fit for duty, and he had been ordered to remain on duty.

Mitchell was found not guilty of these charges, but the reviewing general, John F. Reynolds, was not impressed. Although he confirmed the findings of the Court, he added, "It should not be inferred that the commanding general intends to sanction such irregularities on the part of Assistant Surgeon Mitchell, as the testimony in this case indicates. It is too common for both men and officers to avail themselves of the slightest excuses for their absence, when their regiment is in the presence of the enemy."

Having now been convicted by one court-martial and acquitted by another, Mitchell wrote a long (and often confusing) letter to the President, noting that although he had been dismissed from his regiment, the order had never been promulgated nor had a copy of the order been received at regimental headquarters. He stated that every officer in the regiment had petitioned the governor of Pennsylvania to *promote* (!) Dr. Mitchell, but that the name of his commander, Colonel McLean, had been "withheld." (Apparently, the petition to the governor was successful because on August 15th, Mitchell was issued a commission designating him as a full surgeon, with the rank of major, in the Pennsylvania volunteers.) "However, I was continued under the power of an arrest made more than a month previous, thus rendering the commission inoperable." He also complained that his acquittal in the second court-martial was "practically useless, as I was not then amenable to military law." Mitchell also claimed that, contrary to the testimony received, he was present at the battles of South Mountain and Antietam but not given credit for that.

Two years passed, and Dr. Mitchell was still a surgeon attached to the 88th Pennsylvania. In December 1864 he was court-martialed for the third and last time. The first charge was "fraudulently appropriating U.S. government property to his own use," in which he had ordered eight cartloads of government lumber delivered to his own house for his own private use, along with fifteen pounds of ten-penny nails, one barrel of lime, a bucket, and a broom. He also arranged for the chief carpenter, the mason, laborers, and various patients and employees of Haddington Army Hospital, near Philadelphia, to work on his own home as carpenters. Further, in accounting for hospital funds, the return was $40 short.

The second charge, conduct unbecoming an officer and a gentleman, included his removing from the hospital grounds—using government carts and horses—two cartloads of shingles, twelve cartloads of building stone, two cartloads of sand, and ten cartloads of lumber, all taken to his own home for his own use. Additional charges involved the theft of a pair of window shades and the removal of a barn roof.

The testimony of numerous witnesses confirmed the statements made in the charges and specifications. Dr. Mitchell was found guilty, dismissed from the service, and sentenced to "be forever disqualified from holding any position of trust, honor or profit in the military service of the Unites States." The commanding general approved the sentence and canceled his contract.

In January 1880 Dr. Mitchell, then residing on East Seventeenth Street in New York City, wrote to the Secretary of War about the third court-martial, demanding a review of the records and asserting that the trial was not legal. His sentence had included the forfeiture of his last month of pay, and he wanted that money back. Four months later, the Bureau of Military Justice of the War Department replied, stating that "The forfeited pay has long gone to the Treasury, and there is no way to retrieve it. There is no reason to change the continuing disqualification from Federal service."

Dr. Mitchell died on June 17, 1889, in Los Angeles, California. His widow, Addie, made application for pension, stating that her husband had been discharged from the army on a surgeon's certificate of disability on July 25, 1862. She submitted an affidavit from his family physician, who had treated him after the war for chronic malaria and chronic diarrhea. (Some of these assertions seem at variance with the records. His discharge from the service in July 1862 followed conviction by a court-martial, and his appeal was rejected by Abraham Lincoln.) While the record is unclear, Addie's claim seems to have been rejected.

COMMENT: Mitchell's record speaks for itself. He was quarrelsome, contentious, and self-justifying. He does not seem to have been a man of good character.

Chapter Forty-Seven

Eliab M. Joslin

John C. Frémont bestrode the nineteenth century like a colossus. His 1840s explorations of the West earned him the appellation "The Pathfinder." He was instrumental in tearing California loose from Mexico, served as a senator from that new state, and later as governor of Arizona Territory. In the early days of the Civil War, he was *the* Federal authority in Missouri.

Frémont ran for president of the United States in 1856, on the Republican ticket. During that campaign, the president of the National Republican Association was Eliab M. Joslin. Six years later, Joslin was court-martialed for—stealing a box of candles. What would explain such an apparent fall from grace for this forty-six-year-old surgeon of the 6th Regiment of Missouri Volunteer Infantry?[1]

Jefferson City lies on the south bank of the Missouri River, in the very heart of the Show Me State. There, in July 1862, Joslin (sometimes spelled Joslyn) was tried for absence without leave and conduct unbecoming an officer and a gentleman. His AWOL consisted of taking a steamboat down the river to St. Louis without permission. The latter charge claimed that he had stolen a case of wine and eight bottles of whiskey intended for the sick, and he had used them for himself and his family. He was also charged with stealing and selling thirty pounds of candles. The charges against Joslin were filed by the regiment's other doctor, George S. Walker. Relations between the two surgeons do not seem to have been cordial.

Testimony began with the regiment's commander, Col. Peter E. Bland. "Around the end of July, I was at my house in St. Louis, sick, and the accused came to see me. When I came down the river from Jefferson City to St. Louis, he was in the same boat with me. I have no knowledge of any authority issuing him permission to leave the regiment. He had a letter to that effect, but I know no more about it. He did return to the regiment on August the 7th."

Dr. Walker testified next. "I know that he was absent from the regiment at Jefferson City on July the 29th and I did not see him again until ten days later." Walker had no information at all about the missing case of wine or box of candles. When asked in cross-examination by Dr. Joslin, "Is it not true that there are bad feelings between you and the accused? Is it not true that your system of medicine and that of the accused do not harmonize?" Walker deflected the question, stating, "I am of the homeopathic system and the accused follows the allopathic method. However, we both belong to the same system, it is only that he gives higher doses than I do." (The court did not pursue this interesting oversimplification of the differences between the two schools of thought.)

Hospital Steward H. S. McChessry recalled that a case of wine had been taken away from the hospital and loaded into an ambulance by Dr. Joslin. "The wine was intended for the sick and was marked and addressed to the post surgeon at Jefferson City. The wine was kept in the hospital office, along with other stores. As to the candles, there was a box of them not quite used up. There may have been twenty-five candles left, but I don't know what happened to them. They just went off with the ambulance driver. The candles had been purchased out of the hospital fund by myself, under orders of Dr. Joslin." The hospital steward was queried regarding the mode of caring for patients and of paying the nurses. "Dr. Joslin provides and prescribes for the soldiers at sick call. At that time, we only had two or three men sick in camp. As to payment for the nurses, there seemed to be no way to pay them except out of the hospital fund. The paymaster refused to give her any more than $6.00 a month." (The possibility of a female nurse or nurses is raised by the latter statement but not amplified in later testimony.)

Lt. Col. James H. Blood had command of the regiment at the time that Dr. Joslin was absent. "The accused had come to me for leave to go to St. Louis. I told him that he would have to go through the usual channels, and Dr. Joslin said that would not be fast enough for his purposes. I told him that he would not get a pass. I certainly did not consent or advise that he go to St. Louis. As to our two regimental surgeons, I knew there was considerable feeling between him and the other surgeon, and I thought it would be desirable for Dr. Walker to get a promotion into one of the new regiments."

As testimony came to an end, one exhibit was introduced—a piece of paper stating "Bought of Dr. E. M. Joslin, about three-quarters of a box of candles, more or less, belonging to the hospital department, to be placed to the credit of the hospital fund."

The final piece of evidence before the verdict was the written defense prepared by Joslin, which might best be described as long and rambling. In it, he returned again and again to the concept of malice held by others toward him. The court brought in the verdict, that he was guilty of absence without leave but not guilty of stealing wine or candles. Dr. Joslin was sentenced to be reprimanded by the commanding officer of the regiment, at dress parade.

He continued to serve with his regiment through the siege of Vicksburg; in August of 1863 he was at Camp Sherman, Mississippi. The following month, he was back on duty with the regiment on various transports and in October 1863, was in charge of the Second Division Hospital at Iuka, Mississippi. He spent two more months with the 6th Missouri, but in January 1864, went on sick leave and never returned. In April 1864, he submitted his resignation; however, eight months later he was employed at $100 per month as an assistant surgeon with the provost marshal at Alton, Illinois.

In the early 1880s, he began to make inquiries regarding a pension. In support of Joslin's claim, Warren F. McChesney, who had served with Joslin in the Sixth Missouri, submitted the following statement:

> At the battle of Missionary Ridge on November 25, 1863 [above Chattanooga, Tennessee], Dr. Joslin was in charge of the field hospital on the bank of the Tennessee River in December. The weather was cold and wet and Joslin was afflicted with an attack of bilious rheumatism, and then developed a gastric fever or a malarial fever. He was ever after, during his continuance in the service, unable to do duty. He was carried to the [railroad] cars, and then taken on board a steamer. I did not see him again until April 1864, when the regiment returned to St. Louis. At that time, he was still very feeble, unable to get around without a cane and had chronic muscle problems in the right half of his body, with difficult locomotion.

In 1876, Joslin and his wife Paulina moved to the city of Orange, in Southern California, for his health. Certificates in his pension file indicate that he was too sickly to practice medicine. He died at Orange, at age 73, of "hemiplegia of the right side with other complications."

>⊢⟨•⟩⊶O⊷⟨•⟩⊣⟨

COMMENT: The inchoate condition of medical theory in the 1860s is indicated in the testimony about homeopathy versus allopathy. Homeopaths treated diseases with medications which imitated the symptoms of the disease, but the medications were given in extraordinarily tiny quantities. Allopaths prescribed medicines, in much larger doses, which were antagonistic to the symptoms. Surgeon Walker may only have been trying to smooth matters between himself and Joslin when he said that, "We belong to the same system, it is only a matter of doses."

The matter of candles, which seems to have been more of a supply and accounting problem than theft, reminds us that nighttime in the 1860s was dark. Men and women who needed to write were lucky to have a candle. Surgeons who needed to operate were lucky to have a lamp. Soldiers sat around a campfire not only to keep warm and to cook their food but also to escape utter darkness. On moonless nights the Civil War soldier, whose diet was usually short of eyesight-enhancing of Vitamin A, must have been close to helpless.

While Dr. Joslin appears to have been somewhat cavalier in giving himself permission to be absent without leave, when his request had been denied by higher authorities, no issue was raised as to the quality of his medical work. The regiment seems to have been happy to have him along until he finally left at Chattanooga, apparently partly paralyzed on one side, destined to never be a whole man again. In this he was not alone.

Chapter Forty-Eight

William H. Gominger

During the Civil War, Winchester, Virginia, changed hands dozens of times, in as many battles and skirmishes. Thirty-five miles northwest of Winchester is the town of Romney, now in West Virginia, the scene of nine skirmishes. It was there that Dr. William Gominger (also spelled Gorminger), "having been ordered to take care of the hospital at Romney, Virginia, about May 8, 1862, did, on or about June 6, 1862, leave said hospital, going to Philadelphia without leave from proper authorities, leaving the sick men and hospital supplies in charge of the hospital steward, Henry May, of the 45th New York Volunteers." Since Gominger was part of the 27th Pennsylvania Infantry, the charges seems to add confusion to dereliction.[1]

He was further charged with neglect of duty on two different occasions. In March 1862, at Fairfax Court House, Virginia, he failed to get the medical supplies earmarked for his regiment, supplies being held in a warehouse in Alexandria, Virginia. Two months later, he failed to give the hospital panniers (baskets holding medical supplies) to the hospital steward of the 27th Pennsylvania, Adolph Tafel. Since the regiment was headed for the Shenandoah campaign and the battle of Cross Keys, Virginia, Gominger was considered especially neglectful in leaving his regiment with insufficient supplies.

Finally, he was charged with being drunk at Romney from the day of assuming his new duties until the day he departed for Philadelphia. He was also accused of treating patients very severely during this four-week drunk. Gominger pleaded not guilty to every charge.

The first witness was Henry May, the hospital steward of the 45th New York. His appointment as head of the hospital at Romney came about in an unusual way: He had been a patient there. May recalled that Gominger had told him well in advance of the trip to Philadelphia, that the doctor's behavior had always been good, and that he had always treated the patients in a kindly manner. Furthermore, May had never seen him drunk.

"Dr. Gominger selected me to take charge while he was gone because I had been a medical practitioner for three years before the war and felt confident that I took proper care. There were only nine patients in the hospital and only one was dangerously ill. While I was in charge, no one died. I do not know if Dr. Gominger had official leave or not."

In regards to the former point, Gominger entered into evidence Special Order No. 5, dated June 6, 1862: "During the absence of Dr. W. S. Gominger, Surgeon 27th Regt. Pa. Vol., Dr. [sic] Henry May, Hospital Steward, 45th Regiment N.Y.S.V. will have charge of the Seminary Hospital. By order Col. F. G. d'Utassy, Commanding Post."

(Frederick G. d'Utassy was a piece of work in his own right. A colonel of the 39th New York Infantry—the "Garibaldi Guards"—he spoke seven languages and would acquit himself well in three months at Harper's Ferry, Virginia. However, within a year he, too, would be court-martialed—dismissed in disgrace, and sentenced to a year in prison—on charges that filled dozens of pages.)

Hospital Steward Adolph Tafel was called next as a witness and was questioned about the medical panniers left behind at Romney. "When the 27th Pennsylvania marched south, the panniers remained at Romney, but we had a medicine chest, some medicine in a box, the amputating case, the pocket case and splints. There was sufficient supply for our immediate wants. I was ordered to stay behind at Romney when the 27th Pennsylvania left. Dr. Gominger ordered it and I knew that the hospital director agreed. When we stayed behind at Romney, there were 96 patients in our hospital."

On the subject of neglecting to obtain medical supplies from the storeroom at Alexandria, Tafel's testimony was more damning. "The doctor did not refuse to receive them, but he neglected to do so. We were at Centreville, Virginia, for two weeks, on detached service. It was 28 miles from Centreville to Alexandria. He could easily have got them by rail to Manassas Junction. He made no effort to get the medicines until the day before we left." As to the issues of mistreatment of patients and drunkenness on duty, Tafel had seen nothing improper in the doctor's behavior.

While the 27th Pennsylvania was in the Shenandoah Valley, being mauled by Stonewall Jackson, its medical care was provided by Assistant Surgeon Max Heller, who confirmed that Dr. Gominger had kept the panniers and Hospital Steward Tafel at Romney. "When we left Romney, we had the medicine chest filled as full as possible, but it was exhausted when we got to Franklin [Virginia] eleven days later. When we left Hunter's Chapel [Virginia], we had orders to leave hospital stores behind and then had only a field medicine chest. I could not bring more as we had not transportation. We were two months on the march from Hunter's Chapel to Winchester. The weather was generally bad and detrimental to the health of the men. I did manage to treat my men successfully with what we had in the chest. At the battle of Cross Keys, the enemy took our ambulance, which had the amputating case and the medical supplies."

As to the problem of ordering supplies while at Centreville, Dr. Heller recalled, "Dr. Gominger received the invoice about March 20th, while we were at Fairfax [Virginia]. During the two weeks we were at Centreville, I reminded

Dr. Gominger to send someone to Alexandria, but he did not do so until the day we were leaving."

Lt. Col. Lorenz Cantador of the 27th Pennsylvania contributed little: "Dr. Gominger said that he had permission from the colonel commanding the post to go to Philadelphia. The regiment was completely deficient in medical supplies after the battle of Cross Keys, where our ambulance was lost. Dr. Heller was the medical person during that march."

The court found Dr. Gominger not guilty and returned him to duty, but that is not the end of the story.

Gominger was thirty-eight when he was mustered in on October 12, 1861, for a term of enlistment that would expire in October 1864. However, he was listed as "deserted" on August 27, 1862. A few weeks later, the following exchange of letters took place. Dr. George Rex, Medical Director of the 11th Army Corps (who was himself later court-martialed) wrote to Dr. Jonathan Letterman: "Dr. Gominger was ordered to return to his regiment, but has not. We have a shortage of surgeons and his return is highly necessary."

A doctor whose signature is illegible replied, "Dr. Gominger is a patient at Seminary Hospital, Georgetown [D.C.], and will be ordered to his regiment as soon as he is sufficiently recovered." Dr. Rex then responded, "I am requesting a special inquiry, because I saw him on different occasions and found him in his usual health and fit to return to duty. Both him and his assistant surgeon are absent."

Gominger was discharged from the army on October 14, 1862, and did not apply for a pension. The exact reason for his discharge is not recorded, but we do know that he was almost immediately recommissioned as a surgeon in the 16th Pennsylvania Cavalry, where he served until the end of 1863. Other records show him connected with the Army until 1866.

His difficulties cannot be attributed to inexperience as a doctor—he received his M.D. from the medical department of Pennsylvania College in 1848. Nor was he a doctor nearing the end of his career—he had offices at seven different addresses in Philadelphia between 1868 and 1909, and he lived until 1911.

>─┼◄>─◦─◄>┼─◄

COMMENT: As to his being absent without leave, he had an order, signed by his colonel, authorizing Dr. May to cover for him. However, the order did not explicitly grant leave to Gominger. Whether he misunderstood the order or chose to stretch its meaning is unknown.

There seems to be no direct evidence either for drunkenness or for incompetent care or abuse of patients. However, his procrastination at Centreville in obtaining available medical supplies, his arranging to stay in Romney when his regiment went to meet the enemy, and his apparently unnecessary stay in the hospital in Georgetown all suggest an unwillingness to exert himself much in the service of his original regiment.

Chapter Forty-Nine

John W. Cobb

The only battle at Stoneman's Switch, Virginia, was between Dr. John W. Cobb and the Union authorities. His usual assignment was as assistant surgeon of the 134th Pennsylvania. On December 11, 1862, he was sent on detached duty to the hospital of the 3rd Division, V Army Corps, located at Stoneman's Switch in Stafford County. On December 17th, the medical director of the 3rd Division ordered Cobb to take a group of sick men to the general hospital at Aquia Creek, Virginia. There the patients would be sent by ship to hospitals at Washington, D.C., while Dr. Cobb was to return directly to his regiment.

However, after delivering his patients, around New Year's, Dr. Cobb went to his home in Pennsylvania, via Washington, D.C., and stayed there almost five weeks. On his return to the 134th Pennsylvania, February 8, 1863, he was court-martialed for being absent without leave.[1]

It would appear from the trial record that the doctor was a consummate master of nit-picking obfuscation. First, Dr. Cobb said that he could not be tried for absence from his regiment since he was absent from the division, not from the regiment. Then he said that the charges should be dismissed since they specified that he was absent at home, while he *might* have been elsewhere than home during his absence. Further, Cobb pointed to his orders regarding taking his sick men to Aquia Creek; he was instructed to return to his regiment after delivering the patients, "unless otherwise ordered." Although he had not been "otherwise ordered," Cobb erected an elaborate defense of what ifs.

Then Cobb asserted that the medical officer at Aquia Creek *might* have given him permission to go home for five weeks. Cobb insisted that the burden of proof was on the court to show that the medical officer at Aquia Creek had *not* given Cobb permission to be absent. His next line of defense was his insistence that the Court prove that *some* officer of higher rank had *not* given such permission. (The science of logic tells us that one cannot prove a negative.)

The prosecution witnesses included a Dr. Dailey, the medical director of the division hospital at Stoneman's Switch, who testified that Cobb had been ordered to return to his regiment after delivering the sick to Aquia Creek. The second witness was the adjutant of the 134th Pennsylvania, who showed that Cobb was absent without permission from January 1 to February 8, 1863.

Dr. Cobb presented a written defense, which may say more than he intended. It is dated February 7, 1863.

On December 29th 1862 I was ordered by Dr Dailey, Medical Director of Division to take charge of some 25 sick soldiers to Aquia Creek, on my arrival there I accompanied the sick to Washington [which was against his orders], in that capacity I remained until December 30th when they were sent to General Hospitals by the directions of surgeons detailed for that purpose. Previous to leaving camp I was really unable to attend to my daily duties and the labor, exposure, and anxiety of mind consequent on this duty as above stated brought on a Catarrhal fever causing much pain and suffering, which was seriously aggravated on my arrival at Washington and being a stranger there, I felt utterly inadequate to the physical effort of making personal application for leave of absence, and I suffered myself to be transported to the [railroad] cars that conveyed me home and the only safety to my life. [It may be absurd to quarrel with a man long dead, but the phrase "suffered myself to be transported" reaches into a realm of total abdication of personal responsibility.]

I have Surgeons certificates corroborative of my condition at home and testifying of the same. [These were not entered in evidence, nor do they appear in his service record.] I learn on my return to the Regiment that I have been reported absent without leave. This I admit was the case but I beg leave to disclaim any intention of violating wilfully any rule in the service and desire that my conduct in going home (at which I arrived Jan. 1st 1863) should be regarded as an imperative necessity and hoping this will meet your most favorable consideration.

Surprisingly, the court acquitted Cobb. However, his case was reviewed by a man who also possessed a keenly honed grasp of fine points and minutia: Brig. Gen. Andrew Atkinson Humphreys. While there was no doubt of Humphrey's military prowess (he took part in seventy engagements during his fifty-two-year military career), early in the Civil War, he had court-martialed and dismissed a full colonel who had failed to distribute heavy dress coats, in hot weather, to a regiment that had no means of storing or transporting such coats and had not requested them. The transparent flimflam of Dr. Cobb did not escape Humphrey's analysis.

Does the Court consider the offense with which Assistant Surgeon Cobb is charged to consist in his absence from the division hospital? Or in his absence from duty? If the former, then the accused would be subject to trial for being absent from his regiment during the time it is shown he was absent from it, and could not plead in bar of trial that he had already been tried for that offense. If the Court did not understand the full meaning of the statement of Surgeon Daily, it was its duty to question him. Had it done so, it would have learnt what it appears not to have understood, namely that the nature of the duty Assistant Surgeon Cobb was performing required him to return to his regiment as soon as the sick were placed in General Hospital, unless he was ordered to return sooner. The evidence of Surgeon Daily also proves that Assistant Surgeon Cobb did not return to the division hospital. And as already stated, it is proved he was not with his regiment from the first of January to the 8th of February. Where was he during that time?

The Court cannot intend to hold that the fact, that Assistant Surgeon Cobb was detailed to take care of a party of sick until they reached General Hospital unless he was ordered back to his regiment sooner by a medical officer at Aquia Creek who arranged for the transportation of the sick by water from that point to Washington, conferred upon that medical officer at Aquia Creek any authority to assign Assistant Surgeon Cobb duty separating him from his regiment and division. Or that it is necessary to prove that medical officer did not give Assistant Surgeon Cobb such orders. Or that no medical officer in the service of the United States of higher rank than Assistant Surgeon Cobb gave him orders authorizing him to be absent from his regiment during the time he is proved to have been absent from it.

Having laid the groundwork of analysis, General Humphreys reached his conclusionary statement, one that seems to reflect a state of apoplectic dudgeon. "If such principles were to hold, it would be impossible to prove any officer or any enlisted man absent without leave under any circumstances." Humphreys sent the trial back to the same court-martial board and asked that they reconsider their decision. The president of the court, Maj. Joseph Anthony, of the 129th Pennsylvania, wrote this response. "The proceedings and findings . . . were returned to the Court by the reviewing officer for revision. The review was carefully read to and considered by the Court. On the review, the Court are of opinion that the offense with which Assistant Surgeon Cobb is charged consisted in his absence from division hospital; and cannot consistently with that view of the case and the evidence adduced, alter their findings."

General Humphreys' final note appears to reflect a mixture of annoyance and despair. On April 11, 1863, he wrote, "It is with regret that I find myself obliged to disapprove the findings of the Court. Viewing the offense to be absent from duty without leave, I cannot send Assistant Surgeon Cobb before the Court a second time for what I deem essentially the same offense. Surgeon Cobb therefore escapes the punishment which is justly due. He took advantage of assignment to a duty which removed the physical difficulties of his leaving his post without authority, to absent himself fraudulently, thus betraying his want of that high sense of honor that should characterize the officer."

It must added in Dr. Cobb's favor that, after the trial, two colleagues, a Dr. Knight and a Dr. Kinney, both urged considerate treatment, describing him as a "faithful officer."

Dr. Cobb was discharged from the Army three months after this court-martial and soon began to receive a disability check for injuries sustained when a medical wagon fell on him one midnight, on the passage from South Mountain to Antietam, in September 1862. It is curious that his February 1863 letter, in which he describes his medical problems, makes no mention of any such injury. In his voluminous pension file no witness could be found to the mishap, and, while most dependents described him as "healthy and robust" before the war, at least one entry hints at prewar leg and hip problems. Whatever the origin of his leg atrophy, after having served seven months and twenty-six days, he received a pension until his death in 1915. In 1910, at the age of seventy-one, he married Susan, a thirty-six-year-old teacher. In 1913 she gave birth to Mary Eileen. Before the baby was three, Susan was dead of cancer, and John Cobb was dead from heart disease. Mary Eileen received a pension until 1929, when she turned sixteen. Some member of the Cobb family had received a government check every month for sixty-six years.

COMMENT: In the case of Dr. Cobb, the issues are administrative, not medical. His willingness to cut corners, cheat the system, and make flimsy excuses makes one wonder whether his seven months of service merited sixty-six years of government checks—payments based upon an injury for which there were no witnesses.

Chapter Fifty

Charles Gray

This doctor sounds like a character from the television series *M*A*S*H*. Gray cared deeply about his patients and was little concerned with the formal rigidities of military life. (His attitude may have been formed during his decorated service with the British Army in the Crimea, the Sepoy Rebellion, and a campaign in China, all before he was twenty-eight years old.) He spent time with three different Union regiments and served as a contract surgeon in between. His two contacts with military justice occurred during his year with the 11th New York Infantry.[1]

The 11th New York was not just any regiment. It was recruited mostly from New York City firemen—a rowdy and athletic bunch—and they dressed in the blue and scarlet shirts and jackets of the French zouave troops, hence their name of New York Fire Zouaves. Their first colonel, Elmer Ellsworth (a close personal friend of Lincoln), was killed pulling down a Confederate flag in Alexandria, Virginia, thus becoming the North's first martyr. Like most units at the battle of Bull Run, July 21, 1861, combat experience had been a disastrous eye-opener. In November 1861 the 11th New York was stationed at Fortress Monroe, just to the east of Newport News, Virginia. There, Dr. Gray was charged with absence without leave and with conduct prejudicial to good order and military discipline. The first charge was based upon his unauthorized trip to Baltimore, Maryland, November 3rd through 9th, 1861. The prejudicial conduct arose when his application for a pass was denied at headquarters, and he left anyway. En route, he cautioned two officers of his regiment to say nothing about his leaving without permission. This act led to a third charge: conduct unbecoming an officer and a gentleman. Conviction on this latter charge would mean an automatic dismissal.

The one witness, Capt. Richard Bowerman, began his story:

> I went to the office of Adjutant [William D.] Whipple at Fort Monroe in company with Surgeon Gray. He presented there a request for leave of absence signed by Colonel [Charles] Loeser. Captain Whipple

told Surgeon Gray that he could not grant him a leave of absence because it did not come through the proper authority; that it ought to have been signed by General [John W.] Phelps. (Phelps, a man of violent opinions, was noted for being rabidly anti-Mason, as well as anti-slavery; it was best not to annoy him.) Dr. Gray replied that he tried to see General Phelps, but that the general was not in. Captain Whipple answered that he was very much astonished that the doctor would ask permission without the application coming through the proper hands, that it ought to have been signed by General Phelps at Newport News and by Dr. Augler at Fort Monroe. Dr. Gray and myself then left for the Wharf; on arriving at the boat, the doctor said to me that he had leave from the colonel and he was going to Baltimore. While waiting until the steamboat left, Dr. Gray cautioned me not to say anything to the colonel about his not having obtained leave of absence from Captain Whipple.

Questions by the court demonstrated that Dr. Gray's purpose in going to Baltimore was to obtain lumber to put a floor and a roof onto the log cabin that served as regimental hospital, no lumber being available in Newport News. Captain Bowerman confirmed that Gray had *not* used the lumber to build his own personal quarters.

In cross-examination, Gray established that Bowerman did not know the purpose of the trip to Baltimore and that Bowerman was unsure if Gray was jesting when he said, "Boys, you need not say anything to the colonel."

Then the defendant asked Captain Bowerman, "What is my reputation as a gentleman and as a surgeon?" Speaking of his questioner in the third person, as was the custom in those days, the captain replied:

Dr. Gray is spoken very highly of by everyone who has been under his care, both in camp and in the field. I heard several of our wounded prisoners returning from Richmond [Virginia] say that if they had been under the care of Dr. Gray, they would have been cured.

The Surgeon General of the United States Army honorably mentioned him in his report, for his valuable service at the battlefield at Bull Run. The colonel and staff of a Pennsylvania regiment, I believe it was the Fourth, sent a letter of thanks to Dr. Gray for his services rendered at [illegible] Mill, on the road leading from Alexandria, on an occasion of their Picket Guard being attacked by the enemy, the wounded members of which were under the care of Dr. Gray. They said that if it had not been for his prompt services . . ." [Here, the record is damaged, but the implication is clear.][2]

Dr. Gray was convicted of the first two charges and suspended from rank and pay for a month. "The Court has been thus lenient because of the courage and services of the accused during the summer campaign, as testified by

Captain Bowerman, and also because the services of a medical officer cannot be readily spared for any great length of time."

In January 1862, the month of his court-martial, Dr. Gray was in trouble again, under arrest by order of Brig. Gen. Joseph K. Mansfield. (Not a man to be trifled with, Mansfield had entered West Point at age thirteen, graduated second in his class, and in eight more months would die bravely while rallying his troops at Sharpsburg.)

Gray's fresh legal troubles arose in the following manner: "The Sergeant of the Guard, whom I had treated before for stomach pain, came to me again, at night, with pain in the bowel. My previous prescription had been whisky, ginger, and laudanum. The stores had no whisky or brandy and the Commissary Office was closed for the night. I made out an order to my whisky supplier, Voorhees and Bell. They told me it could only be supplied if signed by the brigadier general. I took the order to his office. When he saw it, he had me arrested. I was not aware I had committed a crime." In the record is a telegram from General Mansfield: "Dr. Gray is under arrest for offending against one of my orders on the sale of liquor. I have not yet made up my mind about charges."

It would appear that no charges were filed because there is no record of a court-martial on the whiskey issue. The Fire Zouaves were mustered out in May 1862, Dr. Gray with them.

He served throughout the rest of the war, with the 7th New York Infantry (November 1862 to May 1863) and with the 11th New York Cavalry (Feburary 1865 to July 1865). In between he was a contract surgeon on David's Island in Long Island Sound, New York, and at Lafayette Hall in New York City. He seems to have mastered the military bureaucracy because he was not court-martialed again. After the war, he did not apply for a pension, and we know nothing further about him.

>+◆>•O•◆+◄

COMMENT: Dr. Gray's crimes seem to be (1) buying a roof and a floor for the regimental hospital which, in the winter of 1861, had neither, and (2) attempting to provide medicine for a sick sergeant when the usual sources were closed for the night. In both cases, he paid, or attempted to pay, out of his own pocket. For these offenses he was twice arrested, once convicted, and fined a month's pay. It is hard not to sympathize with him. The relatively light punishment indicates the Army's dawning awareness that surgeons, especially good ones, could be useful.

The testimony shows him to be a brave, skillful, and compassionate physician. This is a legacy of which any doctor could be proud.

CONCLUSION

Our Civil War surgeons did not exist in a vacuum. They were closely tied not only to the beliefs, customs, and knowledge of their day but also to a matrix of expectations that have influenced doctors and their patients from the earliest years of civilization. We will first consider the factors related to events and experiences of the 1860s.

What did the doctors, soldiers, and officers bring to their encounters? The doctors—at least those with formal training—had eighteen months of lectures plus whatever years of practice they may have accumulated. While this is not much by today's standards, it was the standard of that day and gave them a grounding in anatomy, pathology, and therapeutics that far exceeded the grasp of nonmedical men.

The officers brought the expectation that the regimental surgeon would prevent or cure (or at least alleviate) disease and patch up wounds, and he would aid "their boys" with skill and compassion. The soldiers, mostly country boys, may never have seen a doctor before. Rural care was more likely to rest in the hands of herbalists, midwives, farriers, bone setters, patent-medicine sales-men, and sympathetic mothers than to be through the endeavors of medical-school graduates. The ailing private most likely viewed the surgeon with a mixture of awe, fear, and misunderstanding.

As we have seen, the surgeon was expected not only to patch, sew, ban-dage, and dose his patients but also to locate tent poles, inspect ships, site latrines ("the sinks"), enforce camp tidiness, requisition food and medicine, locate supply wagons, fill out many forms, and even keep medical records—all without the aid of an administrative staff.

In addition to being doctors, the Civil War surgeons were also officers. The usual ranks were major for surgeons, and captain or lieutenant for assistant sur-geons. While we have seen almost no evidence of surgeons "pulling rank" on other men, the records are full of the problems of rank as they relate to dining. The line officers quickly formed "messes," appointed a peer as treasurer, pooled their moneys, and set about the business of buying food and having it prepared.

235

The medical staff of a regiment, either camped or on the march, might consist of a surgeon, an assistant surgeon, a hospital steward, and two "nurses." (The nurses were usually ordinary soldiers, or men convalescing from wounds or disease, with no formal medical training.) This medical staff might possess one set of kettles to be used by both the hospital and the medical staff. Transportation was always in short supply, so there was little room for "extra" cooking gear. To be militarily correct, the surgeon and assistant surgeon, being officers, were to buy their food separately, cook it separately, and eat it separately, while the steward, nurses and patients were to draw regimental rations and cook and consume them separately from the doctors—all of this with one set of kettles. If an army was campaigning nine months of the year, the chances of always following these rules of separation were close to zero.

In 54,000 court-martials, there are no trials of colonels accused of "messing with enlisted men." Many of the doctors tried on such charges seem to have been the victims of circumstance more than criminal offenders.

The surgeons' realistic limitations are seen in cases such as that of Dr. Thomas, who was ordered to "establish a hospital"—in this case in an old church and in an unheated barn, in the middle of a severe winter, without bedding, running water, food, or medicine, while being actively obstructed by insolent supply officers. This at the site of a huge and bloody battle with an ongoing epidemic of various diseases above and beyond the stream of wounded. In all wars events do not go as planned, with medical care as full of the unexpected as combat itself, but the Civil War doctor seems to have been expected to perform miracles, not just in the face of disaster but in an uphill fight against his own army and its bureaucracy.

In addition to these factors, whether in ancient Egypt, the Civil War era, or in modern day America, there is the unique two-level relationship between doctor and patient. One part of any doctor-patient relationship is implied, unspoken, invisible—indeed, close to magical. If it were said aloud, it might be: "I hope he understands how frightened I am, how terrified about the possible disastrous outcome of my condition. I hope he has powers and knowledge beyond my understanding, powers that will not only cure me but relieve my worry/concern/terror." This hoped-for exhibition of magical powers has always been enhanced by props and devices appropriate to the historical era: clouds of incense, grotesque masks, temples of healing, enormous and noisy imaging machines, the removal of bloody feathers during "psychic surgery," the wearing of a white coat, a soothing voice, an imposing title, diplomas on the wall, a touch on the hand, calming eye contact, evil-tasting medicine. At this magical level of medical transaction, doctors vary widely in their ability and willingness to employ its benefits.

The second level of medical transaction is overt, describable, rational, and explicit. It involves tangible medical devices, biologically active medicines, and events that can be measured. It is the stuff of standardized procedures, outcome studies, and peer review.

In the cases presented here, both levels of expectation can be seen: the psychological and the physical. The drunk surgeon loses his credibility, his ability to reassure; the soldier who sees his doctor staggering about is certain to wonder, "If something happens to me, will he be sober enough to help me?" The surgeon in this case will have squandered his capital of "magical" healing, his ability to be a powerful human placebo, a force for recovery beyond the purely anatomic.

The physical, overt level of expectation is also seen in these court-martials, because quite a few line officers set themselves up as judges of medical matters and ordered "their" patients treated ahead of others. The struggle between line and medical officers is seen most strongly in the case of Dr. Webster, where an old-time line officer with years of seniority (and a willingness to ignore direct orders from Washington) ordered a sick patient transferred over the strong protests of the doctor treating him.

Neither the Civil War doctors, nor the politicians, nor the professional soldiers, anticipated the magnitude of the war that came. It was longer, larger, and bloodier than any before in North America. Every doctor involved faced the challenge of a lifetime in trying to provide both the emotional reassurance and the technical skill needed in such a conflict.

Because the fifty surgeons presented here were all in trouble, some for drinking, we may have created an image of Union doctors in general as incompetents. That would be an incorrect picture. To the extent that the existing records can answer such questions, we present here data to show that Union doctors might even have been somewhat better behaved, or at least less court-martialed, than the average Union participant in the war.

The exact number of Union general court-martials is not known thus far, but it is probably close to 80,000. The analysis presented here is based on the first 54,066 court-martials indexed and computerized. In that total number (not counting hospital stewards or nurses) there are 249 medical men: 135 surgeons, 109 assistant surgeons, 1 surgeon general, 1 medical director, 1 civilian contract surgeon, 1 brigade surgeon, and a medical cadet.

We estimate that we have indexed 63 percent of the 80,000 court-martials. Since 12,000 surgeons served in the war (on the Union side), our indexed sample is likely to cover 7,900 surgeons; we have found the court-martials of 249 surgeons and one medical cadet. Thus, approximately 3 percent of all medical professionals were court-martialed.

An estimated 2 million men served at one time or another in the Union army. If 80,000 received a general court-martial, it would indicate that 4 percent of all men were tried, a figure one-third higher than the 3 percent of surgeons who were tried. In that sense, at least, surgeons offended less often than the average man in uniform.

The subject of alcohol in the court-martials is worthy of examination. Alcohol is mentioned as a factor, usually associated with drunk and disorderly behavior, in 9,769 cases—18 percent of the 54,066 cases indexed thus far. In the trial records of 249 doctors, 27 percent mention alcohol as a factor.

However, doctors' relationship with alcohol was unique: Not only might they drink alcohol, but they were responsible for ordering it, storing it, inventorying it, and prescribing it. When the administrative cases that involve alcohol and surgeons are subtracted, the remainder is identical with the general population of defendants: 18 percent of surgeon's trials and 18 percent of all trials charge the defendant with being drunk. In brief, the evidence indicates that surgeons were neither more nor less drunk than their comrades.

Looking back at the fifty doctors whose stories were told in this book, they were just as likely to be in trouble for administrative reasons as for medical shortcomings. As to the former, they cover transgressions that would be unacceptable when done by people of any occupation: drinking, petty turf battles, angry outbursts, improperly disposing of government property, fistfights, absence without leave, failure to keep records, laziness, and association with lewd women. The administrative crime unique to military life—"messing with enlisted men"—covers a wide spectrum, from outright theft of food to a generous and egalitarian sharing of food more palatable than hardtack and salt pork, provided by the surgeon himself.

In the medical cases, one theme stands out: failure to manifest sufficient concern for the patient (a trait perhaps even more prevalent today with "managed care" and HMOs). At least ten cases can be subsumed under this single rubric. With the doctor's limited repertoire of effective treatments, no one really expected him to save all of his patients, but he was expected to appear concerned, not indifferent. A serious failure of "bedside manner" was likely to lead to a court-martial. Sometimes the cause lay in the system itself, such as a doctor with overwhelming casualties and a stingy supply officer. Sometimes the surgeon himself was too physically weak to function, almost as sick as his patients. In a few cases the doctor appeared to be a genuine shirker, the kind of person who should not be a doctor. But fortunately that type of character defect was rare.

Some of the medical issues were unique and fit no pattern. Such cases include those of forced circumcision, controversial autopsy procedures, opium addiction, and failure to diagnose. The issue of jurisdiction over patients, whether line or medical, is seen in several cases. (And it, too, has modern echoes: "I'm sorry, sir, that is not a covered benefit.")

The variety of issues raised in these trials gives unusual insights into the Victorian era in the United States and tells us of subjects as varied as the presentation of a calling card and the techniques of postmortem examination. The stories also once again teach us that the war had little to do with dashing cavaliers, gallant commanders, plumed hats, and noble sentiments—and much to do with grief, pain, pus, shattered bones, diarrhea, and death.

APPENDIX A

A note on plurals: Webster's 1996 *College Dictionary* gives two choices for forming the plural of "court-martial." The first choice is "courts-martial," while the second is "court-martials."

In the process of reading thousands of such records, the authors have concluded that "courts-martial" does not flow trippingly off the tongue, but has instead a fusty, pedantic, antique, and awkward feel about it. On the contrary, "court-martials," which in some eyes may be technically and historically "incorrect," feels more natural and has a less strained quality about it.

Thus, since the accepted reference has given us a choice, we have chosen to choose. Our choice is "court-martials."

APPENDIX B

The court-martials presented here were discovered in the course of preparing a computerized name and subject index of the approximately 80,000 Union general court-martials. During the war, the trial records received by the Judge Advocate General were given arbitrary file and folder numbers and now form National Archives Record Group 153. A typical folder might be labeled MM217. In that folder could be a single trial or a dozen. The filing is not by chronological date of trial, but by date of receipt in Washington, D.C. Thus, two trials conducted on the same day, one in Alexandria and one in San Francisco, might be widely separated in the records because of the transit time of records from across the continent as opposed to across the river. Further, several of the file groupings overlap in time so that a case in LL did not necessarily occur earlier than a case in MM.

Around 1880, alphabetical name indexes were created for group HH through group OO. These indexes are on six rolls of microfilm. A twenty-minute search might yield a wanted name, but there is no way to sort by rank or regiment or location, except by reading every line of every roll of microfilm. There is no way to search other variables either. An effort to create a useful computerized index has been under way for the past four years, conducted by The Index Project, Inc., a nonprofit, tax-exempt corporation, whose researchers are Thomas and Beverly Lowry. As of January 1999, 58,000 court-martials have been cataloged. Current estimated completion date is June 2000.

This study of court-martialed doctors, and a previously published study of fifty court-martialed colonels (*Tarnished Eagles*), reveal some of the possibilities of this index for future generations of academic historians, doctoral candidates, sociologists, criminologists, legal scholars, regimental historians, genealogists, professional writers, and the just plain curious.

Because computer records are written on the wind, vulnerable to magnetic degradation, software obsolescence, rapidly changing fashions in operating systems, and the destructive influence of marketing decisions made by computer "wizards," barely postpubescent, brilliant children with no grasp of the past or vision of the future, The Index Project devotes considerable attention to the question of record stability and continuity. Provisions, both human and technical, are already in place to assure the usefulness of this index for generations yet unborn.

The original court-martial records, written in ink 135 years ago, are still quite readable. There is no reason why this newly created index should not also be usable 135 years after its own naissance.

APPENDIX C

The story of Dr. New and not-yet-mustered Private Hanger illustrates the difficulty of establishing the simplest fact in Civil War history. Let us begin with the information packet provided by the Hanger Orthopedic Group, Inc., of Bethesda, Maryland in 1998, which states that James E. Hanger's leg was shattered at the battle of Phillipi, West Virginia, in 1861; that Hanger was the first amputee of the Civil War, and that on his return home to Churchville, Virginia, he designed and built an innovative artificial leg with an articulating joint. This began a 137-year tradition of fine orthopedic appliances.

The same information packet quotes an article written by Hanger himself, in 1914, which says that his leg was amputated by a Dr. James Robinson of the 16th Ohio. A thorough search of Ohio Civil War records shows no Dr. Robinson in the 16th Ohio.

Dr. Clyde Kerneck graciously provided us with a summary of a speech given in 1961 by Hanger's grandson. This also attributes the operation to a Dr. James Robinson of the 16th Ohio.

The *Civil War Journal of Billy Davis,* edited by Richard S. Skidmore (1989), states that a Dr. New of the 7th Indiana assisted Dr. Robinson of the 14th Ohio in this surgery. National Archives records show no Dr. Robinson in either the 14th or the 16th Ohio.

The *Indiana Medical History Quarterly,* July 1975, page 18, states of Hanger, "His leg was amputated by Surgeon New of the Seventh Regiment." The *History of Indianapolis and Marion County,* page 292, states that Dr. New "dressed the first amputated leg of the war."

These half-dozen versions are an open invitation to anyone with a taste for clarifying small mysteries.

Less open to controversy is the contribution of Mrs. New to the war effort, as described in detail by Peggy Brase Seigel in "Indiana Women Nurses in the Civil War," *Indiana Magazine of History,* Volume 86, 1990, pages 4 through 10.

NOTES

INTRODUCTION
1. Bruce A. Evans, *A Primer of Civil War Medicine* (Knoxville: Bohemian Brigade Bookshop, 1997).
2. George W. Adams, *Doctors in Blue* (Baton Rouge: Louisiana State University Press, 1952), p. 47.
3. Adams, op. cit., p. 52.
4. *Revised Regulations for the Army of the United States* (Philadelphia: J. G. L. Brown Printers, 1861), pp. 281–340.
5. Confederate States of America, Army of Tennessee, Order and Letter Book, August 14, 1862, through May 4, 1864, Samuel Hollingsworth Stout Papers, 1837 (1860–1865) 1902. Center for American History, University of Texas at Austin.
6. Adams, op. cit., p. 64.
7. "Rules for Preserving the Health of the Soldier," *Journal of Civil War Medicine,* October–December 1998, p. 7.

CHAPTER 1
1. National Archives Record Group 153, Records of the Judge Advocate General's Office (Army), entry 15, Court-martial Case File, file MM1664, cited as MM1664.

CHAPTER 2
1. II856.

CHAPTER 3
1. KK682.

CHAPTER 4
1. II914.

CHAPTER 5
1. KK606.

CHAPTER 6
1. NN83.

CHAPTER 7
1. LL1079.

CHAPTER 8
1. LL3199.

CHAPTER 9
1. MM753.

CHAPTER 10
1. LL326.

CHAPTER 11
1. LL1411.

CHAPTER 12
1. MM1293.

CHAPTER 13
1. KK594.

CHAPTER 14
1. LL683.

CHAPTER 15
1. MM3067.
2. Compiled Military Service Record, Benjamin Anderson, 23rd USCT.
3. Pathology opinion graciously provided by William D. Sharpe, M.D., F.C.A.P., Clinical Associate Professor of Pathology, New Jersey Medical School, letter to Jack D. Welsh, 1998.

CHAPTER 16
1. Briggs was charged, but there is no record of a court-martial.
2. Compiled Military Service Record, James Riley, 54th Massachusetts.
3. RG 94, Entry 360, USCT Medical Officers Files, National Archives.

CHAPTER 17
1. II914.
2. United States War Department, *The War of the Rebellion, A Compilation of the Official Records of the Union and Confederate Armies,* 128 vols. (Washington, D.C.: 1890–1902), series I, vol. 11, pt. 2, p. 405, hereinafter cited as *OR.*
3. *OR,* series I, vol. 42, pt. 1, p. 626.

CHAPTER 18
1. LL297.

CHAPTER 19
1. LL382.

CHAPTER 20
1. MM1263.

CHAPTER 21
1. LL457.

CHAPTER 22
1. KK661.

CHAPTER 23
1. KK499.

CHAPTER 24
1. II773.

CHAPTER 25
1. See Appendix C.
2. II528

CHAPTER 26
1. LL80

CHAPTER 27
1. LL375.

CHAPTER 28
1. LL2258.

CHAPTER 29
1. MM3483.

CHAPTER 30
1. MM3676.

CHAPTER 31
1. KK437.
2. KK408.

CHAPTER 32
1. LL1766.

CHAPTER 33
1. II700.

CHAPTER 34
1. LL1621.

CHAPTER 35
1. NN115.

CHAPTER 36
1. II618.

CHAPTER 37
1. II1000.

CHAPTER 38
1. Mary C. Gillett, *The Army Medical Department 1818–1865* (Washington, D.C.: U.S. Government Printing Office, 1987), pp. 129, 168.
2. II547.

CHAPTER 39
1. LL1176.
2. Stout Papers, op. cit.

CHAPTER 40
1. LL850, MM874.
2. LL1108.

CHAPTER 41
1. LL1714.

CHAPTER 42
　1. KK91.

CHAPTER 43
　1. LL930.

CHAPTER 44
　1. LL1980.

CHAPTER 45
　1. LL905.

CHAPTER 46
　1. KK248, KK271.

CHAPTER 47
　1. KK487.

CHAPTER 48
　1. KK207.

CHAPTER 49
　1. LL231.

CHAPTER 50
　1. II556.
　2. *OR,* ser. 1, vol. 2, p. 345.

BIBLIOGRAPHY

BOOKS

Adams, George W. *Doctors in Blue*. Baton Rouge: Louisiana State University Press, 1952.

Evans, Bruce A. *A Primer of Civil War Medicine*. Knoxville: Bohemian Brigade Bookshop, 1997.

Gillett, Mary C. *The Army Medical Department 1818–1865*. Washington, D.C.: U.S. Government Printing Office, 1987.

Holloway, Lisabeth M. *Medical Obituaries—American Physician's Biographical Notices in Selected Medical Journals Before 1907*. Boone, N.C.: Holloway Publishers, 1996.

Directory of Deceased American Physicians, 1804–1929: A Genealogical Guide to Over 149,000 Medical Practitioners, Providing Brief Biographical Sketches Drawn from The American Medical Association's Deceased Physician Master File. 2 vols. Chicago: American Medical Association, 1993.

Revised Regulations for the Army of the United States. Philadelphia: J. G. L. Brown Publishers, 1861.

ARTICLES

U. S. Sanitary Commission. "Rules for Preserving the Health of the Soldier." *Journal of Civil War Medicine*. (October–December 1998.)

MANUSCRIPT COLLECTIONS

Record Group 153, Records of the Judge Advocate General's Office (Army), entry 15, Court-martial File. National Archives, Washington, D.C.

Record Group 94, entry 360, U. S. Colored Troops Medical Officer Files, National Archives, Washington, D.C.

Confederate States of America, Army of Tennessee, Order and Letter Book, August 14, 1862 through May 4, 1864, Samuel Hollingsworth Stout Papers, 1837 (1860–1865) 1902. Center for American History, University of Texas at Austin.

INDEX

Page numbers in italics indicate illustrations.